Gramley Library
Salem College
Winston-Salem, NC 27108

SOPHOCLES'
OEDIPUS

SOPHOCLES' OEDIPUS

Evidence and Self-Conviction

FREDERICK AHL

Gramley Library
Salem College
Winston-Salem, NC 27108

Cornell University Press

ITHACA AND LONDON

Copyright © 1991 by Frederick Ahl

All rights reserved. Except for brief quotations in a review, this book,
or parts thereof, must not be reproduced in any form without
permission in writing from the publisher. For information, address
Cornell University Press, 124 Roberts Place, Ithaca, New York 14850.

First published 1991 by Cornell University Press.

International Standard Book Number 0-8014-2558-1 (cloth)
International Standard Book Number 0-8014-9929-1 (pbk.)
Library of Congress Catalog Card Number 90-55733

Printed in the United States of America

*Librarians: Library of Congress cataloging information
appears on the last page of the book.*

⊗ The paper in this book meets the minimum requirements
of the American National Standard for Information Sciences—Permanence
of Paper for Printed Library Materials, ANSI Z39.48-1984.

FOR
KATHERINE ISABEL
AND
EAMONN SIDNEY AHL

CONTENTS

PREFACE

This book came into being as an attempt to answer questions raised by students, both graduate and undergraduate, in a series of Greek Literature in Translation courses over a period of fifteen years at Cornell and the University of Otago. Unlike classics majors, most of these students were not already steeped in the accepted views of Greek tragedy—and were often only vaguely familiar with the myth of Oedipus. For this reason they could not quite so easily be put off by my protests that they were, as E. R. Dodds would say, asking questions that one is not supposed to ask of a Greek tragedy.

In struggling to cope with the issues students raised, I discovered more questions of my own. So frequently did the translations remove difficulties and "inconsistencies" in the text before they even reached the reader's eyes that I began to wonder to what extent translators were consciously glossing over problems in the text. At the suggestion of two of my students, Lee Carol Owen and Brian Rose, I translated and staged various scenes from *Oedipus,* approaching each episode with a variety of assumptions about the motives of each character, not just Oedipus himself. After all, Owen and Rose contended, it would be naive simply to take for granted that Sophocles created all the other characters only to provide Oedipus with information. As I was preparing the translation and exploring the clues about the play's secondary characters, I thought it would be interesting to find out whether responses to the play would differ if the readers were unaware that they were actually reading Sophocles. So I prepared a second version, in which the names and locations were changed so that the overt face of the myth would be disguised from the audience.

For the next two years I conducted an experiment in which I gave some classes the first (unemended) translation and other classes the second (disguised) version. With both groups I was careful to present only an orthodox interpretation of the text, so that I would not be prompting them to ask questions "they were not supposed to ask." Here was the story of a man who discovered that he had killed his father and contracted an incestuous marriage. There was a marked difference in the responses of the two groups. Those given the disguised version read the play much more carefully than those who knew from the outset that they were reading Sophocles' tragedy. And they asked far more questions and expressed a great deal more skepticism about the conventional interpretation I offered them. It became clear that those familiar with the Oedipus myth were beginning with assumptions about what the play *must* mean, and that they tended to privilege that assumption even when the language of the play did not itself seem to support it. Thus I began to realize that there was a very special tension in *Oedipus* between the "received" myth and the structure of the drama itself.

It seemed worthwhile, therefore, to prepare a detailed study of *Oedipus* primarily for the benefit of readers who know no Greek or do not know it well enough to feel confident in their own disagreement with established views. My goal has been to ask as many questions of the text as I think it can bear and to search for answers as fully as possible. I cannot claim to have resolved all, or even most, of the problems observed, but hope to have shed some new light on them. Yet on one matter I am thoroughly persuaded: in this play, no conclusive evidence is presented that Oedipus killed his father and married his mother. If we decide that Oedipus is the son and killer of Laios and the son and husband of Jocasta, we are doing so on the basis of assumptions external to the arguments presented—doing, in fact, what Oedipus himself does. Perhaps this is precisely the trap into which Sophocles would have us fall.

For me, then, the principal unresolved issue of the play is whether the generally accepted notion of its meaning is the product of our misinterpretation of the text or of Sophocles' dramatic intent to make us follow in Oedipus' path.

Considerations of space have led me to focus on those parts of the play involving Oedipus in interchanges with other characters and with the chorus. The choral songs have been only cursorily treated, even though I am well aware that they are an important part of Sophocles' rhetorical approach to his audience. The chorus of Theban citizens is not just an inner audience; it has its own curious complicity in Sophocles' subtle dramatic persuasion. But full discussion of its role would have made a long book even longer.

On the whole, I have approached the play episode by episode, in a kind of running commentary, since I believe that in a drama it is crucial to maintain a sense of what is known to the characters and audience at a given point. I refer to the play throughout as *Oedipus*—probably its original title—rather than as *Oedipus the King* or *Oedipus Rex*. The text discussed is presented in my own translation of H. Lloyd Jones and N. G. Wilson, *Sophoclis Fabulae* (Oxford, 1990), but with frequent reference also to R. D. Dawe's Teubner text, *Sophoclis Tragoediae* (Leipzig, 1984). Lines are numbered to correspond to the Greek text rather than to the English translation. So there will often be more "lines" in the quotations than seem indicated by the numbering, since my version is expanded where necessary to draw out the nuances of the original. The translation attempts not just to transpose the Greek into English, but to reproduce some of the special wordplays of the original as well as what scholars usually call the "literal" sense. Greek proper names are generally given in the familiar Latinized spelling. I have, however, retained the Greek form for Laios' name to make certain wordplays more apparent. Where it has proved necessary to discuss individual Greek words or phrases, I have transliterated them rather than printed them in Greek. Iota subscripts are written as adscripts on the line, and eta is distinguished from epsilon by a circumflex accent, as omega is from omicron. Detailed discussion of the more complex wordplays and other effects that defy translation I have reserved until Chapter 10, which is the most demanding section of the book for readers with no knowledge of Greek or of Greek history.

Although the principal focus of this book is on the process of argument in the text itself, I have tried to give at least some sense of what issues of his own day Sophocles may be responding to in this tragedy.

The scholarly literature on this play is prodigious and full of brilliant insights. To credit adequately all the various discussions that have influenced my judgment on any given point is not possible. The notes to each chapter provide an indication of the scholarly works I have most frequently consulted on the issues concerned rather than an exhaustive bibliography.

I owe special debts of gratitude to Adele Haft and Robert White of the Department of Classics at Hunter College, where I first presented some of these ideas outside the classroom, in the Earle Lecture of 1985; to the National Endowment for the Humanities, which permitted me an extension of my Translation Grant for my translation of four tragedies of Seneca so I could complete the revisions to this manuscript; to Charles Babcock and the American Academy in Rome, where much of the final text was prepared in 1989; to my colleagues Martin Bernal, Jonathan Culler, Sandor Goodhart, David Mankin, Gordon Messing, Phillip Mitsis, Pietro Pucci, Andrew Ramage, Winthrop Wetherbee, and David Wyatt, who stood by me during the unforgettably painful years when this book was being written, and whose help and kindness I can never repay; to Hanna Roisman and Yossi Roisman of Colby College, who offered so many useful suggestions and corrected so many errors; to Gordon Kirkwood, who first opened up Sophocles for me; to Bernhard Kendler, Victoria Haire, Patty Peltekos, and the anonymous readers for Cornell University Press, whose support, ideas, corrections, and encouragement were invaluable; to Adria Moskowitz, who helped me with proofreading; to my colleague, Jeffrey Rusten, who made available to me his *Sophocles, Oidipous Tyrannos* (Bryn Mawr, 1990) prior to its publication; to my former students, graduate and undergraduate, at Cornell—especially Molly Ierulli, Don McGuire, Martha Malamud, Lee Carol Owen, and Brian Rose—whose persistent questions about Greek tragedy drew my attention to so many of the problems I have attempted to address here. Above all, I thank my wife, Mary, and my children, Kate and Sid, for their patience, love, and understanding.

FREDERICK AHL

Ithaca, New York

SOPHOCLES'
OEDIPUS

INTRODUCTION

$\mathbf{P}$eter Rudnytsky is probably correct in arguing that Sophocles'
Oedipus is "perhaps *the* preeminent classical text in the Western
tradition."[1] Yet we should remind ourselves that its preeminence is
relatively recent. When it was first produced, for example, it did not
even win first prize in the tragic competition at Athens. Sophocles
was defeated by the now forgotten Philocles.[2] Despite Aristotle's
admiration for the play, which we will discuss later in this introduction, the play did not rise to its present preeminence until the late
eighteenth and early nineteenth centuries A.D., when Northern Eu-
ropeans in particular were beginning to discard Latin literary and
intellectual models in favor of Greek: when Homer, Aeschylus, Sophocles, and Euripides began to be preferred over the Roman epicists,
and over Seneca. *Oedipus* gained its hallowed place during the era of
romanticism, during the burgeoning of German letters and scholarship under its muse, Friedrich von Schiller.[3]

Although Rudnytsky's study contains many brilliant insights into
the rise of the Oedipus tradition as we know it today, there is one
issue that I must contest with him. He declares that "until, approximately the 1790s, admiration for Sophocles' *Oedipus the King* was
almost always contaminated by extraneous features, above all the
baleful example of Seneca. Only when German Romantic writers and
philosophers, following the lead of Lessing, were able to clear away
neoclassical and Senecan excrescences, and behold Sophocles' drama

afresh as a tragedy of self-knowledge, do we enter the 'age of Oedipus' that reaches its apogee in Freud."[4]

To dispute this negative value judgment about Seneca—though I believe it mistaken—would take us too far from our immediate task.[5] Instead, let me state that I am less convinced than Rudnytsky that the German romantics were able to cut away these so-called excrescences. They and their successors remained well grounded in Latin poetic and intellectual traditions and in European vernacular literatures that were themselves influenced by—even shaped by—Latin rather than Greek models. The era of the American and French revolutions was one of republicanism, of Cicero, Seneca, Lucan, and Tacitus, rather than of democracy, of Demosthenes, Plato, and Aristotle. Although few critics during the last century and a half have written about Greek tragedy with Seneca in mind, modern criticism of Greek tragedy was born when Senecan tragedy was still widely read, and a Senecan sense of tragedy has been passed on, via scholarly tradition, if not by direct reading of that often maligned Roman dramatist. However little patience nineteenth-century Hellenists had with Seneca, he and other Roman writers provided much of the intellectual substructure for the interpretation of Greek literature. Indeed, many of the religious and philosophical issues that dominate Sophoclean scholarship have not only a very Roman, Stoic flavor but a strong undercurrent of Christian thought. The book remains to be written that researches and describes the formative, latent influence of Roman thinkers on those very romantics who thought they were rejecting Roman models in their generation of the new Greek model of Western civilization. As the Roman epicist Silius Italicus points out, one tends to be defined by what one opposes.[6]

The Greek model for Western culture was fabricated, if I may reappropriate the term from Martin Bernal, during the late eighteenth and early nineteenth centuries to bypass Rome and Jerusalem and establish a direct route between Berlin or London and Athens. Yet although Sophocles' *Oedipus* has become an icon of modern European and American culture, thanks to Freud, who used the Sophoclean hero as a symbol of the repressed incestuous relationship between son and mother and of the son's repressed desire to kill his father, scholars have carried over from Seneca into Sophocles the greater rhetorical certainty that Oedipus actually committed the acts of murder and incest of which he convicts himself.[7] Not only does Seneca's Oedipus explicitly acknowledge that he has killed his father and married his mother, but Jocasta explicitly accepts her guilt and kills herself in as Freudian a self-punishment as one can imagine: by driving a sword into her womb.

The result of negative value judgments about Seneca has been to view him as an imitator of Greek drama, not as an innovator, despite the often startling differences between his tragedies and Greek tragedies bearing the same name. Although Seneca in fact creates a radically different Oedipus, we have tended to see the play as merely a variant on Sophocles'. The consequences have been as misleading for the interpretation of Sophocles as of Seneca, since we have read back onto Sophocles ideas that are really rather Senecan. Our understanding of Sophocles' *Oedipus* has long been shaped, and continues to be shaped, by scholarly understanding of Seneca's *Oedipus*.

Owing to the influence of the Senecan *donnée*, I suggest, we pass too lightly over the troublesome areas where what Sophocles writes is at odds with the synthetic overview of the Oedipus myth prevalent now and in antiquity. We focus even more intently on Sophocles' Oedipus than he does, to the neglect of the other characters in the play, whom we often treat as purveyors of information rather than as individuals with their own proprietary interests in what is happening. We assume, as does Oedipus, that those on whose testimony he bases his judgment speak truthfully and dispassionately. Discussions of guilt and innocence in Sophocles' *Oedipus,* for instance, seem to echo Jocasta's Stoic adage in Seneca's *Oedipus* 1019, as she and Oedipus, blinded, confront each other in full awareness of their unwitting incest: *fati ista culpa est; nemo fit fato nocens* ("Fate is to blame. No one is guilty of what is fated"). Yet even Seneca's Jocasta takes little consolation in the adage. Only a few lines later, she resolves to "pay the penalty for the crimes (*scelerum dare poenas*) in which I am an accomplice" (1024–25) and kills herself (1039).

The Traditional Oedipus

The most crucial and generally unquestioned assumption that remains with us from Seneca, and is applied to Sophocles, is that Oedipus drew the correct conclusion that he was Jocasta's child. Sophocles' *Oedipus,* most would agree, shows Oedipus discovering he has committed two crimes: he has killed Laios, king of Thebes, who proves to be his father, and has married Laios' widow, Jocasta, who proves to be his mother. The play, then, depicts the hero remorselessly uncovering his crimes. When we discuss his guilt or innocence, we focus on whether he acted knowingly or unknowingly, following free will or some inescapable destiny, not on whether he is right in concluding that he has indeed killed his father and married his mother. Since Oedipus finds himself guilty of patricide and incest, most readers accept his judgment against himself as correct, even though it is based on sparse, confused, often anonymous, and occasionally obviously false testimony.[8] Translators reinforce this judgment by presenting *Oedipus* as first play of a Theban "trilogy" or "cycle," with *Oedipus at Colonus* second and *Antigone* last. They generate a close but false thematic evolution from *Oedipus* through *Antigone* which often tricks us into assuming, for example, that Oedipus is exiled as *Oedipus* ends, since he is in exile as *Oedipus at Colonus* begins. *Antigone*, in fact, came first, followed about fifteen years later by *Oedipus* and, about thirty-five years later, by *Oedipus at Colonus*.

An Athenian of the fifth or fourth century B.C. might also have taken for granted that Oedipus was, in the broadest terms, as he is in Seneca, the mythic character who "killed his father and married his mother." A fragment of the comic writer Antiphanes, who began to write in about 386 B.C., makes the point clearly:

> Tragedy is a blessed form of poetry in every way. First the plots are known by the audiences even before the dialogue begins. The poet only has to jog their memories. Say "Oedipus!" They know the rest: his father's name was Laios, his mother was Jocasta, these were his daughters, these his sons, this is what will happen to him, this is what he did.[9]

To disagree with the canonical view invited criticism in antiquity as it does today. Dio Chrysostom, a Greek intellectual of the first and early second centuries A.D., shows the dilemma well. When the Cynic Diogenes questions Oedipus' wisdom (Dio, *Discourse* 10.30), his interlocutor expostulates: "You, Diogenes, are depicting Oedipus as the most unperceptive of all humans. But the Greeks think that, though he was an unfortunate man, he was the wisest of all."

Dio's Diogenes has a point, however. Regardless of what occurs elsewhere in Greek and Roman literature, there is room, even within the boundaries of mythic tradition, for an Oedipus who may not have committed the crimes he comes to believe he has committed. And the purpose of this book is to reexamine Sophocles' play with such a scenario in mind. My approach obviously involves an open examination of the issues raised during the play's various dialogues and the asking of questions that scholars sometimes dismiss as improper.

E. R. Dodds said we have no business considering whether Oedipus could have "escaped his doom if he had been more careful," since "we are not entitled to ask questions that the dramatist did not intend us to ask."[10] But can one know which questions the dramatist did not intend us to ask? *Oedipus* provokes questions in its audiences and readers as profoundly as any play ever written. It is itself a play of many questions asked, and usually only partly answered. Dodds is as unfair in trying to halt the questioning as he is in paraphrasing the question itself. We may ask not only "Could Oedipus have escaped his doom?" but "Is there a doom for Oedipus to escape, and if there is, what is it?" M. S. Silk and J. P. Stern have a point when they contend that Oedipus is "hardly the protestant hero that Schelling makes out. It is not external fate, but rather his own determination to seek out the truth, that brings about his defeat."[11]

Dodds insists that Oedipus' caution—or lack of it—is irrelevant to the accomplishment of his appointed "doom." In a deterministic order, he feels, what "is to be" will happen regardless of mortal attempts to evade that "fate." But there is no evidence that Sophocles "himself" regards Oedipus' fate as determined by a cosmic, essentially divine, destiny. Although some characters, notably Oedipus himself in certain moods, occasionally talk of external, divine forces controlling individual lives, there is no reason to assume that such a fatalistic view is therefore being advanced editorially by the author and shared by him. A dramatist may write about Presbyterian determinists without being a Presbyterian or about Stoics without being a Stoic.

Variations in a Shifting Tradition

Determinism in a kind of Stoic or Protestant Christian sense is not the only kind we must consider. Even in a universe without gods, an individual's destiny may be largely determined by persons or forces outside oneself. One may be chained in prison, living at a jailer's whim. One may be unwilling to make decisions and thus allow one's life to be controlled by others. Finally, like Oedipus, one may be a mythic character, and thus "determined" to some degree by the mythic tradition itself. How, and in what way, does the Oedipus myth determine what Sophocles can or cannot have Oedipus do? If, as some have suggested, *Oedipus* is a dramatized folktale or myth, is Oedipus' fate determined by the myth, if not by "god" or man?

Considering the comic poet Antiphanes' observations, cited above, we may conclude that Dodds was right to suggest, in effect, that Oedipus cannot escape from his mythic (or folkloric, if you will) context and doom. Yet even if we grant that *Oedipus* is a dramatized folktale, the folktale is neither monolithic nor immutable. It undergoes many important variations in detail throughout Greek and Roman literature. In *Odyssey* 11.271–80, for instance, there is no suggestion that Oedipus blinded himself, as in Sophocles. "Myth" does not doom him to lose his eyesight. In Euripides' *Oedipus* he was apparently blinded by Laios' henchmen, according to the ancient commentator on Euripides' *Phoenician Women* 61, who cites a couple of lines to support his contention:

> But in [Euripides], *Oedipus,* Laios' attendants blinded him:
>   "But we threw the son of Polybus to the ground
>   and gouged out his eyes and destroyed them."

We might note, incidentally, that Oedipus' assailants seem to have thought Oedipus the son of Polybus, king of Corinth, not only when they attacked him but when they reported their attack. Precisely when, in the Euripidean treatment of the myth, that attack occurred, we cannot say. But it could even have been immediately after Oedipus' killing of Laios at the crossroads. In other words, Oedipus might even have been blind when he arrived at Thebes in Euripides' *Oedipus*.

Yet in Euripides' *Phoenician Women,* in the very line that prompts the scholiast's comment, Jocasta says Oedipus blinded himself (60–61):

> Oedipus, enduring all one can
> suffer, brutally killed his own eyesight.

So in two different plays, Euripides builds on two different traditions, *modifying and adding to both as he writes.* Not only, then, is myth variable, but playwrights are not consistent in their use of the same myth from play to play. Euripides follows different paths in his *Oedi-*

pus and his *Phoenician Women*. On some issues he is in accord with Sophocles' *Oedipus,* on others not, even within the same play. Doubtless he is making use of his audience's familiarity with Sophocles' *Oedipus,* which was performed around fifteen or twenty years earlier than *Phoenician Women*. *Oedipus* was probably first staged between 429 and 425 B.C., and *Phoenician Women* between 411 and 408. Euripides' Jocasta in *Phoenician Women* reinforces Sophocles' *Oedipus* in one matter (Oedipus' self-blinding), only to undermine it in another: in Sophocles' *Oedipus,* a messenger tells us that Jocasta hanged herself *before* Oedipus blinded himself. In *Phoenician Women,* Jocasta continues to live long after Oedipus destroys his eyesight.[12]

Euripides and Sophocles have various traditions to build on and adapt. In *Odyssey* 11.271–80 Epicaste—as Homer and Pausanias call Jocasta—hangs herself on concluding that Oedipus is her child. But there is no mention of Oedipus' self-blinding or of anything that might make us assume he did not continue as king of Thebes.[13] The version that prevailed in the now lost Greek epic *Oedipodeia,* and that leaves traces in Statius' Roman *Thebaid,* probably lies behind Euripides' *Phoenician Women*.[14] In Euripides' play, Jocasta lives until the later civil war between Oedipus' sons, Eteocles and Polyneices, and indeed delivers the prologue. Pausanias (9.5.10) maintains that, according to Homer, Euryganeia and not Jocasta was their mother. But Euripides' Jocasta kills herself over the bodies of her sons Eteocles and Polyneices (1349 ff., 1455 ff.). In Statius' *Thebaid,* she kills herself before the duel in which the two youths perish (*Thebaid* 11.634–47). But she dies not by hanging, as Homer and the messenger in Sophocles suggest, but by the sword, as in Seneca's *Oedipus* 1034–39.[15]

There is little doubt that our view of the Oedipus myth, and of Greek tragedy in general, would be much different if we had more complete versions of the various dramatic treatments by the Greek tragedians. Our sense of their artistic originality would be enhanced if, for instance, we had Euripides' *Antigone* as well as Sophocles'. For in Euripides, it appears, Antigone did not die in defiance of Creon, along with her betrothed Haemon, but went on to become Haemon's wife.[16] An ancient audience, then, cannot have been as sure as we sometimes think it was about what would happen in a given play, no matter how handily "the plot" might be reduced to a general outline.

Sometimes these general synopses contain surprises. In Aristophanes *Frogs* 1182–94, for example, the ghost of Aeschylus, as he mocks the prologue to Euripides' now lost *Antigone,* gives us a satirical parody of the Oedipus myth:

> *Euripides*: At first Oedipus was a blessed man . . .
> *Aeschylus*: By Zeus he was not so! He was accursed
> the moment he was begotten. How can a man
> be lucky at first who Apollo had said
> even before he was conceived, before
> his birth, would kill his very own father?
> *Euripides*: Then later he became the most wretched.
> *Aeschylus*: By Zeus he did not! For he never stopped
> being wretched! How so? The moment he
> was born, though it was wintertime (*cheimôn*), they put
> him out, inside a piece of pottery (*ostrakon*)
> so he would not be able to grow up
> and be his father's murderer. And then,
> he went in exile off to Polybus,
> with a painful, swollen pair of feet (*OIDôn tô PODe*).
> And then, to top it all, though he was young,
> he married an old woman who turned out
> to be his very own mother. And then,
> he blinded himself.

Some of the Aristophanic Aeschylus' jesting is, of course, at Euripides' expense. The ancient scholiast on the *Frogs* suggested that lines 1184ff. are parodying, specifically, *Phoenician Women* 15ff. But surely the scholiast is wrong. Out of the whole Euripidean prologue, only *Phoenician Women* 53–54 come close to being the originals of such parody:

> *Jocasta*: He marries, without knowing it, poor man,
> the woman who gave him birth. And she
> who bore him shared her bed, unknowingly,
> with her own son.

Elsewhere, Jocasta's prologue has a very different flavor and point. She talks first of *Laios* before going on to *Oedipus* (22–30):

> He, having fathered a child, knowing
> the riddling words and oracle of god,
> gives the child to cowherds to expose
> on Hera's Meadow and the mountain ridge

of Cithaeron, piercing his lower legs
with iron spurs. Because of this all Greece
named him Oedipus, "The Swollen Foot."
Then Polybus' horse-tenders picked him up,
and brought him home and placed him in the hands
of their mistress.

The wordplay on Oedipus' name in the description of his discomfort, *OIDôn tô PODe,* "swollen pair of feet," occurs not only in Euripides' *Phoenician Women* but in Sophocles' more famous and much earlier *Oedipus.* The matter of the swollen feet is no more than incidental to Euripides' play. It is fundamental to Oedipus' self-identification in Sophocles and probably first occurred there. Thus the target of Aristophanes' wit here could as well be the unmentioned Sophocles.

If the Aristophanic Aeschylus is parodying Euripides' *Phoenician Women* here, it is odd that he has nothing to say about the individuals who disposed of and picked up the infant Oedipus. For Euripides' Jocasta makes the exchange occur between cowherds and horse-tenders rather than the more familiar Sophoclean shepherds. Indeed, it would be easier to maintain that *Euripides* is also parodying Sophocles' *Oedipus.* We should perhaps ask ourselves whether the parody in Aristophanes, though overtly directed toward Euripides, covertly mocks Sophocles and even Aeschylus himself, especially since the scholiast is at a loss to explain the most striking part of the Oedipus synopsis as Euripidean.

In Aeschylus' summary, the child is exposed in a piece of pottery, an *ostrakon.* Unable to account for the detail as Euripidean parody, the scholiast resorts to a familiar scholarly ploy: some other commentator (whose name has been lost to us) says these words are an alteration of the original text. Surely, however, the mention of Oedipus' exposure in an *ostrakon* a "piece of pottery," is a joke—not not simply *pars pro toto* for the practice of *chytrizein,* "exposing," children in an earthenware pot (*chytra*). The Aristophanic Aeschylus is alluding to the Athenian reverse electoral process of ostracism (a means of getting rid of politically unwanted *adults*). And the joke is at least partly at *Aeschylus'* expense. Aristophanes is making the dead poet parody himself. From the scholia on Aristophanes' *Wasps* 289, we learn that Aeschylus, in his own lost *Laios,* told how someone, presumably Oedipus, was exposed in an earthenware *chytra.*[17]

The most startling element in the synopsis is, however, almost

certainly a comment on Sophocles' *Oedipus*: the detail about when
Oedipus was exposed. Here again is how it appears in Aristophanes:

Aeschylus: The moment he
          was born, though it was wintertime (*cheimôn*), they put
          him out, inside a piece of pottery (*ostrakon*)
          so he would not be able to grow up
          and be his father's murderer.

Now Sophocles' *Oedipus* 1132–45:

Corinthian: I'm not surprised, master. He obviously
          does not recall; I'll jog his memory.
          For I know that he knows how it was once
          on Cithaeron: he went with two herds. I
          with one, was close to this man for three whole
          six-month seasons from the spring until
          Arcturus rises in the fall. I drove
          my flocks home for shelter in wintertime.
          He drove his off to Laios' cattle-pens.
          Do I speak fact, or do I not speak fact?
Slave: You speak the truth, though this was long ago.
Corinthian: All right. You know the child you gave me then
          to bring up personally, as my own?
Slave: What's this? Why are you telling this story?
Corinthian: This man, fool, was that child when he was young.

Aeschylus has included a minor detail of time in his twelve-line
parody, as Sophocles has at the heart of his play, when Oedipus comes
to accept that he is the killer of Laios and the child of Jocasta. There
is, we will note, a surprising difference between the "original" and
the parody. Oedipus was, the Aristophanic Aeschylus says, exposed
in the *winter*. Sophocles' Corinthian, who claims to have unfastened
the pins from the infant's feet, says he did so when he was grazing
his sheep on Cithaeron (1030–36). He ran flocks there annually for
three years: for six months until the morning rising of Arcturus, from
March through September (1135–37)—until, as R. C. Jebb notes on
line 1136, "about a week before the autumnal equinox, which falls
on Sept. 20–21."[18] We might compare the migrations of the Sarak-
atsani and their flocks in modern Greece. The feasts of Saints George
(May 6) and Demetrius (November 9) "mark the start of the pastoral
summer and winter when the leases for grazing begin and end."[19]

If Sophocles' shepherd returned home from Cithaeron *for* the winter (*cheimôna*), at the rising of Arcturus, at the very beginning of winter, rather than during the winter, Aristophanes' Aeschylus may be suggesting that this herdsman was not on Cithaeron at the right Aeschylean time of the year to unpin the feet of a child exposed in winter. Curiously enough, Seneca's Corinthian talks of being given Oedipus "on the *snowy* top" of Cithaeron by a shepherd who, in contrast, says he grazed his sheep there in summer (Seneca, *Oedipus* 808; 845–46).

Noticeably absent in Aristophanes' parody of the Oedipus myth is any allusion to the Sphinx. In Sophocles, too, the Sphinx and her riddle are alluded to only obliquely. The traditional content of the riddle (what creature has one voice, but two, three, or four feet) is not mentioned at all. The Sphinx had been the subject of a satyr play by Aeschylus, about which we know next to nothing, and was part of his Theban tetralogy, of which only the *Seven against Thebes* survives.[20] To gain a sense, however, of the possibilities that may have lurked for a writer in the story of Oedipus and the Sphinx, let us consider the following passage from Pausanias' *Description of Greece* (9.26.2–4), describing the place where, according to tradition, the Sphinx lived:

> Farther along there is a mountain from which they say the Sphinx, singing a riddle (*ainigma aidousan*), rushed out to destroy those she caught. Others say that she came ashore at Anthedon with a naval force, wandering around for brigandage (*kata lêisteian*), that she seized the mountain and used it for plundering raids until Oedipus overpowered her with a large army he brought with him from Corinth. It is also said she was the bastard daughter of Laios.

> Through fondness for her, he told her the oracle given to Cadmus by Delphi. Apart from kings, no one else knew the oracle. Whenever someone came to dispute with the Sphinx the right to rule—for Laios had sons by concubines and the oracles from Delphi applied only to Epicaste and her children—the Sphinx tricked her brothers with words: if they really were Laios' children, they would know the oracle. When they couldn't answer, she put them to death as punishment, since they had unjustly claimed royal descent and the right to rule. Oedipus then arrived, having learned the oracle in a dream.

Pausanias' sketch of the Sphinx as a female claimant to the Theban throne, engaging in plundering (*lêisteia*), rather than a kind

Gramley Library
Salem College
Winston-Salem, NC 27108

of Egyptian monster, finds reinforcement in the scholiast to Hesiod's *Theogony* 326, who describes the Sphinx as a *gynê lêistris,* "a woman brigand." This tradition is strangely echoed in Sophocles' *Oedipus:* it is rumored in Thebes that Laios was killed by a band of *lêistai* (*plunderers*), as Creon points out in line 122, at the very time when the complex-riddle-singing (*poikilôidos*) Sphinx was at large (130). Other details in Pausanias' account are worth bearing in mind. Oedipus was captain of an *army* from Corinth. He was not traveling alone. And Laios had several sons, illegitimate sons by concubines (presumably to avoid fulfilling the prophecy that he would be killed by his son by Jocasta), who sought to establish their own claims on the throne of Thebes.[21]

Pausanias, though writing in the second century A.D., calls Laios' wife Epicaste, her Homeric name, not Jocasta, the name familiar to us in Greek tragedy. Yet in other details of the Oedipus myth he clearly echoes the tragedians, as in his description of the piercing of Oedipus' feet in 10.5.3, which recalls almost *verbatim* Euripides' *Phoenician Women* 25–26. Pausanias has *diapeirantes dia tôn sphyrôn kentra ektitheasin* ("they expose him, having pierced spurs through his lower legs"); Euripides writes *ektheinai brephos/ sphyrôn kentra diapeiras mesôn* ("to expose the child, piercing his lower legs with iron spurs"). It is Pausanias who gives the famous description of the traditional site where Oedipus killed Laios, the *Schistê Odos,* the "Split Road" (10.5.4), where, he adds, there is a monument not only to Laios but to the household servant (*oiketês*) who accompanied Laios and died with him at the crossroads. Both Euripides (*Phoenician Women* 38) and Sophocles (*Oedipus* 733–34) mention the *Schistê Odos* as the place where Laios was killed. But in Sophocles Creon and Jocasta claim the servant survived.

There were, then, many vastly different variants of almost every aspect of the Oedipus story in antiquity. There was a huge store of folkloric material upon which the poet could draw, material that was (and is) malleable. Poets give themselves much artistic freedom, working and reworking the material in alternative ways. Indeed, what makes writing a mythic tragedy easy—if we concede Antiphanes' comic point—is precisely what makes writing a *great* tragedy difficult. The challenge is to find a way of stimulating and maintaining audience interest in a story whose general outline is already known. The tragedian must either endow his version with a particular relevance to a contemporary social or political issue, or introduce some surprising "twist" in the mythical "plot" variations. In a very important sense, then, "myth" is what the Greek audience knows. The myth, as the Athenian dramatist inherits it, embodies what he can assume about his audience's way of thinking on the moral and other issues the story involves. If he is subtly to redirect or remold his audience's thought, he must do so by unusual inflections of myth—of the world, of social order as people "know" it. He must regenerate myth in a unique and striking way. And usually he does.

Not everyone in antiquity approved of the ways in which poets, particularly tragic poets, reshaped myth. Dio Chrysostom complains (though with tongue in cheek, I suspect) about the secularization of myth among the poets after Homer and Hesiod: they were not so much interested in displaying divine wisdom to humankind as in displaying their own (*Discourse* 36.35):

> Those who came after them at a later date brought their own wisdom
> on stage and into the theaters and often produced imperfect represen-
> tations of religious rites. The uninitiated were addressing the unini-
> tiated. But they were watched and admired by the masses, and they
> personally undertook to ritually "perfect" the people. What they were
> really doing was pitching their stages like tents without veiling curtains
> at some crossroads of tragedy (*en tisi tragikais triodois*).

Dio has much the same criticism of certain philosophers, notably the Cynics who, he declares, post themselves "at the crossroads and in narrow streets" (*en te triodois kai stenôpois* [*Discourse* 32.9]), where you cannot avoid meeting them. They use the places where people converge to sell themselves and their own ideas.

Even if we disagree with Dio's judgment of tragedy, we should note that he is drawing attention to the secular and secularizing nature of the drama. In the fifth century B.C., Euripides was sometimes characterized as an atheistic, intellectual revolutionary. Scholars, however, still find it hard to take the same view of Sophocles, who has been represented to us as a model of conservative piety. Yet Sophocles, even in *Oedipus,* a play that is, above all others, "at [and about] some crossroads of tragedy," provides innovations in matters extending well beyond the more technical details of a poet's craft. He adds new and important dimensions to the Oedipus myth.

The secular elements in tragedy, which we must take care not to overlook in our preoccupation with its ritual aspects, were understood, if not always appreciated, in antiquity. Contemporary thought, as well as contemporary events and personages, seem to have affected the tragedian's treatment of a myth. So too did other literary representations of that myth. The treatments of theme and character in Aeschylus' *Libation Bearers,* Euripides' *Electra,* and Sophocles' *Electra* differ considerably even though they are dramatic variants on the same "story". And when Euripides returns to deal with a further development of the same theme later in *Orestes,* still greater modifications occur. The myth evolves in a continuing dialogue among playwrights reacting to one another. As Victor Ehrenberg notes: "an interdependence can be revealed which is based on a stronger foundation than the more elementary question of the tragic material and the different use of it made by each poet."[22]

Euripides' *Electra* presupposes the audience's familiarity with Aeschylus' earlier *Libation Bearers.* Euripides in fact parodies the Aeschylean Electra's recognition of her brother, as almost all critics would now agree. Electra's feet fit the footprints around her father's grave; her hair matches the tress left on the tomb. So the person who has left the footprints and the hair must be her brother Orestes.[23] Euripides is in effect acknowledging that myth, what the audience "knows" about Electra, is in his day conveniently epitomized by the *Libation Bearers.* So he subverts the Aeschylean original by having his Electra ridicule the idea that her feet would be the same size and her hair the same texture as her brother's. Then he subverts his audience by showing his Electra is wrong: the footprints and hair *are* Orestes'.

Even in plays where one might have thought the myth was immovably fixed, quite drastic reworking was possible and practiced. Euripides, for example, seems to have been the first to establish what is now the canonical version of Medea at Corinth. There is no evidence that in earlier versions of the myth Medea killed her children, as Emily McDermott has decisively shown.[24] Again, it is probably the fact that Seneca seems close to Euripides in his *Medea* that leaves the impression that the Euripidean version was "standard." But clearly it was not the invariable version in subsequent Greek tragedy. In *Rhetoric* 2.23.27 (1400B) Aristotle mentions the lost *Medea* by a fourth-century tragedian, Carcinus (or possibly by his grandfather, the Carcinus Aristophanes lampoons in the *Wasps* and elsewhere). Carcinus was a prolific and successful dramatist, winner of eleven victories in tragic competitions. In his *Medea,* apparently, Medea did not kill her children but sent them away. Nevertheless, she faces a cast of other characters—and possibly an audience influenced by Euripides—predisposed to disbelieve her claim:

> Another variation (*topos*) is to make an accusation or a defense on the basis of previous errors. Such is the case in the *Medea* of Carcinus. People accuse her of killing her children, for she cannot produce them. Medea made a mistake (*hêmarte*) in sending the children away. She answers in defense that she would not have killed her children, but Jason. For it would have been a mistake not to have done this act if she had done the other. This variation on the enthymeme [the rhetorical equivalent of the syllogism] and its like is the whole nature of rhetoric before Theodore of Byzantium.

The comparison of Sophocles' *Oedipus* with Carcinus' *Medea* is a useful reminder of how the dramatist may choose to involve the audience in the false assumptions some of his tragic characters make. Such assumptions, though reinforced by previous versions of the myth, are brought into doubt in the context of a new dramatic situation in Carcinus' *Medea* and, I suggest, in Sophocles' *Oedipus*.

Aristotle treats such variation of myth in tragedy as a feature of *rhetoric,* not of religion: they are, that is, motivated by secular, literary considerations, not by ritual. And rightly so. For tragedies were composed on more or less "set" themes much as were the *suasoriae,* "the persuasion speeches," of Roman declamation. We may also note how common and general Aristotle maintains such rhetorical structures were before the time of Theodore of Byzantium. And this is why I wonder, parenthetically, whether the Carcinus mentioned may not be the fifth-century tragedian rather than his grandson. For Theodore lived in the second half of the fifth century B.C., was ironically praised by Socrates in Plato's *Phaedrus* 266E, and was ranked by Aristotle (*De Sophisticis Elenchis* 183B32) with Tisias and Thrasymachus as one of the most important contributors to the development of rhetoric.

Carcinus' Medea, then, is accused of killing children she has not killed. Similarly, we are told in the scholia on Euripides' *Medea* 264 and 1382 that in Parmeniscus' version Medea's children were killed by the people of Corinth. Thus it stands to reason that Sophocles or any other ancient playwright could have felt free to compose a play whose chief divergence from other versions is as follows: Oedipus does not *discover* that he has killed his father and married his mother. Rather, he *convinces himself* he has done so. His "fate" is determined *rhetorically* by his reliance on the words of others. He *allows,* wittingly or unwittingly, his life to be determined by external human forces and internal fears, which he and others may choose, if they wish, to see as god or immutable tradition.

Aristotle and Oedipus

Many assumptions we have inherited about myth, about tragedy, about Sophocles, and about Oedipus derive, ultimately, from Aristotle. Eckart Schütrumpf observes that "it has often been noted that the tragedy which forms the model for Aristotle's account of the change from fortune to misfortune through a *hamartia* [error] is the Sophoklean *Oidipous Tyrannos.*"[25] Similarly, Cedric Whitman comments: "The *Oedipus Rex* passes almost universally for the greatest extant Greek play—an assumption based, no doubt, on Aristotle's preference."[26] Aristotle has formed our judgment. He made Sophocles' *Oedipus* symbolize the myth as no one has made Sophocles' *Electra* symbolize the vengeance of Agamemnon's children upon their mother. There are other surviving Greek *Electras*; there is no other Greek *Oedipus*.

C. M. Bowra and others, however, have shown that Aristotle does not do justice to Sophocles, although his explanation of tragedy is based on Sophocles.[27] Schütrumpf goes further: "I do not believe," he argues, "that Aristotle expended great effort to analyze this tragedy on the basis of its structure; I would suggest instead that he adopted the interpretation of the actions of Oidipous from the *Oidipous at Kolonos.*"[28] It is not just because, as Bernard Knox contends, Oedipus' "operation in the plot does not fit the Aristotelian formula," but rather that the play corresponds "fairly closely to Aristotle's description of what tragedy should avoid."[29] But whether tragedy is "good" or "bad" in accordance with its degree of conformity to some Aristotelian ideal of tragedy is not the main issue. We need only remind ourselves that Aristotle was in conflict with some critics of his own day when he expressed his preference for tragedies with "unhappy endings" and took exception to those who blamed Euripides for writing "many tragedies that end in misfortune" (*pollai autou eis dystychian teleutôsin* [*Poetics* 1453B]). Modern critics, in contrast, have problems dealing with Euripidean plays that do not appear to end in misfortune, and often deny that they are tragedies at all.

The immediate issue, I think, is how well Aristotle actually remembered Sophocles' *Oedipus*. Does what he says about the play mesh with what is in it?

In *Poetics* 1452A, to illustrate his notion of tragic reversal (*peripeteia*), Aristotle cites the arrival of the Corinthian in Sophocles' *Oedipus* who comes, he says, "to cheer Oedipus up and release him from his fear about his mother (*apallaxôn tou pros tên mêtera phobou*); but when he has shown who he is, he has achieved the opposite." Thomas Tyrwhitt summed matters up well some two centuries ago: "It is just as well we have the tragedy still surviving, for otherwise we would be bound to believe on the basis of Aristotle's statement that the messenger came for the express purpose of releasing Oedipus from fear about his mother."[30] Similarly, R. D. Dawe observes that "the role of the Corinthian messenger is curiously garbled by Aristotle. . . . What the messenger actually comes to do is to offer Oedipus the throne of Corinth now that Polybus is dead."[31] We should perhaps qualify Dawe's remark with the cautionary note that there is no evidence that the Corinthian has any authority to offer Oedipus the throne of Corinth. Dawe himself acknowledges that the man "is not an official representative."[32] Dawe, Tyrwhitt, and others are surely right when they say that what Aristotle says about the Corinthian is flatly contradicted by the play we have.

If we believe, as Carlo Gallavotti does, that to fault Aristotle on this score, as Tyrwhitt did, is just nit-picking, we should glance at another curious error about *Oedipus* that Aristotle makes when discussing dramatic prologues in *Rhetoric* 2.1415A.[33] "The tragic poets," he says, "make things clear about the drama, if not immediately, like Euripides, at least somewhere in the prologue as Sophocles does: 'My father was Polybus.' " Now Aristotle gives us his own definition of a prologue at *Poetics* 1452B: "A prologue is the whole part of the tragedy preceding the entrance of the chorus." In Sophocles' *Oedipus,* the chorus enters at line 151; the first 150 lines, then, are the Aristotelian prologue. But Oedipus does not say "My father was Polybus" until line 774, more than *halfway through the play.*

Again, scholars have bent over backward trying to help Aristotle out. Lane Cooper translates: "Yet somewhere in the earlier part ('prologue' in a very loose sense), like Sophocles . . . " Similarly E. M. Cope: "It seems that Aristotle has here used *prologos* in a more comprehensive sense than that which it usually bears."[34] The problem is that Aristotle is so using the term prologue in his discussion of dramatic prologues, not in some other context where it might pass as simply a casual aside.

Perhaps Aristotle was confused because Oedipus' statement looks as though it *should* be in a prologue. The Oedipus myth was sufficiently popular with ancient tragedians that Aristotle may have confused the Sophoclean *Oedipus* with a play in which Oedipus does claim Polybus as his father in the prologue. In the only other *Oedipus* that survives to us from antiquity, that of Seneca, in fact, we find precisely such a statement in the prologue, at line 12: "how successfully I had escaped my father Polybus' realm of power!"

There is, of course, a more radical explanation, raised tentatively by Frederic Parsons, as he was writing about Aristotle's puzzling attribution of "My father was Polybus" to the prologue of the *Oedipus*. There might be "some variation or omission in our present editions."[35] Parsons presumably meant variation or omission in editions of Sophocles. But there is also the possibility that Sophocles' *Oedipus,* as we now have it, is structurally different from the play Aristotle read. We cannot pursue this possibility, since there is no means of knowing the answer. I raise the point only to remind the reader that unless we allow for such a possibility, we must concede that Aristotle's recollection of Sophocles' *Oedipus* is not very good, and that his judgments on the play are not definitive.

But as always with the *Oedipus,* observing one issue tends to blind us to others. We should not be so distracted by discussion of Aristotle's attribution of the declaration "My father was Polybus" to the prologue that we neglect the curious nature of the statement itself. Why does Oedipus not say "My father *is* Polybus"? There is no indication that Oedipus has learned of Polybus' death until Jocasta relays news of it to him from the Corinthian almost two hundred lines later (956).

Detection and Dialectic

To note that Aristotle is inexact in some of the many external references he makes to other works is a very different proposition from suggesting that a passage in Sophocles or Euripides is "flawed" because there is a conflict between it and other internal statements on the same subject. No good artistic reason exists for assuming such conflicts are there without the knowledge of the writer. For drama *is* conflict, and part of the special quality of Oedipus, both play and protagonist, is the frequency with which conflicting statements occur. To assume the writer either did not notice them or thought they were unimportant is to assume if not a modern, at least a very unclassical, sloppiness of composition, as unflattering to a fifth-century poet as to a fifth-century sculptor.

Many "contradictions" we see in Greek tragedy highlight what is wrong not with the poet's work but with out interpretation of it. We often ascribe something to artistic oversight or structural flaw when accepting its intentionality forces conclusions we find personally distasteful. In satirizing Anthony Fitton-Brown's explanation of some "inconsistencies" in how Sophocles deals with Oedipus' feet, Dawe observes: "It is better to accept the inconsistency... as typical of Sophoclean technique than to invest the author with the attributes of a paediatric (not to say podiatric) Agatha Christie."[36] Dawe's resentment, in this case, is ostensibly directed against what he calls "arguments from real life," based on analogies between the stage world and the world of common experience. In practice, scholars use such arguments from the real world whenever it suits them, regardless of how much they criticize others for doing so. Dawe employs the popular terminology of modern medicine to provide his own explanation on the same page he attacks Fitton-Brown: "Sophoclean characters in other plays besides this one seem at times to suffer from dramatically convenient transitory amnesia."

This statement is a severe indictment of Sophocles' dramatic skill. It is used to justify dismissing as insignificant major contradictions in matters of memory, evidence, and testimony that arise in *Oedipus*— even though the play deals with the attempt to discover past crimes and is about memory and the mind.

E. R. Dodds went further than Dawe. He denied that Sophocles' *Oedipus* is a drama of detection—although it has numerous elements that make it precisely that, however much it may be based on myth or folktale. Undermining Dodd's contention is the ubiquity of legal language in the play. A. A. Long, writing of the changes in Sophoclean language in the later tragedies, notes: "The atmosphere of the lawcourts still pervades central scenes in the *Oedipus Tyrannus* and *Electra*."[37] Knox observes: "The action of the play is a characteristically Athenian process: it is a legal investigation."[38] In that sense, of course, the play is quite likely to refract fifth-century "real life." We may compare J.-P. Vernant, who cites Louis Gernet's unpublished lectures: "The tragic writers' use of a technical legal vocabulary underlines the affinities between the most favored tragic themes and certain cases which fell within the competence of the courts. . . . the tragic poets make use of this legal vocabulary, deliberately exploiting its ambiguities, its fluctuations and its incompleteness."[39] Knox's stress on the play's *Athenian* nature is appropriate, as we will see later. But I would suggest that Oedipus' actions seem designed to convey the *flavor* of a legal investigation rather than actually to be one. True, the language is that of the Athenian court. There is a search for evidence, cross-examination of witnesses, passing of judgment, and sentencing. There is even the inner audience, the chorus, before which most cross-examinations occur, and to whose opinion the protagonists both refer and defer. Yet the single man who plays prosecutor, judge, and agent of punishment quickly comes to regard himself as the accused. In the final interrogations, Oedipus is no longer interested in the plague and in Thebes, only in his own guilt and his personal crimes.

A more useful comparison may be made between *Oedipus* and Plato's *Apology* rather than between *Oedipus* and a surviving speech actually delivered in an Athenian court. Sophocles, like Plato, allows us to be present, as it were, at the "trial" of a famous wise man. And both their wise men claimed a special relationship between their investigations and responses received from the Delphic oracle. Plato's Socrates (*Apology* 20E–21A) says his admirer Chaerephon asked the shrine whether there was anyone wiser than Socrates.[40] And Socrates, though doubtful of the oracle's correctness, spent his hours trying to find out in what sense the oracle might be right. Oedipus does much the same. But whereas Socrates is found guilty by the judges at his trial, not by himself, Oedipus finds himself guilty.

A verdict of "guilty" is final in most legal systems if no appeal is lodged. In Socrates' case, Plato makes an extralegal, posthumous appeal. But there again, the Platonic Socrates clearly considered himself innocent to the end. Since the Sophoclean Oedipus, in contrast, comes to accept his guilt, it is obviously difficult to appeal a judgment that the accused makes against himself and finds proven. But we do have the evidence presented: the play itself. And if we do not examine conflicting statements in the play, we do not examine the evidence. For the only "evidence" the play has to offer is verbal.

The Nature of the Evidence

Plato's *Apology* is a work of dramatic reenactment. The real trial is over. What is at issue is not whether Socrates will be acquitted or condemned but whether the judges were right to condemn him—or even permit his trial on the charges brought against him. When we read the *Apology,* then, we allow for the possibility that the verdict was mistaken, even unjust. In contrast, we approach the trial of Oedipus with the assumption that the verdict is correct. We rarely concern ourselves with how convincing the case against him is, or with the fact that no *evidence* is brought against him such as would have been accepted in an Athenian court of law.

The charges against Oedipus are based entirely on his own testimony against himself and unsupported hearsay. On the first matter, Athenian law made clear that "a litigant could not be his own witness."[41] On the second, Oedipus could not have been convicted on the basis of hearsay in an Athenian court. Although under some circumstances hearsay was admissible as evidence in a Roman court of law, it was inadmissible in *Athens.* A. R. W. Harrison points out: "Hearsay evidence was ruled out by law, the only exception being in the case of what a dead man was alleged to have said."[42] Demosthenes provides the proof for this rejection of hearsay in two passages. First, *Euboulides* 4: "Nor do the laws allow hearsay as evidence, not even on the most serious charges." Second, *On the Crown* 2.7: "They do not permit hearsay evidence from a living witness, only [a deposition] from one now dead."[43] A particularly relevant example of such testimony for the dead occurs, by the way, in Plato's *Apology* 21A, where Socrates asks for a deposition by the deceased Chaerephon's brother to be accepted as evidence about Chaerephon's consultation of the Delphic oracle. Accepted forms of evidence are *nomoi* ("laws"), *martyres* ("witnesses"), *synthêkai* ("agreements"), *basanoi* ("tortures"), *horkoi* ("oaths")—and not, we will note, either hearsay or oracles.[44]

Unlike Plato, who presents Socrates' trial only through Socrates' eyes, Sophocles gives us all the testimony on which Oedipus bases his judgment and lets us see the situation through a number of different eyes. We have the chance to make some objective assessment of the information Oedipus has at his disposal and to note what he does not take into account. To decline that chance is to fail to interpret the play. There is no sound reason not to read the play with the same critical attention to argument that we would accord a Platonic dialogue or a modern play, much less a trial.

Questions and Answers

Playwrights both comic and tragic realized that audiences notice and understand—or think they understand—matters that elude the characters in a play. And since one ancient comedy makes particular fun of dialectic, it is worthwhile drawing our example from it.

In Aristophanes' *Clouds* 658–66, Socrates asks his would-be student Strepsiades to list the male quadrupeds, then berates Strepsiades for including the word *alektryôn,* which, he says, can be applied to both a rooster and a hen. To keep Aristophanes' jest, I have translated *alektryôn* as "chicken":

> *Socrates*: There are other things you need to learn first:
> the right names of the male quadrupeds.
> *Strepsiades*: But I know the males, unless I'm out of my mind: the
> ram, the buck, the bull, the hound-dog, the chicken
> (*alektryôn*).
> *Socrates*: See your mistake? You use the same word for the
> male chicken as you do for the female.
> *Strepsiades*: How do you mean?
> *Socrates*:   You'd say "chicken" and
> "chicken."
> *Strepsiades*: By Poseidon, you're right. What should I call them?
> *Socrates*: The female's a cockette (*alektryaina*), the male a cock
> (*alektôr*).[45]

Not only is Socrates' final answer absurd, but nobody, not even Socrates, points out that neither cock nor bogus "cockette" is a quadruped. The fact that no one explicitly notes the oversight does not mean that Aristophanes neither intends nor expects his audience to notice the omission—though some modern readers do miss the point. Nor does it mean the poet himself thought cockerels were quadrupeds. Rather, we are seeing a rhetorical phenomenon well known to ancient critics and not altogether different from what we have nowadays come to call subliminal suggestion. It involves letting the "facts" speak for themselves—a mode of argument that, according to the ancients, made the effect of one's criticism more formidable (*deinoteros*). Demetrius states it this way in *On Style* 288 : "The effect is more formidable (*deinoteros*) because it is achieved by letting the fact make itself manifest (*emphainontos*) rather than having the speaker make the point for himself." The figure of speech was called *emphasis* in antiquity—but how different it is from what we mean by "emphasis." When we "emphasize" something, we proclaim it to our readers, leaving no doubt that we want its presence known. The ancient writer does precisely the opposite. Quintilian defines *emphasis* as a figure of speech in which "something latent is 'dug out of' something said" (*ex aliquo dicto latens aliquid eruitur* [*Instructing the Orator* 9.2.64]).[46] It is, in short, a kind of hidden meaning, innuendo, or double entendre. Unfortunately, classicists are uneasy with double entendre and sometimes assume that unless writers underscore a point, they are not making it at all.

Emphasis in the ancient sense is the technique Aristophanes uses in the discussion about cocks and coquettes in the *Clouds*. The poet *himself* does not explain to us that Socrates and Strepsiades have both missed the crucial point: that roosters are not quadrupeds. He leaves the reader to deduce this independently. Here the *Tractatus Coislinianus* 4 may help. The writer observes: "Comedy differs from *loidoria* (reproach, abuse) in this way. *Loidoria* goes over the bad things it adduces without disguise. But comedy needs what is called *emphasis* ('double entendre, innuendo')." Aristotle in *Nichomachean Ethics* 1128A20 makes much the same point as he draws the distinction between the *loidoria* and *aischrologia* (foul language) of old comedy, and the *hyponoia* ("underlying meaning") of new comedy. *Emphasis,* then, is an alternative to outright abuse. And it is often preferred not only by ancient comic writers but by other kinds of critics too.

Demetrius, in *On Style* 288, cites a passage from Plato's *Phaedo* 59C in which he says the philosopher wishes to reproach (*loidorêsai*) Aristippus and Cleombrotus for not visiting Socrates in prison. He does not wish to attack the men openly, for this would commit him to reproaching them. Instead, Plato has Phaedo enumerate those present when Socrates died. When asked whether Aristippus and Cleombrotus were there, Phaedo answers: "No, they were in Aegina." Everything, Demetrius concludes, is revealed in (*emphainetai*) the expression "They were in Aegina."

For some readers, however, the facts do not speak for themselves. This is the notorious difficulty with many such double entendres, as Aristotle points out in *Rhetoric* 2.1412A–B when citing Theodore's jest about a Thracian harp player called Nicon. Theodore said: *Thratt' ei sy* ("You Thracian slave") while pretending that he meant *thratteis sy*("you play the harp"). "But," Aristotle adds, "if you don't know that he was a Thracian, there will be no evidence of a joke." In similar fashion, we may not be aware that Aegina is not far from Athens and that passage from Aegina to Athens by boat cost only two obols, as Plato himself tells us in *Gorgias* 511B. Editors of the *Phaedo* usually ignore Demetrius' interpretation of *Phaedo* 59C or dispute it.[47] Callimachus says in *Epigram* 24 that a Cleombrotus (possibly the one mentioned in the *Phaedo*) committed suicide after reading the *Phaedo*. R. Hackforth, presumably following Cicero's *Tusculan Disputations* 1.84, suggests Cleombrotus may have done so because he was convinced by the arguments it contains on the immortality of the soul.[48]

Emphasis was already in common use as a rhetorical term before the end of the fifth century B.C., and several ancient writers other than Plato were judged most expert in it. Dionysius of Halicarnassus (*Thucydides* 16) points out that there are some passages where Thucydides failed in his perfect economy and craftsmanship, "or reeled off easily without the slightest lurking trace (*emphasis*) of his famous forcefulness (*deinotês*)." And the verbal form *emphanizô*, "reveal," often used in contexts where the figure of speech *emphasis* occurs, finds a particularly striking instance in the following passage from Euripides' *Philoctetes* found in the *Rhetoric to Alexander* 1433B12 (fragment 797 Nauck): "Even though he reckons he has annihilated my arguments by conceding that he has acted unjustly, I shall make them. So you will hear and know the facts from me, and his own words will reveal (*emphaniei*) him to you as what he is." *Emphasis* could be at its most lethal in courts of law. Quintilian talks of persuasive speech in court as follows *(Instructing the Orator 9.2.71–72)*:

> The facts themselves should lead the judge to suspect. Our job is to remove everything else so that only this conclusion remains. Use of the emotions helps a lot. It's good to break the flow of your speech with silence, to hesitate. Then you may be sure the judge will search out that certain something which he probably would not believe if he heard it actually stated. You may be sure he will believe what he thinks he himself has discovered. . . . In sum: *the judge is most likely to believe what is figured in our speech if he thinks we are unwilling to say it (sic maxime iudex credit figuris si nos putat nolle dicere).*

To return, then, to Strepsiades and Socrates: Aristophanes' parody of dialectic leaves the error in Socrates' cross-questioning for the reader to discover, in an ancient, "emphatic" manner. His poetic technique becomes, in Demetrius' terms, more *deinos* ("formidable"). Its "formidable" quality in this context is particularly delicious since it is directed against one of the great experts in formidable speech: Socrates himself. Indeed, one of the accusations leveled against Socrates at his trial, and the very first one he seeks to refute, as we see in Plato's *Apology* 17B and elsewhere, is that he was *deinos legein* ("formidable at speaking"). Aristophanes shows us that this famous master of refutation, *elenchos*, the great questioner, can become so intent on proving one point that he fails to observe, and thus incorporates into his argument, an error on another.

Not only does Aristophanes' Socrates produce, in the name of grammatical analogy, a nonexistent "cockette"; he inadvertently classifies cockette and cock as quadrupeds. The error is absorbed as fact by Strepsiades. One of the few lessons he remembers from his Socratic education is that female cocks are "cockettes." It is not unlikely that Aristophanes chose the confusion over feet in this scene to allude to the Oedipal nature of Socratic inquiry which is so heavily based on the "true" definition of words and which leads in the *Clouds* to a justification of flogging one's father and mother. After all, Plato's man, defined as a "wingless biped," resembles a plucked rooster, as Diogenes the Cynic noted (Diogenes Leartius 6.40).

Knox suggests that "Oedipus' methods of investigation are those of the critical spirit of the age which he represents."[49] How correct an assessment is this? True, Oedipus uses the *vocabulary* of such investigation, and he poses as a cross-examiner in the Socratic manner. But like the Aristophanic Socrates, he focuses so intently on one area of inquiry that he overlooks important details and ambiguities in other areas. The result is that it is not Oedipus himself, but an old slave of Laios, who finds himself on the "formidable brink of speech" (*pros autôi . . . tôi deinôi legein*) in the final stages of the investigation in *Oedipus* 1169. Sophocles' Oedipus, like Aristophanes' Socrates or Herodotus' Croesus in *Histories* 1.53 ff, is as likely to reach dubious, possibly wrong conclusions on the basis of testimony as to reach conclusions that are arguably right. Socrates' dialectical weakness in Aristophanes' *Clouds*, his missing the point in his interchanges with Strepsiades, is the ruination of Oedipus and of other characters in Greek tragedy and in Herodotean history who overlook ambiguities in situations they confront and in responses received not only from other humans but from divine sources, particularly the oracle of Apollo at Delphi.

At this point a vast chasm appears to open up between literary convention and documentary evidence for oracular consultations. If Joseph Fontenrose is correct in maintaining that genuinely "historical" responses given to seekers of oracles at Delphi were *not* ambiguous, then Greek (and Roman) literature has left us an image of Delphic ambiguity that is at odds with Delphic practice. "Ambiguous and obscure commands or prohibitions, conditioned commands and predictions, and extraordinary future predictions are characteristic of Legendary oracles, and are not found among Historical oracles," Fontenrose contends.⁵⁰ He thus concludes that all Herodotus' oracles are either quasi-historical or legendary, and admits no historical responses before 440 B.C., curiously enough Chaerephon's consultation of Delphi on Socrates' behalf, mentioned in Plato *Apology* 21A–C. Be this as it may, oracular responses are at least as ambiguous as those of the most wily and evasive human speaker throughout the literary tradition. For Plato, as for all ancient authors, oracular utterances (including those of Delphi) are proverbially difficult to fathom and multivalent.

Oedipus' ultimately self-destructive career of investigation was approved, like Socrates', by the Delphic tripod—*triPOUS,* the "three-footed" stool upon which the priestess of Apollo sat. Indeed Oedipus, like Socrates in Aristophanes' *Clouds,* shows himself both ignorant and knowledgeable in matters of feet, of bipeds and quadrupeds no less than of tripods. His fame lies in his solution of the Sphinx's riddle, which at its most simplistic level is the ability to explain that man walks first on four feet, then on two feet, and finally on three feet. The Sphinx is herself simultaneously a woman, that is to say a biped, and a lion, that is to say a quadruped. But he himself is ruined when he accepts that his name, *OIDiPOUS,* can be appropriately etymologized as "Swollen (*OIDi*) Foot (*POUS*)" to explain the riddle of his *own* feet. He assumes his destiny must be in his name and in effect rejects the several other possible (in terms of ancient theories of language) explanations for his name that arise elsewhere in the play such as "He who knows (*OIDe*) the foot (*POUS*)" or "is known to everyone (*PASI*)." In short, he is destroyed when he settles, like Herodotus' Croesus, on the "wrong" interpretation of an ambiguity.

Oedipus may know how to *answer* questions, but he has little sense of how to *ask* questions and listen to other people's answers, or of how to prevent his interlocutor from sidetracking him or avoiding points at issue. Yet, as Knox comments, "the characteristic tone of Oedipus in the first two thirds of the play is that of an impatient, demanding questioner." Knox goes on to reckon up some of the numerous questions Oedipus raises. He poses eleven to Creon in forty lines (89–129), some nineteen to Teiresias, and so forth.[51]

Oedipus in fact asks too many questions too quickly. He rarely digests the answers to one question before asking another. When he went to Delphi to inquire who his parents were, Apollo sent him away "not honored" with an answer, he tells Jocasta; rather, the god told him that he would kill his father and have sexual intercourse with his mother (787–93). From this point on, his actions are based on the assumption that his father and mother are the people about whom he had been so uncertain in the first place, even though he concedes that the oracle did not answer his question. In short, he behaves as if the oracle had said: "Yes, your parents are those who claim to be your parents; but you will kill your father and have intercourse with your mother."

No less important, Oedipus has little sense of how to determine the credibility and truthfulness of those he asks for advice and information. He is not strong in dialectic or even in the practical techniques of cross-examining witnesses. Such a failing would have been apparent to many Athenians who participated in trials, attended comic plays, such as Aristophanes' *Wasps* and *Clouds* which presuppose familiarity with trials, or heard the famous "conversations" of Socrates.

Assessing the Evidence

Sophocles' Oedipus is unable to discern, or unwilling to make, the case for his own defense. He is similarly unwilling to hear counterarguments once he has decided on someone else's guilt. He charges his brother-in-law, Creon, with criminal conspiracy and sentences him to death without adducing any evidence of his guilt, much less putting him on trial. He acts in a most high-handed and tyrannical way. Creon, however, can at least respond to Oedipus' charges. But Oedipus does not respond to the charges he makes against himself.

Oedipus' trial is extraordinary in that we, the audience, do not find his guilt or innocence dramatically confirmed on stage, as is the guilt of Phaedra and the innocence of Hippolytus in Euripides' *Hippolytus*. For Euripides shows us the world through Phaedra's eyes as well as through Hippolytus'. In Sophocles' play, however, we are left to decide for ourselves whether Creon, Teiresias, the Corinthian, and Laios' slave are telling the truth. There is no written statement, such as Phaedra's false deposition in *Hippolytus*. There is no physical evidence such as the tokens mentioned by the scholiast on Euripides' *Phoenissae* as identifying the infant Oedipus. Our sureness that Oedipus is an incestuous parricide is based, first and foremost, on our external "knowledge" of the myth. But equally significant, it is based, like Oedipus' own self-conviction, on spoken statements, on hearsay pertaining to events that occurred long ago. And those whose testimony convinces Oedipus of his guilt often have vague identities and questionable motives.

Above all, Oedipus' conclusions are based on words and their interpretation. And words are notoriously elusive and prone to ambiguity. Yet Oedipus takes for granted that there can be a *verbal* (rather than a medical) solution to such problems as the plague afflicting Thebes as the play opens. He tells priest and people that, after much thought, he has sent Creon to Corinth to consult the oracle of Apollo at Delphi. This he considers the *only* cure (*iasin monên*) for the plague (68).[52] He must find out what to do, *drôn*, or what to say, *phônôn*, to protect the city (72). *Phônôn* does not, I think, mean "tell others to do."[53] It means Oedipus thinks that words may solve the problem, perhaps because, according to common tradition, he disposed of the Sphinx with words, not actions, by solving the riddle of the feet. Logically he, like the Sphinx, is destroyed when someone "solves" the riddle of his own feet.

Oracular responses, cross-questioning of witnesses, examination of testimony will reveal the answers; and Oedipus is sure that the *verbal* curse imposed on the killer or killers and anyone who remains silent about their identity will have its effect (231–43). Oedipus' trust in the power of words is curiously offset by his careless use of them and his careless listening. Jocasta complains publicly (914–17) that her husband is vulnerable to manipulation by a speaker who plays on his fears:

> For Oedipus upsets himself too much
> whenever stressed or pained. He turns not where
> the rational man turns, to evaluate
> the new against his past experience.
> No: he's owned by the man who speaks to him,
> provided that man says things that cause fears.

Jocasta's comments about Oedipus are interesting in several ways.

First, she suggests that Oedipus is "owned by [literally: is of] the man who speaks to him," that he *esti tou legontos,* that he is the orator's dupe. In fact, in Aristophanes' *Knights* the Paphlagonian slave (who may well caricature the Athenian demagogue, Cleon) begs Dêmos (i.e., the Athenian people) not to be the dupe of whoever happens to be speaking to him and uses exactly the same expression (*Knights* 860): "My good fellow, do not be owned by [literally: of] the speaker" (*mê isthi tou legontos*). The chorus echoes the charge later in the play (*Knights* 1111–20):

> O Dêmos, you have marvelous power.
> All humans live in fear
> of you, just as if you were
> a tyrant.

> But how easily you're led.
> You love to be flattered,
> to be totally deceived.
> You always listen gaping
> to anyone who speaks (*pros ton . . . legonta aei*) to you.
> You have a mind,
> but it is on vacation.

Second, Jocasta's contrast between Oedipus and "the rational man" is a comparison between someone controlled by anxiety about the future rather than knowledge derived from the past. Here is Aristotle's definition of fear in *Rhetoric* 2.1382A: "Let fear (*phobos*) be some pain or disorder stemming from fantasy (*phantasia*) about a future evil which will cause pain or death." The orator is supposed to manipulate the response of fear in his listeners, not they in him. The good cross-questioner should be in command of his interlocutors. So if Jocasta is correct, Oedipus has some major rhetorical weaknesses and is particularly vulnerable to suggestions that come from someone he fears or who tells him something that frightens him.

The most obviously formidable voices for Oedipus are the following: the oracle of Apollo, his brother-in-law, Creon, and the prophet Teiresias. All three affect his public and political life, and, ironically, they are precisely the sources he turns to during the crisis in Thebes. Yet Oedipus is not totally naive about the threats they could pose to him. On the contrary, his most violent outbursts of anger on stage are with Creon and Teiresias whom he quickly comes to suspect of treason. As we will see, he both trusts and distrusts Creon, believes and dismisses the prophetic powers of Teiresias and Delphi. It is not going too far to say that he trusts and believes them *because* they *are,* potentially or really, his rivals: because they do threaten him. And that is why it is so important for us to examine the characters other than Oedipus within the play, to discover what we can of their motives and ideas.

Characterization

Roland Barthes takes issue with what he perceives to be a tendency among scholars to speak of a literary character "as though he existed, as though he had a future, an unconscious, and a soul." "What we are talking about," he continues, "is his *figure* (an impersonal network of symbols combined under the proper name)."[54] One might almost conclude from his remarks that there is no human author penning the words, no human actor speaking them, no human eyes and ears seeing them and listening to them: that language can exist on its own, without the human faculties, senses, and without the human mind.

It is interesting to compare Barthes' assessment of dramatic characters with that of two very different and influential dramatists: W. S. Gilbert and Luigi Pirandello. Both dramatists wrote plays in which they describe characters, *personaggi,* either rebelling against the roles and destinies the author has selected for them (as in Gilbert's *A Sensation Novel*) or struggling to make their way into a playwright's and theatrical director's consciousness (as in Pirandello's *Six Characters in Search of an Author*) like souls demanding bodies.

Scholars, however, are inevitably more interested in what other scholars have to say about characters than in what dramatists have to say. The extent to which Barthes' criticism has taken root can be seen in a recent essay on character in Greek tragedy where Pat Easterling observes that we no longer find anyone "naively supposing that . . . stage figures can be studied as if they were beings with a continuing off-stage existence."[55] It is, of course, true in a rudimentary, formalistic way that a theatrical character in tragedy is a text performed before a human audience by a human actor who assumes a traditional mask: he or she is a visual image, a *prosôpon,* to take the Greek term in its most literal sense, or a *persona,* a "mask through which sound is made," as the Latin term is sometimes taken to mean.

Yet herein lies the irony of our own terminology of the *person* in modern literary discourse which Barthes defines, in the context cited above, as "a moral freedom endowed with motives and an overdetermination of meanings." For although we have settled on the Latin word for a dramatic mask to represent the "real" man or woman in "real" life, we sometimes forget that our term for a "real person" is itself borrowed from the terminology of the stage—and first attested in Latin in something approaching this sense by Tertullian in his discussions of the "persons" of the Trinity.

We may also overlook the aptness of such a theatrical metaphor as applied to life. As Easterling points out, it is more difficult than literary critics sometimes acknowledge to define "what constitutes a person in the real world."[56] A real "person" is himself or herself involved in complex patterns of role playing which often shift quite radically in different situations and in response to different stimuli. For if it is fair to say, as Simon Goldhill does, that the representation of a fictional character is "(over) determined by the fictional narrative in which the figure plays a part," we might add that much the same is true of living beings in "real" life.[57] People speak, express ideas, and behave in accordance with the varying languages, countries, societies, and life "scenarios" in which they are placed and defined. Since there are themes and conventions of human behavior offstage as well as on, we might wish to accord a certain validity to Ovid's remark in *Metamorphoses* 3.158–89 that nature imitates art as well as to the scholarly assumption that art imitates nature. For, granted that the human being is perhaps above all else a language-using animal, as Colin Renfrew emphasizes, we define ourselves and our roles in the various societies among which we move in verbal terms.[58] Hence the artistic convention that enables us to ascribe human qualities to anything that speaks or appears to speak.

Since we are also clothes-wearing animals and define ourselves with costumes appropriate to the roles that we choose or are pressured to adopt in different circumstances, we not only distinguish ourselves from one another within the various hierarchies of our societies, but participate in societal conventions that enable us to be acknowledged in terms of the clothes we wear. Although more numerous and varied than the masks and costumes of Greek tragedy or comedy, our clothes serve a similar enough function to make those masks a generally valid convention for representing role-playing human beings. As Aeschylus' Xerxes in *The Persians* reassures himself (and reminds the Athenians) of his continued kingship by donning new royal robes, so we, after a humiliation, may restore our status and our spirits by reasserting them in terms of our outer trappings. What complicates matters further in Greek tragedy is that two or three actors wear all the masks. Behind Creon and Teiresias lies the same *actor's* voice, not only the same author's.

Literary characters wear many masks. In the *Odyssey* Odysseus ensures his survival—and others' destruction—by disguising himself both physically and verbally, by representing himself in so many different ways to the different people he encounters that the notion of who or what the underlying man is becomes increasingly difficult to track as the epic proceeds. Crucial to the pathos of Patroclus' death in the *Iliad* is the fact that he is wearing Achilles' armor but is not Achilles: because he is thought to be, and masquerades as, the best of the Achaeans, although he is not. More ambiguously: in *Aeneid* 2.386–412, Trojan Aeneas tells Dido that he put on Greek armor during the fall of Troy.[59] In Statius' *Thebaid* 7.474–533, the distraught Jocasta cannot distinguish her son Polyneices from the other soldiers surrounding her because he is wearing armor and a visored helmet: "Under what helmet, tell me, will I find my son?" (491–92). Beneath the steely facade of the soldier is hidden another of Polyneices' many masks: that of the son. And Polyneices' tears of joy on seeing his mother become shockingly incongruous as they dampen the metal covering his face, and as he presses Jocasta to his armored bosom. There is no one "real" Polyneices: he is (among other things) the soldier, the loving son (to his mother), the hating son (to his father), the beloved brother (to Antigone), the hated brother (to Eteocles), and the loyal friend and brother-in-law (to Tydeus). The plurality of his *personae* adds to the illusion of his reality.

Just as ancient authors maintain the illusion of reality by showing the multiplicity of *personae* that may lie behind a given mask, so too they often broaden characters by alluding to their activities outside the scope of their masks within the text. In *Aeneid* 4.422, for example, we discover that Aeneas' closest confidante is not Dido but her sister, Anna, to whom, Dido says, he entrusts all his hidden, inner feelings (*arcanos . . . sensus*). But what these hidden feelings are and what is the nature of Aeneas' relationship with Anna we never learn in the *Aeneid*. If we do speculate about them on the basis of what we know from elsewhere in the tradition, we discover that sometimes Anna, rather than Dido, was Aeneas' lover.[60] Since this scenario adds more than most scholars wish to cope with about Aeneas' "offstage" existence, it is usually ignored.

What happens offstage in Greek drama can be equally perplexing. Not only does almost all violent action (killing, for example) occur beyond the audience's sight, but so do abrupt shifts in a character's mood. In Sophocles' *Oedipus*, we find Jocasta leaving the stage with Oedipus quite calmly at line 762 only to return in despair over Oedipus (911–23) after the chorus finishes its song. What happens offstage to change her mood we do not learn. Nor is this an isolated instance of such shifts in mood and character in *Oedipus*, as we will see. For *Oedipus* differs from other surviving Greek tragedies in that the central character is so focused on past memories, on events that took place offstage and at some distant time in the past, that he gradually loses track of the environment in which he exists dramatically. And the information available to the audience about what actually "happened" is fragmentary and contradictory.

I would contend, then, that not only *can* literary characters be studied "as if they were beings with a continuing off-stage existence," but that in ancient literature they *must* be so studied when the author makes it clear that they are involved in actions extending beyond the compass of the narrative and from which we, as readers, are excluded. Greek and Roman writers often supply verisimilitude by allusion, rather than by outright description as many modern novelists do, leaving us to figure out what their characters' inner thoughts and feelings are. We are thus invited, or rather forced, to make of them what we will, as we are in the case of Vergil's Aeneas or of Sophocles' Oedipus.

It is at this point we are returned to ancient *emphasis* as defined by Quintilian, with which we must come to terms if we are to cope with the rhetoric of Sophocles' *Oedipus*. Sophocles' language is at least as informed by ancient rhetoric as is that of his intellectual contemporaries in poetry, history, and philosophy. And to be informed by rhetoric, as Aristotle's *Rhetoric* makes abundantly clear, it is to be informed about the emotions and how they can be used by the speaker to his or her advantage. Rhetoric, then, is psychology. It is worth reminding ourselves of this since Freud rediscovered it, renamed it, and made it his own at that historical moment when traditional scholars were beginning to assume that rhetoric was nothing other than a means of ornamenting something essentially simple, straightforward, and classical.

1. ORACLES AND PLAGUES

Sophocles' association of Oedipus' self-discovery with a plague in Thebes is his innovation. Subsequent treatments of the myth that make the same link, notably Seneca's *Oedipus*, follow what Sophocles began.[1] The poet's Athenian audience could hardly have avoided thinking of the epidemic in the play in terms of the devastating plague of their own recent experience, in 430–28 B.C., with a recurrence in 427.[2] Although the exact date of *Oedipus'* production is not known, there is a consensus that it was produced after the Athenian plague began, somewhere between 429 and 425 B.C. Thus Sophocles' innovation endowed the myth with a very contemporary color. Victor Ehrenberg comments:

> We should not forget another aspect of the relations between the poet and the world around him. Actual persons or events may have been before the tragedian's mind when he was working on one of his plays. Men and institutions of mythology were frequently made by the "maker," or *poietes,* in the image of men and institutions directly known to him. This can go far beyond individual allusions and thus become a very substantial part of the poet's material.[3]

Sophocles' association of the Oedipus myth with the Athenian plague probably surprised his first audience more than it surprises us, exciting questions as to whether the play was primarily about contemporary Athens or remoter myth. Was there, then, a public dimension to the issues of the play itself, not just a literary and moral dimension? For plague is closely linked with war for the Athenians who, two years before the plague began, embarked on the Peloponnesian War with Sparta, Corinth and Thebes.

Apollo and Plagues

To mention a plague in Greece is to invite mention of Apollo. H. W. Parke and D. E. W. Wormell observe: "Ever since the *Iliad* the Greeks had associated Apollo particularly with epidemics, of which he could be sender and averter. At this time the specially severe incidence of the plague at Athens, due primarily to overcrowding, was obviously regarded as a special dispensation from Apollo."[4] Whether the Athenians also regarded the end of the plague as a blessing from Apollo is disputed. Certainly some believed thanks were owed to the god. Pausanias (1.3.4) says the Athenians dedicated a statue made by Calamis to Apollo Alexikakos, "Averter of Evil," because he had stopped the plague in the Peloponnesian War.[5] And the temple of Apollo at Bassae, Ictinus' work, was dedicated after the plague.[6]

But there was not universal agreement. The Athenians' attitude toward Delphi was complicated. Although—or perhaps *because*—Delphi produced political oracles and was under the influence of Athens' enemies, the Athenians insisted when they concluded the Peace of Nicias in 421 that they should have free access to the oracles and other Pan-Hellenic shrines. They certainly did not like to be excluded from Delphic services. And they went to considerable ritual effort in 426–5 B.C. to secure Apollo's favor by purifying the island of Delos, Apollo's great Ionian sanctuary, which, unlike Delphi, was under their control and accessible by the seaways which they controlled. They wanted to show gratitude for the ending of the plague, Thucydides suggests (3.87 and 104).

The literary evidence, however, suggests that resentment ran high against the Delphic oracle as an institution. Parke and Wormell conclude: "one could suppose that Athenian feeling became embittered against Delphi during the first part of the Peloponnesian War."[7] Similarly John Burnet comments on Plato's *Apology* 21B8: "The fact is that the ordinary Athenian had no great respect for the Pythian Apollo. The oracle had taken the Persian side and the Spartan side and generally opposed the Athenians who were allies of the Phocians.

When, finally, it took the side of Philip, the Athenians gave it up altogether and sent to Dodona instead for oracles."[8]

There is certainly no lack of adverse criticism of Apollo and his oracle among fifth-century poets, most notably Euripides, whose *Ion*, *Andromache*, *Electra*, and *Orestes* lash out at Delphi's corruption and the oracle's lack of wisdom. Criticism appears in the mouths of ordinary people, such as Euripides' messenger who describes the brutal murder of Achilles' son Neoptolemus in *Andromache* 1160–65. In *Electra* 276 and 972, Orestes blames Phoebus Apollo for ordering Clytemnestra's death. And in the same play the divine Castor openly blames Phoebus for Clytemnestra's murder (1296–97) and, still more stingingly, suggests that the god's oracular responses were lacking in wisdom, *asophoi* (1301–2):

> What had to be (*chreôn*) drove her to fate—
> And unwise words from Phoebus' tongue.

Castor adds a similar comment in *Electra* 1245–46:

> Phoebus, Phoebus . . . But he's my lord, I'm silent.
> Though wise, he spoke no wise advice to you.

It is not just in Euripides—the "atheistic" poet as Aristophanes suggests him to be—that we find attacks Apollo. When Plato wishes to show his displeasure with poetic representations of the gods, he selects a passage from Aeschylus. Aeschylus earns Socrates' special wrath in *Republic* 2.383A–C for having Thetis suggest that Phoebus Apollo proved false in his prophecy of family happiness for her at her wedding feast (*fragment* 350):

> Since Phoebus was a god I thought his mouth
> would not speak lies, that its prophetic skill
> would bring his words to promised flowering.
> He sang these songs himself, came to the feast
> in person. And that selfsame god who spoke:
> he killed my son.[9]

Trusting the Gods

The possibility that prophets and gods, including Apollo, might be wrong arises in Sophocles' plays too. Although Oedipus does not at first express distrust of Delphi—much less appreciate the danger of trusting the oracle—his faith is counterpoised by an almost atheistic contempt for it as the play proceeds. Oedipus has spent much of his life trying to prove the Delphic oracle wrong on another personally terrifying matter: his relationship with his parents. He even declares triumphantly, but fleetingly, that he has shown the oracle to be wrong (964–72):

> Well, well, dear wife! Who now would give a glance
> at Pythian prophecy or ominous birds
> cawing above our heads? Allegedly
> they showed I'd kill my father. Now he's dead,
> buried beneath the earth. And I, this man,
> am here and did not touch my sword.

Oedipus oscillates violently between faith and skepticism. Scholarly critics tend to assume his faith is correct and his skepticism unjustified, taking an evangelist's joy in his return to the acceptance of god. It is, of course, hard to be sure of the extent of religiosity among the Athenians, but we need not suppose an Athenian audience would have been shocked or would have disapproved when Jocasta and Oedipus disparage Apollo and his oracles in *Oedipus*.[10] It might rather have puzzled some of them that the traditionally intelligent Oedipus should believe the politicized Delphic oracle could cure the epidemic afflicting Thebes.

Sophocles' contemporary, the historian Thucydides, knew the Delphic oracle loomed large in the political maneuvers involving Athens and Sparta at the time of the plague—and the outbreak of war between the two cities a couple of years earlier. Charges and countercharges of blood-guilt were exchanged between the combatants. Thucydides, Plutarch, and Herodotus make particular mention of an ancient curse of the goddess Athena which the Spartans demanded that the Athenians expiate. The curse stemmed from an incident occurring around 600 B.C., related in Thucydides 1.126: Cylon, an Athenian athlete, attempted (and failed) to establish himself as tyrant of the city on the Delphic oracle's advice. (Let us note that the oracle prompts a political action whose aim is to overthrow the Athenian government.) The survivors of Cylon's debacle took sanctuary with the gods: in front of the altar of Athena Polias on the Athenian acropolis. They were then lured out by a promise of safety from the Athenians besieging them but were killed when they emerged.

The Spartans of Sophocles' day, during the plague and during the war between Athens and the Peloponnesian League which Sparta headed, claimed that the descendants of those who killed Cylon's allies—the members of the noble Athenian family of the Alcmaeonids—were polluting the city by their presence and demanded that they be thrown out to expiate the curse. But, Thucydides adds (1.127), Spartan motivation was recognized as not only religious but political: one of the people affected would have been the leading Athenian military and political figure, Pericles, who was related on his mother's side to those under the curse—the Alcmaeonids. Plutarch, in *Solon* 12.1–3 and *Pericles* 33.1–2, tells the same story. It was not, says Thucydides, that the Spartans expected the Athenians to banish Pericles. Rather, they hoped the scandal that made him a "religious" cause of war would lower him in Athenian eyes. Pericles, incidentally, died of the plague in 429 B.C.

It is instructive to compare the Spartan demand for the removal of blood pollution with the Delphic oracle's demand as reported to Oedipus in Sophocles' play. Thucydides supposes a patently political purpose in such dredging up of ancient curses. Similarly, in *Oedipus,* when Teiresias declares Oedipus is the blood pollution on the city, Oedipus immediately assumes Teiresias is involved in a political plot to overthrow him and gain his position as tyrant (380–89):

> Riches, tyranny, and skillfulness
> surpassing others' skill makes for a life
> much coveted. The envy that stands guard
> upon you is so great! I did not ask
> the city to put in my hands the power
> to be first lord. The city gave it me,
> this power for which Creon, a trusted man,
> a friend from my first days of lordly rule,
> now yearns to throw me out. He secretly
> creeps on me from behind, quietly works in
> a plot-weaving, king-making charlatan,
> a treacherous liar who sees personal gain
> but was born sightless in the trade he plies.

Unlike Thucydides, Oedipus does not consider the next possibility: that a political purpose may underlie the oracle's apparent demand for the banishment of those causing the "pollution." He never questions the truth of the oracle reported to him, although it is reported by a man he comes to suspect of plotting against him: his brother-in-law, Creon. Nor do most critics of the play. Yet only a person who believes that the murder of kings causes plagues is likely to believe that plagues can be cured by finding the murderers of kings.

The oracles and verbal inquiries that obsess Sophocles' Oedipus do not have much of a role in Thucydides' account of the Athenian plague. On the contrary, the historian says oracles and prayers were no help against the epidemic (2.44): "Similarly ineffectual were prayers to the gods, consultations of oracles, and suchlike activities; it finally came to the point that people were overwhelmed by the disaster and gave up on them all." Thucydides leaves no doubt that he and others thought the plague arose from "natural" circumstances, originated overseas, and was passed on by contagion. Similarly the chorus of the Theban people in Sophocles' *Oedipus* 181 comments that "unlamented children lie pitifully dead upon the plain, bringing death (*thanatophora*)." The remark suggests that the contemporary audience "must have been aware of the dangers of infection and contagion, otherwise Sophocles' one-word allusion to the ideas would not have been understood."[11]

Nowhere does Thucydides suggest that an unsolved crime might really be the cause. Indeed, Fontenrose's analysis of Delphic responses argues that Delphi was not much consulted on such national catastrophes: "Though plague, famine, and other catastrophies . . . account for 41 Legendary consultations and the maladies of individuals . . . for 9 more, only one Historical is said to have been made for such a reason."[12]

There were, of course, recollections of old prophecies at the time of the plague. Thucydides (2.54) says the Athenians "understandably recalled a verse which the old men claimed had been delivered in the past, and which said: 'There will come a Dorian war and plague (*loimos*) with it.' " Others, he adds, disputed the text and thought the word was *limos* ("famine"), not *loimos* ("plague"). It was, Thucydides says, a case of people "adjusting their memory to suit their experiences." Perhaps it was their memories of reading or hearing Homer or Hesiod. The *Iliad* begins with the dilemma of the Achaeans faced with war and a plague. And in Hesiod, *Works and Days* 242–43, Zeus punishes errant humanity by bringing upon them "famine and plague together (*limon homou kai loimon*), and the peoples perished." Similarly, Herodotus links *loimos* and *limos* in 7.171. Such juggling with words in search of an explanation was not limited to the superstitious, but applied by the witty to make pungent modifications of familiar phrases. Peiraeus, for example, was the *limên* ("harbor") of Athens. Pericles, according to Aristotle *Rhetoric* 1411A, observed that the island of Aegina was the *lêmê(n)*—not the "harbor" but the "eyesore"—of the Peiraeus.[13]

Oedipus' belief that consultation of the Delphic oracle was the *only* possible way to deal with the plague would have struck many of Sophocles' contemporaries as old-fashioned, not efficacious, and politically suspect. Oedipus too may be "adjusting . . . memory to . . . experiences."

In more than half the consultations of the Delphic oracle that Fontenrose accepts as historical, "the motives of consultations are mainly religious or political."[14] Such political and religious consultations were common and were even approved by notable intellectuals. Fontenrose reminds us that Plato's Socrates "would have his ideal state refer to the Delphic Apollo . . . foundations of cults, sacrifices, and other worship of gods, daimones, and heroes"—and, we should add, "services for the dead," though not plagues, as we can see from *Republic* 4 (427B).[15] Nonetheless the very first genuinely "historical" consultation of Delphi, according to Fontenrose in his study of the oracle, is that by Socrates' friend Chaerephon a decade or so before the *Oedipus* was written and which is first mentioned in Plato's *Apology*. Chaerephon's embassy involved a personal and intellectual question: "Is anyone wiser than Socrates?" (*Apology* 21).

Although I think Fontenrose too skeptical about the historicity of earlier consultations, most notably in his unwillingness to accept as authentic any of Herodotus' numerous references to embassies to Delphi and their responses, let us simply assume, for the moment, that he is right: historical occasions for consultation were usually priestly. The opening of Sophocles' *Oedipus*, then, sets the right atmosphere.

Public and Private Questions

As the play begins, Oedipus publicly confronts a gathering of citizens led by a priest and asks why they are sitting at his threshold. The priest responds to Oedipus' question with one of his own: the petitioners wish to know what Oedipus proposes to do about a plague afflicting Thebes. Oedipus replies that he has sent his brother-in-law, Creon, to consult the oracle of Apollo at Delphi. The play, then, begins with two questions: Oedipus' question to the assembled people ("What are you doing at my palace?") and the priest's question to Oedipus ("What are you doing about the plague?").

The priest, the public he represents, and Oedipus, whom priest and public approach as if he were an oracle, are all invoking a higher authority they can defer to in this time of crisis. The dilemma of the plague is passed on from people through priest to tyrant and thence, by means of an ambassador, to the god Apollo. The problem of the plague is, of course, indubitably a public issue. But the public questions raised at the outset soon fade. As the play proceeds, the information—or apparent information—about the plague and its "cure" that Oedipus gathers in a series of conversations and arguments raises a second and entirely personal question, which he nonetheless discusses publicly and which becomes progressively more important to him. That question is: "Who are my parents?"

At the best of times there are dangers in asking—much less in trying to answer—two or more apparently separate sets of questions simultaneously, as Seneca's Corinthian messenger tells Oedipus (Seneca, *Oedipus* 829–32). Most obviously, there is the risk that one will come to associate the two lines of inquiry, to blur the boundaries of distinction between them. The public question of the plague, though it arises in the narrative before Oedipus' private question about his origins, is, we gradually discover, the more recent in Oedipus' mind. As the play proceeds, we learn that Oedipus has spent much of his life trying in vain to discover who he is. But the extent of his preoccupation with his identity is not evident in his apparently confident statements during the opening scene of the play. In fact, we get only a slight inkling of his anxiety about his origins before it is dragged out openly in the midst of a public quarrel between Oedipus and another religious leader: the seer Teiresias. Nor do we appreciate the degree to which his origins preoccupy Oedipus until an anonymous stranger arrives from Corinth announcing the death of the man who certainly regarded himself as Oedipus' father: Polybus, king of Corinth. From then on, the search for his identity obsesses Oedipus to the exclusion of all else.

Oedipus' obsession with his origins leaves him curiously vulnerable to an interlocutor. For if the interlocutor is (or becomes) aware of the obsession, he may use it against Oedipus. Like Socrates in the *Clouds,* Oedipus becomes so intent on establishing one point that he makes critical errors or oversights in his inquiry about the other and thus commits a compound error. Oedipus' mingling of private questions about his past with public investigation of the plague allows personal and public inquiry to merge—with disastrous consequences for himself, others, and indeed for the state as a whole. Whenever Oedipus encounters someone who knows or senses his private anxieties, he is easily distracted from public business and even lured into establishing links between the public and the private questions on his mind.

Let us examine the steps by which Sophocles proceeds. A priest asks Oedipus for help; Oedipus says he has sent Creon, his brother-in-law, to Delphi for oracular advice; at Creon's suggestion, Oedipus has also summoned the prophet Teiresias. Oedipus is, then, at the center of a priestly world—and a priestly world mediated by Creon who, as we will see, is at least potentially his political rival. Oedipus seems to believe what priestly people say. The way he addresses Teiresias in 300–304 suggests that he honors the prophet; he even calls him, as he calls Creon, *anax* ("king" or "lord" [304]). Oedipus, for all his professed skepticism later in the play, clearly accepts the principle that oracular sources, particularly Apollo, can predict the course of events and resolve problems. The priest addressing Oedipus calls the plague (as does Thucydides' oracle) a *loimos* (*Oedipus* 28). And Oedipus, in responding to him, takes it for granted that there can be a *verbal* solution to the problem the *loimos* poses. Here he goes beyond even the Platonic Socrates, who claims in *Symposium* 201D that by making sacrifices the prophetess Diotima of Mantineia ("Prophetville") was able to put off the disease (*nosos*) for ten years before the plague (*loimos*) actually occurred.

Oedipus makes it clear that he regards Delphi as the obvious recourse at this critical juncture (65–77):

> You are not waking me from sleep.
> No: understand that I've wept many tears,
> and traveled many roads in wandering thought,
> I looked thoroughly. I kept finding
> only one cure, and I've acted on it.
> I've sent Menoeceus' son, my brother-in-law
> Creon, off to Phoebus' Delphic (*Pŷthika*) shrine,
> to delve into (*pythoith'*) what I might do (*drôn*) or say (*phônôn*)

to guard this city. It's time. He's due.
I'm pained, worried about what he's doing.
He's been gone more than the usual time,
the needed time. Still, when he does arrive,
I'd be an evil man if I did not
do everything suggested by the god.

As we have seen in the Introduction, *phônôn* does not mean "tell others to do."[16] It means, rather, that Oedipus thinks there is a verbal solution to the problem. And, much in the style of Plato's Cratylus, he finds, as a riddler might, answers within the scope of what scholars are pleased to call "folk etymology." Oedipus' turn to Delphi seems reinforced by his wordplay between *Pŷthika* ("Pythian") and *pythoith'* ("might try to learn").[17] I have approximated a translation with an English play between Delphi and "delving." Oedipus is doing much the same thing as we find in *The E at Delphi* (385B), where Plutarch—himself an official of the Delphic shrine—explains Apollo's epithet "Pythian" as follows: "He is *Pythios* for those who are trying to learn and ask questions (*diapynthanesthai*)."

Modern scholars, often uncomfortable with wordplay, argue that Sophocles' audience would not connect "Pythian" with *pythoith'* ("inquiry"), since "apart from anything else there is a difference in quantity" between the long *y* of *Pŷthika* and the short *y* of *pythoith'*.[18] But aside from the fact that ancient authors routinely disregard differences in vowel quantity when making wordplays, several other adjectives meaning "Pythian" have short vowels exactly like that found in *pythoith'*: *Python* in *Oedipus* 152, *Pythios* in *Oedipus at Colonus* 1049, and *pythomantin* in *Oedipus* 965.[19]

We should not be surprised that Oedipus has a little of Cratylus in him. After all, he disposed of the Sphinx with words, not actions. Here R. G. A. Buxton's comments on "the connection that was felt to exist between professing medicine and professing rhetoric" are helpful. Buxton adduces a passage from Antiphon mentioned in Plutarch's *Lives of the Ten Orators*: "He [Antiphon] advertised that he has the power of curing those that were in trouble by means of speech (*dia logon therapeuein*); and discovering the causes of their sickness by enquiry he consoled the sick; but thinking that the profession was beneath his dignity he turned to rhetoric."[20]

Oedipus' turn toward Delphi distinguishes him from Thucydides' Athenians, who, when talking of their plague, almost all gave up on oracles and religious acts when the epidemic peaked. Oedipus becomes convinced that the city will be saved if he can find the killer or killers who, according to the Delphic oracle (as reported by Creon), are responsible for "polluting" the city. He will discover the guilty by cross-questioning witnesses and examining verbal testimony and is sure that by imposing a *verbal* curse on the killer or killers and anyone who remains silent about their identity, he will force them out into the open (231–43). That is why it is incomprehensible and exasperating to him that a seer and priest, Teiresias, should claim to know who is the "accursed one" but refuse to tell. Teiresias, in Oedipus' terms, is not only jeopardizing the well-being of the city but, ineluctably, placing himself under the curse Oedipus has pronounced.

Here, perhaps, another comparison between Sophocles' own world and that of Theban myth may be helpful. Although the Athenian plague ended and Pericles died of it within a couple of years of its onset, the wars associated with it did not. They continued, on and off, until after Sophocles' own death in 406 B.C. Similarly, the horrors afflicting mythical Thebes do not end with Oedipus' self-punishment. True, Oedipus concludes that he is the pollution on the city. He finds himself guilty of murder and incest, blinds himself, and urges Creon to banish him. True, the chorus, with the wise air of a Herodotean Solon addressing Croesus, intones in the disputed lines that are found at the end of the play: count no man happy until he is dead.[21] But Oedipus is not yet dead; his sufferings and those of Thebes are not yet over.

Will the plague that besets the city end with Oedipus' self-conviction and self-punishment? Will all be well once Creon is ruler and Oedipus in exile? The play does not answer these questions—though the unanimous verdict of other mythic accounts does. Thebes' troubles will not abate; on the contrary, they will worsen. But Sophocles' characters, chorus, and audience become so involved in Oedipus' sufferings that they, like Oedipus, ultimately forget the city's suffering. After the opening interchanges, none of the main characters seems much more concerned about ending the plague than does Oedipus. Even Teiresias, who claims to know its cause, acts as though it is better not discussed.

If we are believers and assume the Theban plague does end with Oedipus' self-punishment, we must still recall that Greek tragedians, including Sophocles in his *Antigone* and *Oedipus at Colonus,* insist that fratricidal civil war ensues, followed by the tyranny of Creon, and finally the annihilation of Thebes in the generation of Oedipus' grandchildren. Much of this horror is treated by dramatists as the legacy of curses Oedipus imposes on those who he believes have done him wrong.

Tyranny Within and Without

Nosos is the most common word for "plague" in Sophocles' *Oedipus* and in Thucydides, but its use is not restricted among writers to physical illnesses. When Oedipus addresses the assembled petitioners, he talks of his own mental suffering as *nosos* (58–64):

> My poor sad sons, I know what you yearn for
> as you come here. It's not unknown to me.
> I'm well aware that all of you are sick (*noseite*);
> Yet, sick as you are (*nosountes*), not one of you
> has sickness (*nosei*) to match mine. Your suffering
> comes to each one individually,
> to no one else, whereas my soul moans
> for city, self, and for each one of you.

The meaning of *nosos* may also be extended into a political metaphor. Plato describes in book 5 of the *Republic* (470C) the conflicts among the Greek states not just as civil wars but as themselves a kind of *nosos*, "sickness": "in such a situation Greece is sick." Many in Sophocles' audience may have shared Plato's view that the internecine wars among Greeks are "the ultimate sickness (*nosêma*) of the *polis*" (*Republic* 8.544C)—a point Plato makes several times elsewhere in the *Republic*, especially in book 8 (563E, 564B). Indeed, as we can see from a statement attributed to Alcmaeon, disease arises from the supreme rule, the *monarchia*, of one of the body's powers. Health lies in the balance, the *isonomia*, of the body's powers.[22]

The preceding observations are important to Sophocles' play since Oedipus is himself described on several occasions as the tyrant of his city. When Creon challenges Oedipus, Oedipus tells him, as T. B. L. Webster notes, "that the tyrant can use any law he pleases, like the Zeus of the *Prometheus*. . . . The tyrant denounces the elementary rights of free speech and equality of opportunity."[23]

Despite the occasional argument by modern scholars that "tyrant" and "tyranny" are not necessarily bad words for a fifth-century Athenian, the majority of ancient Greek writers disagree. In fact, when Creon's herald appears in Athens (Euripides, *Suppliants* 399) asking "Who is the tyrant of the land?" he is rebuked sternly, if not without dramatic irony, by Theseus, king of Athens (*Suppliants* 403–5):

> First, stranger, you began your words upon
> a false assumption: seeking a tyrant here.
> No one man rules this city, it is free.

The champion of Athens and critic of tyranny, Theseus, is himself king of Athens. And it is only a matter of moments before the wily Theban herald exposes at least something of Theseus' own autocratic nature.

Euripides, like Sophocles, knew that the Athenian democracy of his own day had some features of tyranny about it. His *Suppliants* was written and performed somewhere around 424 B.C., possibly during the lifetime of the popular leader Cleon who, many thought, exercised an almost despotic control over Athens. Cleon himself had succeeded Pericles, about whose political power Thucydides (2.65.9) remarked: "it was in theory a democracy; in fact it was government by the most important man." More outright statements to the effect that Pericles was indeed a tyrant were common enough, as Plutarch shows in his *Life of Pericles,* and as Ehrenberg has discussed to great effect.[24] One man's great popular leader is another man's tyrant. "Tyrant" was a common, dirty political word in Athens. That is why we should not privilege it by translating it as "king"—which, in modern English, is a neutral, even a positive and respectful, word for a ruler.

The process whereby a popular champion (*prostatês*), such as Pericles or Cleon, moves from being a leading citizen to a tyrant preoccupied Plato, who in *Republic* 8.565D–566B asks why and how such a transformation occurs:

> "How does this process of turning him around from being champion of the people (*prostatou*) to tyrant begin? Or does it become obvious that the champion (*prostatês*) begins to do the same thing as the man in the myth told about the shrine of Lycaean Zeus in Arcadia . . . that anyone who has tasted human flesh, even though it is only a morsel

sliced up along with all the others from the consecrated foods, must become a wolf?

"It is the same, then, with someone who, as champion of the people, gains a hold on the people whom he has persuaded and who now obey him. He does not keep away from the blood of his own folk. He brings someone to court on crooked charges—a favorite ploy—and kills him. He blots out a man's life; his tongue and his profane mouth get the taste of killing a fellow man. He sends men away from their homelands and murders them—while hinting at redistribution of lands and cutting up records of debt . . .

"Isn't the sequel to this inevitable and predetermined? He will either be destroyed by his enemies or rule tyrannically and change from man to wolf. . . . This is the man who stirs up hostility against the propertied classes. If he is thrown out and comes back despite the hostility of those that hate him, doesn't he return as an absolute tyrant? . . . If they don't have the power to turn him out or kill him after they have turned on him verbally and publicly, don't they get together and plot to kill him secretly?"

"That's the way it usually occurs, I think," he said.

We will return in Chapter 3 to the significance of the word *prostatês,* "champion," for Plato and for Sophocles. For the moment we must notice that Plato describes not a particular *prostatês* turned tyrant, but the *habitual* metamorphosis of democracy into wolflike despotism, and the consequences of that metamorphosis—a theme which dominates *Republic* 7–9.526A–76B. Plato notes in particular the transition from the tyrant's gentle and well-meaning facade, his denial that he really has dictatorial powers, to his subsequent and vicious persecution of his opponents (565D–567E). Similarly, in book 10 of the *Laws* (906C) Plato establishes an equation between "what we call in living bodies (*sarkinois sômasi*) a *nosêma* (disease) and what we call a plague (*loimon*) in the seasons of the years and what we call in cities and states . . . injustice (*adikian*)." In book 4 of the *Laws* (709A) he notes that the danger always exists that diseases (*nosoi*) will lead to revolution, when plagues (*loimôn*) occur.

As usual in Plato, the issue of justice in the state is indissociable from that of justice within the individual. The theme of metamorphosis symbolizes the political brutality of the tyrant and of tyranny as well as the division in the soul between the rational and the animal instincts. As the metamorphosis of the state brutalizes the state, so man is brutalized by the dominance of the despotic elements in the soul over the rational, a correspondence that makes real the grotesque desires and fanstasies of the dream (571C–D):

> "Those that awaken when we sleep," I said, "when one part of our soul is at rest—the part that approaches things reasonably and verbally, with gentle clarity, the part that rules the other element of the soul. That other element is like a wild and ferocious animal, gorged on food and drink. It leaps up, pushes sleep away from it, and goes off on a lively search to satisfy the call of its particular nature. You know it is bold and stops at nothing at these times, for it is freed from—and unburdened by—morality and thought. Its lust, people think, does not shrink at intercourse with its mother or anything human, divine, or animal. It will kill anything and has no taboos against any kind of food. To put it in one succinct statement: it will stop at nothing we would regard as mindless or disgusting."

The part of our nature that awakens when reason sleeps is nocturnal and wolflike: the Mr. Hyde in us, our propensity for lykanthropy. In short, both the individual and the state have their werewolf forms. To put it in more Sophoclean terms, the irrational soul is Oedipal. Perhaps that is why, later in Sophocles' *Oedipus,* Jocasta, concerned that Oedipus is behaving irrationally, appeals to Apollo *Lykeios* (*Oedipus* 911–23). As in *Electra* 7, Sophocles may be emphasizing the "wolf" etymology of the god's epithet. The battle waged in Sophocles' *Oedipus* may well be, like Plato's, against the wolflike tyrant within as well as the tyrant without.[25]

Here again there is a point of contact between Sophocles and Plato. Jocasta, talking to the tyrant Oedipus who fears he may marry his mother, reassures him that it is commonplace for men to dream of having sex with their mothers (*Oedipus* 980–82):

> Don't fear this marriage with your own mother.
> Many a mortal before you has slept
> with mother in dream fantasies as well.

It is not just in later antiquity, then, that "undisguised Oedipal dreams . . . were common," as we see from the long discussion of them in the second-century A.D. writer Artemidorus of Daldi's "Interpretation of Dreams," *Oneirocritica* (1.79).[26] Robert White comments:

> Artemidorus' surprisingly detailed treatment of them could be taken to imply a less rigorous repression of incestuous longings than is usual

in modern societies. But it seems more reasonable to assume that since the forbidden impulse was not disguised in the dream images themselves, this was subsequently and necessarily accomplished through an interpretation which attached an innocent symbolic meaning to' it.[27]

Oedipal dreams in ancient literature are generally associated with people in major positions of military and (or) political power—in other words with "tyrannical" types. Julius Caesar dreamed that he slept with his mother the night before he crossed the Rubicon to make the Roman empire his own. His mother, then, was Rome, whom he was to possess (Plutarch, *Caesar* 32.6). Similarly Herodotus (6.107) tells how Hippias, the last member of the tyrant Peisistratus' family, after dreaming that he had slept with his mother, took this to mean that he would return home to Athens as tyrant. The Messenian Comon even dreamed that he slept with his dead mother and that she returned to life, indicating the recovery of his conquered homeland, Messenia, from Sparta (Pausanias 4.26.3).[28]

What distinguishes Sophocles' Oedipus from Hippias or Caesar is that he takes the fantasy quite literally, rather than allegorically and politically as they do. He is afraid, whereas they, on the whole, are confident. He assumes the prophecy *must* have a negative, literal force. So do his readers. His literal interpretation of the oracle, and ours, distinguishes his tale from that of most other mythic (or mythicized) figures confronted by oracles or prophetic dreams.

Polyphony and Plague

Tyranny is not the only cause of sickness in the state, according to Plato. So we must now turn briefly to a passage in *Republic* 3. 399E–401A where Socrates talks of removing pollution, of "thoroughly cleansing again (*palin*) the city (*polin*)." His words, especially the wordplay on *polin* and *palin*, curiously recall *Oedipus* 100–101, where Creon announces the gist of the Delphic oracle's response with a similar wordplay as he replies to Oedipus' inquiry about how the plague must be ended:

> By banishing or paying out again (*palin*)
> killing for killing. Death's a hemorrhage
> whose rage makes stormy days for the city. (*polin*).

Creon, in a series of responses which we will examine in detail shortly, goes on to suggest that the pollution was caused by the death of the

former king, Laios, and that investigation of the killing was hampered
by unusual circumstances. When Oedipus asks "what trouble was
afoot (*empodôn*) to stop the search?" (128), Creon replies: "the riddle-
singing (*poikilôidos*) Sphinx forced us to drop things past and gone,
see what was at our feet (*pros posi*)" (130).[29] The riddle of the Sphinx
which Oedipus, *Oidipous,* solves has a poetic form; the Sphinx, we
recall, is a singer of songs, a "rhapsode bitch" (*rhapsôidos kyôn* [*Oedipus*
391]), and the song she sings involves "foot" and "feet," *pous* and
podes. Pous, "foot," of course may be either an animal or a metrical
foot (as in Aristophanes *Frogs* 1323). The riddle is: what creature is
first four-footed, *tetrapous,* then two-footed, *dipous,* and finally three-
footed, *tripous*? Oedipus, then, "knows" metrical measure as well as
mankind's feet, even if he does not pay much attention to his own.
Hence the multiple irony in Creon's excuse for not investigating
Laios' murder.

If the idea of knowing metrical feet and purging the city of a blight
seems too farfetched—Dawe calls it "tasteless" in his comment on
line 130–the words from Plato *Republic* 3 (398C–399E), cited above,
should give us second thoughts. When Socrates talks of "thoroughly
clensing (*diakathairontes*) again (*palin*) the city (*polin*)," he is talking
of banning the use of complex musical forms and the instruments
used to express them. He continues (399E–400A):

> "Come on then," I said, "let's cleanse the rest too. Following on from
> scales (*harmoniais*) would come the matter of rhythms. We should not
> aim for those that are too complex (*poikilous*) or for manifold variety
> of steps in phrasing (*baseis*) but look to see which rhythms suit an
> orderly and manly life. When we have seen these rhythms, we must
> compel the foot (*poda*) to follow the rationale (*logos*) of such a life—
> and the melody too. The rationale (*logos*) should not follow the foot
> (*podi*)."

In destroying the "complex-riddle-singing," rhapsodic Sphinx,
Oedipus destroyed something, which, in the opinion of the Platonic
Socrates at any rate, was capable of causing disease within the city.
Socrates does not want "many-stringedness" (*polychordia*) or "pan-
harmonious (*panarmoniou*) music" in his ideal state, but, rather, music
characterized by *haplotês*: "oneness, simplicity." And *panarmonia* in
Republic 3.404D is compared to Sicilian food, noted for its intricate
variety (*poikilian*). Food and nourishment of this kind is, Socrates
observes, like music made in *panarmonia* and not to be encouraged.

No doubt he considered the state already complex enough without such "panharmony." In *Republic* 8 (557) he compares the state "decorated with all its different life-styles" (*pasin êthesin pepoikilmenê*) to an ornately decorated tunic (*poikilon himation*) decorated with (*pepoikilmenon*) all the flowers in existence.

However odd all this may seem to the modern reader, as Edward Lippman observes, "concepts of the ethical force of music are a characteristic feature of the Greek outlook."[30] Hence Socrates' argument in *Republic* 2.377D–3.403C and 10.606C–608B that Homeric poetry must be banished from the ideal state, as well as complex rhythms and musical scales *because they produce licentious behavior* (*akolasian*) as dietary excess produces disease (*noson*) (*Republic* 3. 404E). Of poets, Homer was throughout antiquity thought to be the most "polyphonic." Dionysius of Halicarnassus (*De Compositione Verborum* 16.42) calls him "the most many-voiced (*polyphônotatos*) of the poets," as does the Homeric commentator Eustathius (on *Iliad* 4.76 and 414, and on *Odyssey* 2.317). His "polyphony" appears to be why Plato saw his polyvalence and pluralism as threatening to the moral of the state, and therefore something to be banished. So too the riddle-singing Sphinx of Sophocles' *Oedipus* plagued Thebes before Oedipus solved its enigmatic riddling.

When Socrates asks his interlocutor Glaucon which rhythms are conducive to the good and brave life (*Republic* 3.400A), Glaucon confesses himself unable to answer the question. He knows that there are three kinds of rhythm from which steps in phrasing are made, just as there are four such steps in harmony. Cicero explains the first idea in *Orator*, 56 (188):

> For the foot used to make rhythms is divided into three classes: part of the foot must be (1) equal to the other part; (2) twice as big as the other; (3) fifty percent larger. Hence we have (1) the dactyl where the parts are equal; (2) the iamb, where one half is twice as long as the other; (3) the paean, where one part is half as long again.

The three different kinds of foot available to the writer correspond, curiously, to the three different stages of "footedness" in human life alluded to in the poetic riddle of the Sphinx. And the sorrows of Oedipus' house are intimately linked with the Delphic tripod, *tripous*. To speak "from the tripod" was to ancient Greek usage much as "to speak *ex cathedra*" is to ours (Athenaeus *Deipnosophists* 2.37F).[31]

The complex music of a Homer, a Sphinx, or a Sophocles could, in the opinion of some, be a disease blighting the city. But Oedipus, who was able to rid Thebes of its musical plague, does not seem to grasp that he himself represents that other Platonic plague of the state: tyranny.

2. AMBASSADOR CREON

If Athenians were puzzled by the apparent connection between their
own plague and Oedipus', they were doubtless equally puzzled by
Oedipus' choice of ambassador to Delphi: Creon. Yet in sending
Creon to consult Apollo, Oedipus has taken, Bernard Knox suggests,
"the only remedy his careful reflection suggested to him."[1] Knox
intends his comment as a compliment to Oedipus, whom he regards
as a "great man, a man of experience and swift courageous action,
who yet acts only after careful deliberation, illuminated by an analytic
and demanding intelligence."[2]

If the only remedy Oedipus' careful reflection can suggest is to
leave the enigma of the plague to be solved by an oracle, he is doing
no more than any unimaginative, but superstitious, ruler might do
under the circumstances even if his consultation is a last resort. He
is backing away from action rather than acting. He is in effect setting
his own judgment second to that of the oracle and whoever reports
it, allowing external forces to provide answers he might himself try
to provide. If we call such resignation "action," we should contrast
it sharply with Oedipus' more obviously active, traditional role in
solving the enigma of the Sphinx, where the initiative and the solution
to the riddle are his own achievement.

"This initial action (carried out in full before the play begins),"
Knox continues, "Sophocles has defined by striking dramatic means
as the free action of a free agent." This contention is very important

to Knox, who wishes to demonstrate that *Oedipus* is not a "tragedy of fate," as many have argued. While I agree with Knox that Oedipus is "fully responsible for the catastrophe," I would add that Oedipus is responsible because he places himself in the hands of other powers, because his use of freedom is actually a resignation of freedom.[3] In subdelegating the problem of dealing with the plague to Apollo and to Creon, Oedipus gives the god and his brother-in-law immense power over both his own future and that of Thebes. He subjects himself and the city to the control of others. He generates a kind of "fate," a fate that does not, at least initially, exist independently of himself. And he becomes the victim of that fate. Yet he acts of his own free will. Indeed, no other character in Greek tragedy is more wholly and personally responsible for the disaster that befalls him than is Oedipus.

Oedipus' opening response to the priest, in short, underscores the play's spiraling circularity. A religious leader asks the state's secular leader what he plans to do about a national catastrophe, and the secular leader announces that he has already referred that question to a religious source outside the state. Apollo, through the intermediacy of his oracle and of the secular Creon, is expected to provide the necessary answer. And the oracle Oedipus is about to receive as the play opens comes to him at *second hand*—as indeed does all the other information on which Oedipus bases his self-conviction. Not only does Oedipus fail to confront the enigma of the plague personally, but he does not even consult the oracle himself on this occasion. So there is a double distance between himself and the answers he seeks.

In Greek tragedy, characters named Creon tend to be rather unlovely people. The Creon of Sophocles' own *Antigone,* produced around 442–41 B.C., some fifteen years or so before *Oedipus,* is no exception. He is the unjust, tyrannical ruler of Thebes. In some traditions—Apollodorus 3.81 and Hyginus, *Fable* 67, for instance—Creon was king of Thebes *before* Oedipus but was displaced by Oedipus when the latter solved the riddle of the Sphinx. Our dilemma deepens when we see how quickly Oedipus comes to suspect—and convict—Creon of treason a little later in the play. If Oedipus allows himself to be guided by the reports other people give, why does he not take more careful account of the credentials, motives, and reliability of those whose word he accepts? Why does Oedipus send Creon, a man whom, we discover, he fears as politically unreliable, to Delphi to consult an oracle whose prophecies he both doubts and fears? Further, why does Oedipus, on Creon's advice, send for the prophet Teiresias, whose skills he similarly both admires and despises, believes and distrusts, even as a last resort?

The only viable answer would seem to be a paradox: Oedipus consults Apollo and employs the advice of Creon and Teiresias *because* he both trusts and distrusts them. Curiously, his subsequent conviction that Creon has behaved treasonably never leads him to suspect that Creon's report from Delphi may be false.

The Oracle as Reported by Creon

To resolve a public dilemma Oedipus has turned to the voice of his anxiety in private life, the Delphic oracle. And his choice of the potentially threatening Creon as ambassador is consistent with this paradox. He listens to the speakers he fears. Sophocles carefully sets the scene for Creon's entrance, inviting us to join with the priest and Oedipus in looking closely at his personal appearance and mien for clues (80–81):

> Lord (*anax*) Apollo, I pray he comes with news
> as promising and bright as is his eye.

The priest, in contrast, looks for a more obvious ritual token of a successful consultation than Creon's facial expression (82–83):

> To take a guess, it's fine. For otherwise
> he'd not be crowned so well, he'd not have wreathed
> his head with laurels loaded with berries.

Creon, then, enters, with the special symbol of a successful consultation of Delphi, a laurel crown, which invests him with an importance superior to that of the others on stage. Oedipus now becomes Creon's petitioner just as much as the priest and the assembled crowds were his own petitioners only a few lines earlier. When Oedipus moves on to question Creon, he hails him with the same honorific title *anax*, "Lord," he uses of Apollo, and others of him (85–86):

> My lord and kinsman, Menoeceus' son,
> what statement (*phêmên*) do you bring us from the god?

It is an ominous moment, considering that at the end of the play
Creon will actually be "lord" over Oedipus.

Creon replies not with a report of the oracle's words but with an
evaluative adjective: *esthlên* ("A good one"). His very next word is
legô (not "he says" but "I say"). The passage reads (87–88):

> A good one. For I say things that are hard
> to bear could all turn out quite happily
> if they ultimately turn out straight.

As John White, among others, noted long ago, this response "shows
that Creon, and not the oracle, is the authority for the statement."[4]
Oedipus hears not the oracle but the oracle as consulted, alluded to,
and interpreted by Creon. And Creon speaks as enigmatically as an
oracle, thereby becoming an oracle Oedipus must consult. Oedipus
is instantly at three removes from the god himself: between them
come the voices of the Pythian priestess and of Creon.

Creon's enigmatic response distracts Oedipus. Instead of asking
what the oracle actually said, Oedipus asks whether Creon's words
mean he should hope or fear. He thus invites Creon to become the
interpreter as well as the reporter of the god (89–90):

> What kind of a report (*epos*) is this? What's said
> now neither makes me bold nor frightens me.

Instead of explaining, Creon offers a further distraction by asking
Oedipus whether the announcement should be made publicly or pri-
vately (91–92):

> If you want to me speak with all these men
> around, I'm willing. Or we can go inside.

Oedipus answers (93–94)

> Tell everyone. These people's suffering
> weighs more upon me than my own life does.

Creon is, of course, perfectly within his rights to demur at this
moment. In fact, it was the privilege of those who went to Delphi
to disclose or keep the oracle secret until an opportune moment should
occur. Hence Creon's question need not be suspicious in and of itself.

But Oedipus' reaction is interesting: he seems to sense that his own life may be at stake in inviting the public to hear the proclamation of the oracle. For Creon's enigmatic preamble hints at something disturbing about the god's response. "This decision [not to go inside] is important," Knox observes, "for it makes it more difficult to stop the enquiry or suppress the result later in the course of the action."⁵ Dio Chrysostom has the Cynic Diogenes make much the same point about Oedipus in *Discourse* 10.29: Oedipus erred in relying on Teiresias' prophecy instead of going to Delphi himself. Oedipus thus suffered "terrible misfortunes on account of Teiresias' prophecy and his own ignorance." White states the matter succinctly: "Oedipus by this command seals his fate. The oracle is made public, and the first step taken that leads to his overthrow."⁶ Precisely. Sophocles *Oedipus* is not just about an individual's self-discovery but about a major change of power at Thebes that will depose Oedipus and leave Creon as ruler.

Oedipus' open gesture affords Creon a chance to present an interpretation of the oracle before the assembled people. Creon has put him in a rhetorical jam. If Oedipus were to opt for a private presentation of the oracle which he has publicly declared may affect the lives of everyone and solve the enigma of the plague, he would invite public suspicion and ill will. But the alternative proves more devastating. His decision to deal publicly with Creon and the oracle—and indeed with all the others he questions—is a tactical error in an erroneous strategy. By the time Oedipus acknowledges he is involved in a rhetorical, political battle, he has been outmaneuvered.

It is instructive to contrast the oracle of Apollo as reported by Creon in Seneca's *Oedipus* with the oracle as reported by Sophocles' Creon. First, Seneca, *Oedipus* 233–38:

> Gentle to Cadmean Thebes will the stars return in their motion
> If the fugitive guest slips away from Ismenian Dirce.
> He did harm by killing a king, was marked down by Phoebus from
>   childhood.
> You killed as a villain; you will not enjoy your pillage much longer!
> You'll fight in a war with yourself, leave war to your sons as their
>   portion,
> For you vilely returned once again to the womb of your mother.

Although Seneca's Oedipus does not ask what the oracle says, his Creon appears to cite it verbatim and in oracular hexameters.

Sophocles' Creon, in contrast, does not cite the oracle; he gives a summary in interpretive indirect speech introduced by a conditional optative along these structural lines: "[If I were permitted to speak] I would tell you that the god said that . . . " (95–98):

> I'd then say what I heard from god–his shrine.
> Lord Phoebus clearly ordered us to drive
> away our land's blight; that we've nurtured it
> upon this soil, that we must not persist
> in nurturing it all untreated here.

What Creon would announce is already known. Thebes is aware of the plague upon the land. The problem is how to discover and eradicate its cause, not to know that it is present.

Creon's lack of precision does not bother Oedipus. He neither asks for, nor gets, the oracle's exact words. He simply asks Creon what suggestions the god *might have* about how to accomplish the purification (99): "By what ritual? How must we deal with it?" As Creon responds, again we cannot tell whether he is reporting what the oracle said or his own interpretation of it (100–101):

> By banishing or paying out again (*palin*)
> killing for killing. Death's a hemorrhage (*haima*)
> whose rage makes wintry days (*cheima-zon*) for our city-state (*polin*).

We have already discussed in Chapter 1 some of the resonances of these lines in connection with Plato's *Republic* 3.399E–401A, where Socrates talks of removing pollution, of "thoroughly cleansing again (*palin*) the city (*polin*)," and we will return later to Sophocles' extensive soundplays on *palin* ("again"), *polin* ("city"), *palai(os)* ("of old"). The effect is oracular enough. Creon plays the sounds of "blood" (*haima*) and "again" (*palin*) against "wintry going" (*cheima-zon*) and "city" (*polin*). Banishment or death, a kind of sacrificial death of retribution—this is what Creon is conveying about the oracle's sense. And those in the audience who knew the Theban myth well in its many variations may have sensed an irony in the oracular wordplay. In the epic tradition of Oedipus, Creon had to offer his son Haemon as a sacrifice to the Sphinx.[7] Although Sophocles does not use this tradition in his extant works, he is well aware of, and employs, the wordplay between Haemon's name and *haima* ("blood") in *Antigone* 1175 when the messenger says: "Haemon (*Haimon*) is dead and shed his blood (*haimassetai*) himself."[8]

Let us assume Creon's words are not just oracular but part of the oracle. The reconstructed response so far, then, is something like the following:

> There is a blight upon this land which has been nurtured in it. It must be driven out. It cannot be nurtured here in its incurable state. It is to be removed either by driving into banishment whoever was involved or by killing in return for killing, since blood makes wintry weather for the state.

On the basis of this information Oedipus *immediately* assumes that a single individual is responsible for the plague (102): "What man does he declare (*mēnyei*) has earned this fate?"[9] He takes it for granted that a plague can be caused by unpurged blood-guilt—an idea about which Thucydides and others would have had doubts. He also calls on Creon to state the oracular response he has brought. Creon's reply, however, draws on information from his own recollection, not from the god's mantic utterance (103–7):

> Creon: We had a ruler once called Laios
> before you set our city on its course.
> Oedipus: I've heard the name, but never seen the face.
> Creon: He's dead. God clearly now instructs a hand
> to act as agent of revenge upon
> those who killed him, whoever killed him.

Creon undermines the definitive "those who killed him" by tacking on the indefinite *tinas,* "some," whose force I have rendered with "whoever." Perhaps more significant, the Suda, a Byzantine compendium of comments and notes on ancient texts, uses instead the singular indefinite *tina:* "some killer." For the singularity or plurality of Laios' assailants becomes an important issue in Oedipus' mind.

We should now add to what Dio's Cynic observes. Oedipus allows not only Teiresias but Creon to be his prophet. He fails to register fully that it is *Creon's interpretation of the oracle, not the oracle itself, that connects Laios with the pollution that, he is told, has fallen on Thebes.* In two lines charged with syllabic echoes of his own name and of Laios', Oedipus asks (108–9) and Creon responds (110–11):

Oedipus: But who'd know where they are (*hOID' eisI POU gês*)?
    Faded footprints,
    The crime's antiquity (*paLAIAS*) would delay us
    in our search. Where will we find them now?
Creon: In this land, he insisted (*ephaske*). What is sought
    can be caught, what's neglected gets away.

Creon replies that the god insisted that the tracks are to be found in
Theban land. The relatively uncommon verb *ephaske* has an imperfect,
iterative sense: "he kept on saying, he was insistent"—an unusual
word to describe an oracular utterance which is normally densely
compact. He uses it again soon. No less important, he reverts to the
singular to utter his maximlike observation that what is sought can
be caught.

Another question and answer follow (111–14):

Oedipus: Is Laios in his home or in the wilds
    or in another land when he is killed?
Creon: He went off, he insisted (*ephasken*), to consult
    the oracle. He left. Never came home.

Oedipus does not pick up on Creon's point that the tracks begin in
Thebes. Instead he tries to learn where Laios actually died. Creon
does not tell him and implies he does not know.

Oedipus, remarkably and publicly, accepts Creon's interpretation
of the Delphic oracle without challenge. The latter's answer is com-
prehensible but vague and again, curiously, uses the rare verb *ephasken*
("he insisted"). "He went off, he insisted, to consult the oracle,"
presumably, at Delphi, thus leaving open the possibility that Laios
might in fact have been going somewhere else. Creon does not add
the particulars of Laios' death: that the killing happened on the Split
Road in Phocis, as Jocasta and, presumably, others, know quite well.

In cross-questioning, the respondent may try to "lead" his interrogator by including in his answer information designed to prompt
or guide the next question. Answers, as Pentheus complains to Dionysus in Euripides' *Bacchae* 475, can be so phrased as to excite the
questioner's curiosity.

Creon perhaps wants Oedipus to follow up Laios' pilgrimage to
Delphi. Since the dramatic focus is now on Delphi and its oracle, and
since Creon himself has just returned from Delphi, it would be natural
enough for Oedipus to ask why Laios wanted to consult the god.
But Oedipus does not nibble. He will have deduced most of what he

wants to know from Creon's reply: Laios died somewhere between Thebes and Delphi.

Oedipus' failure to elicit more specific information about where Laios died does not necessarily mean Creon's response has gone unnoticed. For, as we later discover (800–813), he himself once killed a man between Delphi and Thebes at the Split Road.

Instead Oedipus asks if there were any witnesses (116–17):

> No messenger or fellow-traveler—
> from whom one might inquire and learn—saw him?

Creon replies (118–19):

> They died—apart from one who fled in fear
> at what he saw, and could say not one thing
> about it—well, apart from one detail.

Creon so phrases his response that the uniqueness of the single piece of information communicated by the single survivor stands out clearly. This time there is a follow-up question (120–127):

> *Oedipus*: What? We might find many in this one
> if we grasp onto this short strand of hope.
> *Creon*: He insisted (*ephaske*) that many brigands (*lêistas*)
> waylaid him: many hands, not one man's force.
> *Oedipus*: The brigand (*lêistês*)—how would he have come
> to dare this, without bribery from here?
> *Creon*: This was suspected. But, with Laios dead,
> there was none to help us in trouble.

Four points deserve special comment here, some of which have already been highlighted in Sandor Goodhart's brilliant discussion.[10]

First: Creon has already used the verb *ephaske*, "he insisted," twice before. The god "insisted" that the traces of the crime were to be found "in this land"; Laios "insisted" he was going to consult the oracle. Now the man who ran from the scene of the killing "insisted" that not one, but many brigands attacked the former king. In each case, Creon is reporting news at second hand: hearsay. In each case, the statement's accuracy depends not only on Creon's truthfulness but on the reliability of his source. The witness who ran away in fear is most obviously suspect, not only because cowardice apparently caused him to flee but because if Oedipus really did kill Laios, as he later becomes convinced he did, there really was only one assailant. As we will see in Chapter 5, Oedipus recalls that he acted alone when he killed an old man at the crossroads and that he killed everyone who was with that old man.

Second: the use of *lêistês*, "brigand, bandit," to describe Laios' assailants. The word carries curious resonances of the Sphinx. The scholiast on Hesiod, *Theogony* 326 says: "the Sphinx in reality (*pragmatikôs*) a female brigand (*lêistris*) and had many fellow robbers with her." And we will recall that Pausanias (9.26.2–4) also describes the Sphinx as a woman who lived off brigandage (*kata lêisteian*).

Third: the number of brigands involved in the attack. Their plurality, although Creon says it is the one sure thing known, is the *only* element in Creon's account that Oedipus doubts. Oedipus, quite remarkably, makes Creon's plural bandits singular. He shows his doubt again later, when addressing the Thebans and placing a curse on anyone involved with the crime (246–47): "whether just one man has eluded us or whether there were more." Then, six hundred lines later, in 845–46, he declares that the surviving witness' testimony as to the singularity or plurality of bandits will determine whether he himself is Laios' killer. Oedipus, then, accepts from the start the truth of everything that points to himself as the killer of Laios and the cause of the plague, and doubts only the detail that would ultimately show his innocence. He gives us no clue immediately as to why he regards this aspect of Creon's report as dubious. We have only a sense of his unease: that something not clear to us is troubling him. We see in operation the literary technique discussed in the Introduction: a kind of reverse dramatic irony, where something known to the characters in a play or epic is withheld from the audience.

Fourth: Oedipus' assumption that the brigand could not have acted without some bribery or collusion from within the city itself. In other words, Laios must have been the victim of a political plot. The rationale for this assumption is hard to fathom. But it is the first indication that Oedipus thinks in terms of conspiracies. And his concern about conspiracies will bubble to the surface very soon. Creon's response to Oedipus' conspiracy theory is brilliantly affirmative and

negative at the same time suggesting, if I may paraphrase lines 126–
27: "yes, that's what we thought too, but we lacked any capable
leadership once Laios was dead." The man who stood most obviously
to benefit from Laios' death was Creon himself, who would have
been heir apparent. But the "proof" of his own innocence, and the
refutation of the conspiracy theory, is his suggestion that no one
(including himself) was capable of taking over—until Oedipus
arrived.

Creon's last response defuses Oedipus' conspiracy theory by hinting at the helplessness of both himself and the government once Laios
was dead. Yet it provokes Oedipus' outrage that there was no proper
investigation (128–32):

> *Oedipus*: What trouble was afoot to stop the search?
>   The tyrant and his power (*tyrannidos*) were overthrown!
>   *Creon*: The riddle-singing Sphinx forced us to drop
>   things past and gone, see what was at our feet.

In line 128 we find the first of many references to the ruler and
rulership at Thebes as *tyrannos* ("tyrant") and *tyrannis* ("tyranny").
To render *tyrannis* by "royalty"—as Jebb and others have done—is
to mute the strident suggestions of usurped power and absolutism
into those of an inherited and essentially harmless constitutional monarchy.[11] Oedipus seems concerned not just about the fate of a particular tyrant but about the fate of tyranny itself. Oedipus is, after all,
Laios' successor, a tyrant himself. Curiously, it does not occur to him
that a tyrant's death might prompt celebration, not investigation.
Creon, of course, would hardly want to correct his tyrant on this
point, given Oedipus' suspicions of conspiracy, and his anxiety about
tyranny as an institution.

Creon again silences the objection with brilliant *emphasis,* in the
ancient sense. He picks up Oedipus' use of the word *empodôn,* "afoot,"
and points out that the Sphinx and her riddle were "at our feet" at
the time. There was, then, a legitimate excuse, since the Sphinx's
riddle (which was of the feet) was not solved until Oedipus came
along. Creon's answers have now set Oedipus on the road to Thebes
at a time when he might meet Laios coming in the other direction.
And obviously that thought sticks in Oedipus' mind. But we, if we
are more cautious, might note that Creon is also telling us that the
Sphinx, the *lêistris,* the female brigand with large band of robbers in

some traditions, was still around when Laios died. Put her together with her troops and you have the plural *lêistai,* perhaps even the same *lêistai* whom Creon and his alleged sole survivor claimed were the killers of Laios.

Creon has discreetly moved the focus from himself to Oedipus. He does not mention Oedipus' arrival, only the circumstances that prevailed when he arrived. But his allusion to the Sphinx and her riddle (which everyone knew was solved by Oedipus) reminds the Thebans that Oedipus is unable to resolve the present crisis as he resolved that of the Sphinx. Oedipus himself senses that he is being challenged with the recollection of his past success and rises to the bait. He abandons further questions, fluffs his own feathers, and takes center stage. Oedipus will repeat, he claims, his tour-de-force as savior of the state (132–46):

> So, once again, I'll start right from the top
> and shed light on the darkness. How rightly
> Phoebus and how rightly you have drawn
> all this attention to the dead man's cause.
> You both will see that, as is only just,
> I am your ally, *agent of revenge*
> for this land, yes, and for the god as well.
> I shall dispel this poisoned cloud not for
> some distant friends, but really for myself.
> Whatever man killed him might want to use
> his hand like that as *agent of revenge*
> on me. Therefore, in doing right by him,
> I help myself. Now, quickly as you can,
> my sons, up from the altar steps, stand up
> and take away these branches you have left
> in supplication! Let someone convene
> the Theban laity (*laon*), the people, here—
> aware that I'll do everything I can.
> For we will be revealed, with the god's help,
> either as blessed or already ruined.[12]

Oedipus here publicly commits himself to Apollo as interpreted by Creon and links the god and his brother-in-law in a flattering union of righteousness. But he sees his action as self-serving rather than simply in the public interest. He is already beginning to turn away from his concern about the state to concern about himself. Oedipus' anxiety that the hand that struck Laios may also strike him is, of course, ironic. But there is a curious half-consciousness about it too. His use of the verb *timôrein*, which I have rendered as "to act as agent of revenge," is applied both to himself as inflicter of punishment on the killer and to the killer's potential strike against him. It is also the verb Creon uses when reporting the oracle in line 107:

> to act as agent of revenge upon
> those who killed him, whoever killed him.

But we will notice that Oedipus, in summing up, talks of a single killer. And Creon does not contradict him.

Oedipus began this scene by calling the Thebans not fellow citizens (which they are not, since Oedipus is not a citizen of the city he rules) but children, *tekna*, of Cadmos. At line 58 he called them *paides oiktroi*, "pitiable sons." Now he calls them just *paides*, "sons," assuming a more personally paternal tone which the priest echoes as Oedipus leaves the stage (147–50):

> Come, sons, let us depart. This man proclaims
> in public what we came here to obtain.
> And may Phoebus who sent these prophecies
> come as savior to rid us of disease (*nosou*).

The priest, like Oedipus, seems satisfied with what has been accomplished. Creon is probably satisfied too.

3. OEDIPUS AND TEIRESIAS

Not only has Creon served as Oedipus' ambassador to and interpreter of Apollo's oracle, he has also advised Oedipus to consult Teiresias (287–89, 555–56). Oedipus, in relying so heavily on Creon's advice and on his interpretations of the oracle, places himself squarely in Creon's hands. Yet not until Teiresias appears do we begin to realize that Oedipus' reliance on Creon is counterbalanced by fear and distrust of him. What he most trusts is that which he also most suspects, distrusts, and fears.

The Preamble

After Creon leaves the stage, the play's chorus enters. The chorus, we have been specifically told, represents the Theban people and gathers in response to Oedipus' injunction at line 144 that the *Kadmou laon*, the "laity" of Cadmus, convene. The first two-thirds of their song (151–89) is a complex of prayers addressed not only to Apollo but also to Athena, and reinforces the priest's comments about the plague at the play's opening. But there is an added sense that the singers are reaching out to the ancient audience's own circumstances in their special appeal to Athena, Athens' very particular goddess. The final third of their song (190–215) moves even further into the writer's contemporary world, appealing to Zeus, Apollo, Artemis, and Bacchus in the hope they will strike down with their various weapons and emblems of power—thunderbolts, arrows, and Bacchic *thyrsus* ("staff")—"the god who is dishonored among gods"—Ares, the god of war.

In the chorus' thoughts, then, the plague is accompanied by a war, and it is above all the war that they want ended. The verb they use to ask Zeus to destroy Ares, *phthison* (201), is the same verb the priest uses twice to describe the destructive effects of the plague upon Thebes in lines 25–26 (*phthinousa*).¹ What war could the chorus have in mind? There is nothing in the mythic context of Sophocles' play to suggest that Thebes is currently at war with anyone. The great wars of Theban tradition *follow* the reign of Oedipus. On the other hand, the great war between the Athenians and the Peloponnesians (who were allied with Thebes) was well under way as Sophocles wrote. The chorus, then, in its first utterances, has assumed a very fifth-century Athenian identity.

Oedipus and the Chorus

Oedipus' opening words after the choral song indicate that he has heard at least the last part of the chorus's prayer. He must either have remained onstage throughout, as I suspect, or have reentered in time to catch the final words of the choral song. Oedipus begins his speech (216–20):

> You are praying. Now regarding your prayers,
> if you're willing to listen to my words,
> to use them on the plague, you could achieve
> strength—and reduction of your suffering.
> I will speak them as an outsider
> both to what was reported and to what
> was done.

Oedipus adopts an authoritative, oracular tone, as if he really has an answer to offer the chorus. He also specifically dissociates himself from Laios' death and the reports of it that he has just heard. He then goes on to explain his inability to act on his own in an investigation (220–26):

> I could not track things by myself,
> and get far. I lack evidence. But now,

a latecomer and fellow resident,
I proclaim to all you Cadmeans:

If any of you knows the man who killed
Laios, the son of Labdacus, I command
that he communicate it all to me.

He demands information from the chorus to get his investigation
under way. But notice that he has not revealed any particular plan of
action to cope with the problem; that he again refers to the killer in
the singular; and that his description of Laios as son of Labdacus (the
first mention of Labdacus in the play) shows that he knows more
about Laios than was evident from his earlier conversation with
Creon. There he said only that he had heard of Laios.

Oedipus mentions various categories of people who might give
information. He starts by allowing for a confession by the (singular)
killer himself, with a promise of clemency (227–29):

If he fears for himself, he shall evade
full penalty if he just brings the charge
against himself. He will suffer nothing
unpleasant. He will leave the land unharmed.

He continues by allowing for the possibility that the murderer was
not a Theban (230–32):

Or, if someone knows the man who struck the blow
came from elsewhere, let him not be silent.
I will reward him; he'll be duly thanked.

But no one has yet interrupted. So Oedipus proceeds to threaten
(233–45):

But if you're silent, if someone holds back,
fearing for a friend, or for himself,
then he should hear from me what I shall do.

I proclaim that no one must receive
this man, whoever he may be, within
this land whose throne I now control,
no one must speak to him, no one take part
with him in prayers or sacrifices, none
share with him the cleansing holy font.

> No, everyone must shun him from their homes.
> He's the defilement on us, as the god
> of Delphi has just now revealed to me
> in prophecy. I thus ally myself
> with the god's will, also with the deceased.

Oedipus offers, as yet, only words—a proclamation that the murderer (still singular) must be shunned. More curious, he speaks as if he personally had received the word from Apollo at Delphi. He does not allude to Creon's intermediacy, much less to the fact that it was Creon's *interpretation* of the oracle that established the connection of the plague with the death of Laios.

Finally Oedipus proceeds to his action: a ritual curse on the murderer (or murderers, this time) and those who harbor him (246–48):

> I lay a curse on him who did this deed,
> whether just one man has eluded us
> or whether there were more to help him out:
> May this wicked man in wickedness
> wear down a wretched, homeless path through life.

There is no strong threat of punishment, only whatever power may reside within the imprecation itself.

Now Oedipus assures the people that, if the killer lives in his palace, he himself does not know it. He is not necessarily alluding only to himself. Creon, for instance, might have a motive for killing Laios. Jocasta might also have a motive, as we will see. He continues (249–54):

> I lay a curse, if he is in this house
> and shares the hearth, my very own,
> with my full knowledge: may what I just prayed
> for others fall upon me with its spell.
> I set responsibility on you
> to do just as I ask on my behalf,
> on god's, and for this land so ruined now,
> deprived of fruitfulness and god's presence.

It is worth at least passing notice that Oedipus places himself first in the order of those on whose behalf he asks the chorus to act. Had he stopped here, we might have summed up what he says as a vain and ineffectual gesture that tries its best to be evenhanded. But this ap-

parent peroration is in fact the prelude to the most astonishing part
of his declaration (255–64):

> Even were this a matter where the gods
> made no demands, it would be like leaving
> a moral stain uncleansed, to overlook,
> not hunt, its cause. A noble man, a king (*basileôs*),
> has perished. Now, since I am in control,
> possessing the power he once possessed,
> possessing his marriage, the woman who
> drew semen from us both, some common bonds
> would surely have been born between us from
> children, had there not been such bad luck
> in terms of his own offspring. Since, then,
> Luck came crashing down upon his head, I'll take
> their place, as if he were my own father.

Oedipus avows a moral responsibility quite independent of specific
oracular demands. A king's death demands a inquiry, especially since
Oedipus is himself that king's successor. It is worth noting that on
this occasion, as opposed to his earlier comment to Creon in line 128,
he refers to Laios as a king, *basileus*, rather than as a tyrant, perhaps
because numerous people in Sophocles' Athens would find the killing
of a *basileus* more morally reprehensible than the killing of a tyrant.
The *basileus* at Athens was an important figure in the religious functions of the state and was not the subject of antityrannical legislation.[2]

Oedipus goes to such pains to establish virtually a blood relationship between himself and the dead monarch that he represents himself
as charged with the duty to avenge kindred blood. This claim, like
his representation of Laios as a *basileus*, not only intensifies the demand
that an important, unresolved crime be cleared up, but attempts to
bolster his own rights to act as litigant. As R. G. Lewis points out
in connection with the procedures in the prosecution of a case of
homicide at Athens, "a litigant had to be a citizen and (normally
anyhow) kin of the victim."[3] Further, an Athenian homicide trial
(*dikê phonou*) required a proclamation not only by the litigant but by
the *archôn basileus*, the "king" archon, who "retained the responsibility
for many of the older religious ceremonies of the city throughout his
year of office."[4]

When Oedipus declares that he will act as if Laios were his father
and describes Laios as a *basileus*, he is drawing himself, rhetorically,

within the citizen and family community of the state so as to justify his proclamation. And his stress on the fact that he is now the husband of the former *basileus'* wife, whom Athenians called the *basilinna*, "queen," seems designed to authorize his own acting as both litigant and "king" archon in making his proclamation. For the *basileus* shared important ritual duties with his wife.[5] Thus Oedipus, who is neither a citizen nor a *basileus*, seeks to justify his religious authority by virtue of his relationship to the *basilinna*, Jocasta, and the *basileus*, Laios, whose place he has taken.

In justifying himself as the man entitled to bring a curse upon Laios' killer, of course, Oedipus is describing himself both as Laios' son and as Jocasta's son and husband. He has created enough of a figured description of his relationship with Laios by this act of speech that the mere discovery that he had killed the old king would, in terms of most Herodotean oracles, show him as having killed his father and married his mother.

Oedipus reveals something else of importance here: that he knows more about Laios' personal life than he has indicated earlier: either Laios and Jocasta had no children, or something unfortunate happened to them. But what is surely most troublesome is his metaphor of Laios' death as "Luck crashing down upon his head." For, we later learn, Oedipus remembers striking down an old man at a crossroad with a lethal blow from his staff (810–12). He also claims himself to be "a child of Luck" (1080–81). Our sense that Oedipus knows more than we at first assumed about his predecessor's family is firmly reinforced by the complete genealogy of Laios he gives in the following lines (265–68):

> I'll fight for him, I will go everywhere,
> laboriously seeking how to catch (*labein*)
> the man who killed the son of Labdacus,
> son of Polydorus, Cadmus' son,
> the child of Agenor from long ago.

Of course Oedipus will not really go everywhere in the search. He stays in Thebes and will conduct his investigation from just outside the palace. Others will come to him.

Finally, we have the real peroration, both curse and benediction (269–75):

To those who do not act: I pray the gods
no produce may sprout from the land for them,
that their wives bear no children, but that they
will wither with the doom that strikes them now—
and even worse than this.
                              But then for you,
you other Cadmeans who do approve,
may justice be your ally, may the gods,
all gods, be with you and be kind always.

The chorus, representing the citizen body of Thebes, promptly dis-
avows either killing or knowing who killed Laios, and takes exception to Apollo's vagueness—a point on which Oedipus agrees with
them (276–81):

> *Chorus*: As you have made me subject to a curse,
>   my lord, I'll state outright: I did not kill,
>   I can't point out the killer. But Phoebus,
>   since he sent us on the search, should then
>   explain just who it was who did the deed.
> *Oedipus*: You're right, that would be just. But no one man
>   can force the gods to do what they don't wish.

It is worth noting that the chorus says it can't point out, rather than
that it does not know, the (singular) killer. So Oedipus is left with
the possibility that someone unknown—or at least offstage—is (or is
harboring) the killer, or that he himself may be (or be harboring) the
killer.

The chorus realizes it has just deflated Oedipus' grandiloquent announcement of his nonexistent plan to deal with the plague and offers
its own suggestion for a course of action, which Oedipus avidly
accepts (282–83):

> *Chorus*: Then could I say what I judge second best?
> *Oedipus*: If there's a third best, don't miss telling me!

Oedipus, who began by pompously advising the chorus to listen
attentively to him, awaits the chorus's response with almost childlike
eagerness. And the response is crushing (284–86):

> As lord (*anakt'*) equal to lord (*anakti*), identical
> in sight to Phoebus is Teiresias:

> this I know, absolutely. Anyone
> who looked to him, my lord (*ônax*), in this matter
> would learn deeply. He'd make things very clear.

Apollo will not give the answer, but Teiresias, who is Apollo's equal
in foresight, can and will. The use of *anax* ("king, lord") to describe
both Teiresias and Apollo sets them above Oedipus. Calling him *anax*
too seems merely formal courtesy, if not irony. There is nothing the
citizens of Thebes can now learn from the man who destroyed the
Sphinx.

Oedipus responds with something like pique (287–89):

> I did not consign even this to lists
> of what could be put off. When Creon raised
> the subject, I twice sent him embassies.
> He's long past due and so amazes me.

There is a strange confusion in Oedipus' phrasing which critics have
imputed to Sophocles' (rather than to Oedipus') haste or loss of balance. The verb I have rendered "consign," *epraxamên*, does not yield
the meaning editors want the sentence to carry, namely: "I did not
leave this among things neglected" or "Well, I have not neglected this
point either."[6] The verb suggests to me, rather, that Oedipus is taken
aback a little by the chorus's response, that he shows a hint of reluctance to deal with Teiresias. Note how carefully Oedipus points out
that Creon suggested consulting Teiresias. In contrast, he takes all the
credit for the mission to Delphi himself and does not even mention
Creon's role to the chorus. Oedipus also notes that his approaches to
Teiresias have been made through unspecified emissaries rather than
directly—and that they have been sent twice without success.

The chorus hurriedly changes the subject (290–93):

Chorus: Then there's the silly talk of times long past.
Oedipus: What was it? I'm surveying every word.
Chorus: Word was he got killed by some travelers.
Oedipus: I heard so too—and someone saw it all.
But no eyes see the man who saw it all.

Oedipus instantly takes the bait when the chorus mentions ancient
rumor. Then he gives a biting retort when he assumes that he is
hearing a reiteration of what Creon had just told him. But the last

word before Oedipus takes over again is not "brigands" but "travelers." Perhaps, as Dawe suggests obliquely on line 292, "travelers" (*hodoiporôn*) might have some sense akin to "highwaymen" in English.[7] Oedipus does not follow up this difference, which is at least as marked as that between the singular and plural of the word "brigand" which so bothers him, because he is too quick to assume he knows what they are going to say and too eager to point out, in a snide manner, that what he had expected to hear after his proclamation has not emerged: the identity of the supposed witness who could presumably say who killed Laios.

Oedipus has in fact noticed something important. Why does no one point out the man who saw the killing, despite the fact that Creon and, later, Jocasta imply that what the witness said was publicly stated and thus general knowledge? At the same time, however, Oedipus himself has not yet made a single move to ascertain the identity of the alleged witness, much less summon him, other than by this proclamation.

The chorus adopts the attitude that the man (witness or, more likely, the killer) will probably go away (294–96):

> *Chorus:* Well if he's subject to portentous fears,
> he won't stay when he hears curses like yours.
> *Oedipus:* If deeds don't scare him, words won't frighten him.

These three lines undermine many assumptions on the basis of which Oedipus invokes his curse on the killer and those shielding him. The curse will have effect only *if the killer fears such pronouncements,* and Oedipus admits that someone who does not stop at killing will not be deterred by a mere verbal formula.

In short, Oedipus' grandiloquence has led him only toward a close association of himself with Laios, to whom he now plays the role of avenging son. The Thebans have given him no information. Although they treat him with formal respect, they make it clear that they admire and value Teiresias much more. The blind seer, like Creon, will be the center of attention as he comes onstage.

Teiresias *Anax*

As Teiresias arrives, he is hailed by the chorus as the person who will be able to cross-question and refute (*houxelenxôn*) the killer (297–99):

> The man who will cross-question and refute
> the killer has arrived: the godlike seer
> these men are leading in before us now,
> the only human in whom truth is born.

Skill in cross-questioning and refutation seems more rhetorical and Socratic than prophetic. The guard who arrests Antigone, for instance, tells Creon (*Antigone* 399) to "judge and cross-examine (*ex-elenche*)" her to assure himself of her guilt. In what sense would we imagine that Teiresias is such a master of *elenchos*, of dialectic? *Elenchos,* to use Aristotle's definition in *De Sophisticis Elenchis* 170B1, is "the proof of the contradiction of a given thesis." Similarly, in the Aristotelian *Rhetoric to Alexander* 1431A7–8, *elenchos* is "that which cannot be otherwise." Dawe, commenting on *Oedipus* 297, finds it odd that the chorus should talk of refuting the killer since the killer's identity is unknown. "Until it is known," Dawe observes, "examining, cross-questioning, refuting, have no place."[8] Unless, of course, the chorus suspects or knows that there is going to be an argument. For Teiresias is Oedipus' cross-questioner and refuter in the dialogue that follows: the only person in the play to accuse Oedipus outright of killing Laios, and to suggest that he was the child of Laios and Jocasta. He turns Oedipus from principal investigator into the accused. And such is his success that by the end of the play everyone, including Oedipus, accepts the full sweep of Teiresias' charges.

True, Oedipus *attempts* both to cross-question and to refute Teiresias. But in the hostile interchanges that follow, Oedipus is verbally routed. Teiresias earns the chorus's title of the great refuter. We should ask ourselves, however, why the chorus feels so sure at the outset that Teiresias, rather than Oedipus, merits this honorific. Although it was Oedipus who solved the verbal riddle of the Sphinx, who refuted her, the chorus is absolutely confident that Teiresias is "the only man in whom truth is born (*pephyken*)" (298–99).[9]

To engage in public debate with such a man before a choral audience already disposed to believe that one's interlocutor has some inborn access to the truth could be most dangerous. To augment Teiresias' stature, Oedipus himself delivers a flattering introduction to the seer, extending from line 300 to line 315, which reinforces the chorus' high opinion, endowing him with a Delphic prophetic authority, and casts aside, albeit temporarily, the uneasiness he seemed to feel about the seer when talking to the chorus a few lines earlier. No less important,

Oedipus' words immediately inform everyone (including Teiresias) that Oedipus makes no distinction between Phoebus' prophecy and Creon's interpretation of it. Again Oedipus shows he has accepted that it was Phoebus, rather than Creon, who connected Laios and his death with the plague:

> Teiresias, observing everything
> that can be taught and all things that defy
> expression, what is in the skies above
> or walks upon the earth! You cannot see,
> and yet your reason shows you our city,
> and the plague afflicting it. My lord (ônax = ô anax),
> we are discovering that only you
> can be her savior, champion (prostatês), and spokesman.
> Phoebus—in case you have not heard the news
> from messengers—sent us his answer.
> For we had sent to him for his advice.
> The only release from this disease
> could come if we clearly identified
> those who killed Laios and then killed them
> or drove them out in exile from this land.
> Don't grudge us what the auspices have said,
> or any other pathway that you have
> which yields prophetic insight, and protect
> yourself, the city—and protect me too—
> from all the blight this dead man brings on us.
> For we are in your power. To help a man
> with all your might is real nobility.

The extravagant admiration expressed for Teiresias' rhetorical prowess, insight, and truthfulness deserves close attention, because such praise commits those who give it to a rhetorically inferior position either real or, as with Socrates, feigned. The chorus and Oedipus give all outward signs that they expect Teiresias to be able to provide truthful answers. Oedipus not only calls Teiresias *anax*, "king, lord" as the chorus just did, but even acknowledges: "we are in your power." Events prove the assessment correct. Oedipus and the chorus are transferring to Teiresias the power to decide what actions are appropriate.

Rhetoric and Decisions

"The purpose of rhetoric," Aristotle observes, "is to control decision making" (*heneka kriseôs estin hê rhetorikê* [*Rhetoric* 2.1377B]). Our ability to control decision making is affected by how we are perceived by others. Aristotle continues (ibid.): "One must look not only toward one's speech so it will demonstrate one's point and be believable, but set both oneself and the decision maker in the right perspective."

Aristotle here assumes that the speaker, that is, the rhetorician, and the decision maker are not one and the same. The speaker's task is to control, by rhetorical skill, the reactions of the decision maker. So, as Aristotle makes absolutely clear in the second book of his *Rhetoric*, rhetoricians must understand what the emotions are and how they work. They must know how to play upon the emotions of their audience; and they cannot play upon emotions until they learn what these emotions are and how they can *predict* the circumstances under which a given emotional response will be triggered. Thus rhetoric is as much a matter of what we would nowadays call psychology as it is of the artifices of speech. The most persuasive rhetorician must have a good sense of what the object of manipulation will do when subjected to given stimuli.

There is no question, then, that Oedipus has put the chorus and the audience in a very receptive mood toward Teiresias by giving him what we would call a good "buildup." He has also put himself at a rhetorical disadvantage by making himself—the tyrant, the decision maker—dependent on the rhetorician. Thus the chorus' description of Teiresias as the "cross-questioner" or "refuter" is fundamentally valid. Teiresias can say anything he wishes. He, not Oedipus, controls the dispersal and interpretation of information. And he does so with Oedipus' consent.

Teiresias the Rhetorician

Teiresias' first statement is oracular in its ambiguity and apparently addressed to himself (316–18):

> Alas: reason's power! How formidable (*deinon*)
> when reason does not pay. I know this well.
> But I forgot it, or I'd not have come.

He berates himself for having come at all. Or perhaps it is wiser to say that he conveys the appearance of berating himself. For precisely what he means is not at all clear. His first word in the Greek text—

after his exclamation of grief—is *phronein* (to have "reasoning power"). *Phronein* is also his last word as he departs in line 462. Could the formidable quality of the rational mind to which he refers be somehow akin to the great speaker's traditionally formidable tongue? Is Teiresias *deinos phronein* ("formidable in reasoning"), as Plato's Socrates was apparently *deinos legein* ("formidable in speaking") according to his accusers (*Apology* 17A)?

Formidable power in speaking, as in thinking, is potentially devastating to rhetorical adversaries; but it can also mean trouble for its master. Socrates, after all, was brought to court and ultimately put to death on charges of being, among other things, *deinos legein*. There is, then, a sense in which one can suggest that what is fearsome (*deinon*) is the ability to speak (*legein*) or think (*phronein*). And this is how Teiresias begins: with a comment on the drawbacks of intelligence under certain circumstances. Critics usually assume that he is reacting to his own dilemma, and that he wishes he did not have the intellectual power that is his. But it is surely no less possible that Teiresias is reacting to the irony of Oedipus' laudatory introduction—that he is commenting on the drawbacks of Oedipus' rationality rather than on the drawbacks of his own intelligence. Such an interpretation might make better sense of the extraordinary observation Teiresias adds: that he knew how formidable a thing powerful reason was but had forgotten until this moment.

Oedipus either fails to hear or fails to understand Teiresias' words. He notes only that the seer seems depressed (319): "What *is* this? You come in so listlessly." Teiresias responds (320–21):

> "Send me home. Do as I say, then you'll
> cope best with your affairs and I with mine."

Teiresias' response is curiously phrased: he does not say "I'm going home" or "Let me go home," but "Send me home." Oedipus has assumed responsibility for summoning Teiresias. Teiresias is now leaving him the responsibility for his dismissal—something Oedipus seems hardly likely to do. Further, Teiresias adds that such a dismissal would be in their mutual interests—though he makes no mention of the interests of Thebes.

Oedipus understandably responds by rebuking Teiresias for his lack of concern for the city; but Oedipus in turn is knocked back into

place by the blind seer's needling and personal retort, ironically introduced by the verb "I see" (322–25):

> *Oedipus*: What you suggest runs contrary to law,
> and is not kind to this city. It nourished
> you, yet you deprive it of wise words.
> *Teiresias*: I see you voicing words not right for you
> or the occasion. Let me not do so too.

Oedipus lets the insulting innuendos slip by and resorts instead to
the humblest statement he voices in the play (326–27):

> Since reason rules your mind, don't turn from us.
> We are your suppliants; by the gods we all
> beg you, shower kisses at your feet.

The dramatic image of a tyrant so humbling himself before a seer
might well elicit a gasp from most ages and societies other than our
own. Certainly nowhere else in surviving Greek tragedy does an
unconquered ruler prostrate himself before another person. But Teiresias, instead of acknowledging Oedipus' gesture of self-humiliation
with at least a courteous refusal, turns on the prostrate monarch with
withering condescension (328–29):

> Precisely. *All* of you lack reason. I myself
> will never give my best advice. I'll thus
> avoid revealing your bad news to you.

Again, Teiresias says nothing about the city's suffering. Nor does he
comment this time on any troubles to which he himself might be
susceptible. He alludes only to his own knowledge of *Oedipus'* misfortunes and thereby sets up a dialectical opposition between himself
and the tyrant from which the city is pointedly excluded.

Oedipus manages to contain himself somewhat and still insists on
linking his inquiries to the city's interests more than to his own (330–
31):

> What's this you say? You know, and will not speak?
> You plan to sell out, ruin the city?

Oedipus' multiple questions, however, show more than a trace of
anger and indignation. Teiresias' next haughty response could hardly
fail to make things worse, when he intones (332–33):

I cause myself no pain and none to you.
Why cross-question (*elencheis*) me further on this?
You could not find the answer out from me.

Teiresias' selection of the word *elencheis* is especially effective, given our recollection of the chorus' observation that the seer is himself "the great refuter." I won't let you play the role of the cross-questioning attorney, Teiresias is saying. But is this his statement or his challenge? The seer certainly does not maintain his uncommunicative pose very long. Seventeen lines later he starts to level charges against Oedipus—to say all the things that he now avers could not be drawn from him.

The Angered Oedipus

The immediate result of Teiresias' condescension is an explosion of anger on Oedipus' part. Oedipus expects answers from Teiresias. Yet he has created a situation in which his requests and unparalleled self-abasement have been met with rudeness. Here is their exchange (332–49):

Oedipus: You evil man, you'd temper a heart of stone!
You just won't speak? You will appear, yet be
inflexible and leave things unresolved?
Teiresias: You mind my temperament yet have no eyes
to see your own. And you despise me for it.
Oedipus: Who could control his temper when he hears
your words which now dishonor this city?
Teiresias: Fate comes, though I wordless and quietly go.
Oedipus: Since it comes, don't you *have* to let me know?
Teiresias: No sense in saying more. So counter that
with all the wildest temper of your heart.

Oedipus' expectations have been frustrated. Predictably, he becomes angry. Aristotle observes that we are liable to be specially angered when "things turn out the opposite from what one expects" (*tanantia tychêi prosdechomenos* [*Rhetoric* 2.1379A24]). Indeed, the first emotion he treats in the second book of his *Rhetoric* is anger. After discussing the mental disposition of those who are angry, the objects of their anger, and the reasons for their anger—the *pôs* ("why") the *tisi* ("at

whom"), and the *dia poia* ("on account of what kinds of thing")—
Aristotle points out that people, when angry, are always in some kind
of pain. "And the person who is in pain is in search of something"
(*ephietai gar tinos ho lypoumenos* [*Rhetoric* 2.1379A]); "whether a person
is deliberately getting in your way, preventing, say, a thirsty man
from drinking, or whether he is not doing so deliberately but *appears*
to be; he could be working against you—or not working with you."

One of the orator's tasks may be precisely "to arrange what he is
saying so as to make his hearers inclined to anger" (*kataskeuazein tôi
logôi toioutous hoioi ontes orgilôs echousi* [*Rhetoric* 2.1380A]). But if so,
the orator in this scene between Oedipus and Teiresias is Teiresias.
We surely cannot miss the very overt challenge in Teiresias' last words
in the passage cited above: "So counter that with all the wildest temper
of your heart." Unfortunately, it takes Oedipus a disastrously long
time to realize that he has played into the refuter's hands. By appearing
to force Teiresias to speak in public against the latter's own declared
better judgment, Oedipus endows in advance whatever the seer says
with public authority. And the seer's professed reluctance to speak
undermines Oedipus' later contention that Teiresias has conspired
with Creon against him.

We cannot rule out, then, the possibility that Teiresias' opening
words are part of a deliberate strategy rather than a bumbling confession of absentmindedness, particularly if he is, as the chorus suggests,
the master cross-questioner and refuter. Teiresias leaves the impression that he has the answers everyone in seeking but does not want
to reveal them. And by pointedly focusing on Oedipus' problems,
he implies that his reticence arises from unwillingness to get his ruler
in trouble.

Teiresias' words and conduct arouse Oedipus' curiosity as well as
his anger. They may well be designed to do precisely that. If so,
Teiresias has adopted a powerful rhetorical strategy, given both the
chorus's and Oedipus' avowed respect for the accuracy of his prophetic skills. Further, Teiresias' words make it quite clear that the
news he has for Oedipus is bad. So if Jocasta is right about Oedipus'
vulnerability to someone who speaks to his fears, Oedipus is in Teiresias' power from this point on.

Teiresias creates an opposition between himself and Oedipus in
almost every utterance early in the scene. He refers to his *own* misfortune in contrast to Oedipus' (e.g., 321, 329, 331). In his first seven
interchanges with Oedipus, none more than three lines long, Teiresias

uses the emphatic personal pronoun "I," *egô,* six times, and both "me" and "my" in the one response where he does not use *egô.* Oedipus, in contrast, uses a first-person singular pronoun only once in these interchanges: as the very last word of line 342 when he has lost his temper with the reticent seer: "You must tell me (*emoi*)."

Oedipus concludes, ironically, that Teiresias is setting himself above ruler and country. I say ironically, because Oedipus does not comment on the fact that both he and the chorus—the country, if you will—have placed Teiresias on that very platform above them on which he now stands, abusing his monarch. Oedipus comments only on the arrogance of Teiresias' insistent and apparently haughty *egô* and on his refusal to take any account of the city itself.

Oedipus now finds himself facing an especially difficult task. He must reestablish his authority and his status as tyrant not by rising from his throne in anger but by rising from the floor where he has been groveling at the feet of the man he now realizes is his adversary. So he resorts to the tyrannical and authoritarian first person. Once Oedipus' angry, tyrannical, and egotistical response occurs, Teiresias does not use *egô* again for, roughly, the next fifty lines. He has, I suspect, elicited the angry response he sought. He, like the chorus, has the opening advantage of knowing there would be an argument with Oedipus.

Oedipus' Accusations

In response to Teiresias' challenge to get angry, Oedipus exclaims (345–49):

> Yes! Such is my temper that I'll hold
> nothing that I know back. For you should know
> that I suspect you helped father this act,
> indeed, you did it—all but with your hands.
> If you had eyes, I'd claim you worked alone.

Teiresias' refusal to speak drives Oedipus to declare with passionate religious logic that Teiresias must have planned Laios' murder. For if Teiresias has known the criminal and has not spoken out as bidden, he is not only under the curse that Oedipus has placed on the murderer or murderers of *Laios* and on those who may be sheltering him or them, but also responsible for the destruction of the Theban people, the *laos*, who will continue to perish until the murderer is found.

Teiresias must therefore be responsible for the murder of Laios—though his blindness at least means that he did not actually commit the crime himself. Oedipus' conclusion is perfectly logical for someone who believes first that an unsolved murder really has caused the plague and second that Teiresias really knows who the killer is. Oedipus probably assumes that Teiresias, as a holy man, accepts the same religious logic too. But there is no reason to assume that Teiresias the rhetorician does.

It is no less ominous that Oedipus talks of Teiresias "fathering" or "begetting" the crime (*xymphyteusai*). It may be more than coincidence that Oedipus' mind seems yet again, as when he invoked the curse on the killer and those who might be harboring him, to be linking Laios' death and fatherhood, an association that becomes quite critical later in this scene.

Oedipus, then, lets anger get the better of him and unleashes upon Teiresias charges that have neither basis nor substantiating evidence. Is Oedipus simply being irrational and foolish, or is there rhetorical method in this apparent madness? If Oedipus has suddenly realized that Teiresias is about to point the finger at him, it could be quite advantageous to forestall Teiresias' accusation with one of his own. For any accusation from the seer would then appear to be only a retaliation in kind.

Indeed, Teiresias, who seconds earlier was saying that Oedipus did not have the power to drag his secret from him, does in fact retaliate with accusations of his own: he declares that Oedipus is the pollution upon the city (350). And we should note that this is also the first time Teiresias makes any reference to the city and its suffering (350–56):

> *Teiresias*: Is that true? I bid you now honor
> your proclamation: from this very day
> speak neither to these people nor to me!
> You are this land's unholy, sickly curse!
> *Oedipus*: You see no shame in starting such rumors?
> Where do you think you'll get away to hide?
> *Teiresias*: I've got away. I nurse the truth—it's strong.

Oedipus is understandably enraged at the accusation and the public humiliation, for the people, we recall, are present during the interchange. Yet Teiresias never offers a shred of evidence—now nor later—to substantiate his claim that Oedipus is guilty. Instead, he reiterates the words *alêthes,* "true," and *alêtheia,* "truth" (350, 356, 369). And the chorus, we will recall, has praised Teiresias as "the only human in whom truth is born" (299).

Teiresias and the Truth

Oedipus now faces the much more difficult task of assailing Teiresias' credibility as a purveyor of truth. To do so, he falls back on the conventional arguments which we find again and again in fifth-century Greek writers on the fraudulence of prophecy. The case would have more rhetorical merit had Oedipus not prefaced his interrogation of Teiresias with a speech that seemed to show traditional honor and respect for the seer's profession. Here is Oedipus' attack and Teiresias' response (358–59):

> *Oedipus*: Who taught you it? It's not part of your trade.
> *Teiresias*: You taught me, made me speak against my will.

Oedipus' taunt does not elicit a defense of prophets and prophecy from Teiresias as Pentheus' taunt draws out Teiresias in Euripides' *Bacchae* 248–327. The Sophoclean Teiresias simply hurls the insult back in his accuser's teeth, just as he does when Creon insults the prophetic trade in *Antigone* 1033–90. The Sophoclean Teiresias will not let his interlocutor escape from the personal nature of the conflict.

But angered as Oedipus is, he is still listening. Nothing Teiresias says is lost on him (359–60):

> *Oedipus*: Speak what? Say it again, so I'll learn more.
> *Teiresias*: You did not catch it—or you're testing me?

Why does Oedipus ask Teiresias to repeat his accusation? Dawe suggests (on line 359) that it is an authorial device "so that the audience may fully grasp some important point . . . or because the demands of stichomythia [the rapid interchange of single lines of verse] require a line to be delivered but the sense really requires nothing."[10] This explanation leaves me uneasy, since both alternatives assume there need be no dramatic justification from the speaker's point of view. I find it hard to see how the audience would not have caught the point the first time around and think it does Sophocles little credit to suggest he resorted to "filler." So we must explore alternatives.

Teiresias has just suggested, sarcastically, that he has learned the truth from Oedipus who forced him to speak. Now Oedipus is feigning not to understand the drift of Teiresias' words; he places himself in the position of a slow learner at Teiresias' feet, thus subtly undermining Teiresias' contention that he learned from Oedipus. Oedipus' words are not hostile but matter-of-fact: he is not, as tyrant to subject, *forcing* Teiresias to speak; he is, as student to teacher, requesting him to repeat what he said before. Oedipus' response throws Teiresias off balance for the first time in this scene. Confused and suspicious, he must be reassured by Oedipus before continuing (361–63):

> *Oedipus*: Not to my best knowledge. Say it again.
> *Teiresias*: These murderers you hunt: I say they're you.
> *Oedipus*: You'll not say this a second time scot-free.

Teiresias rephrases his original accusation with greater precision. We note that it assumes the connection between the plague and Laios' murder which was not made by Apollo's oracle but suggested by Creon, then given definitive form by Oedipus himself in his opening address to Teiresias. It is, of course, possible that Teiresias had heard news of Creon's consultation before Oedipus summarizes its outcome for him, as Oedipus concedes at the beginning of the scene (305). But we do not have to make this assumption.

A conflict of testimony now exists between Creon and Teiresias, as the chorus and Oedipus should realize. Creon insisted that Laios was assailed by many attackers: Teiresias implies that Oedipus was the only killer. And general opinion on this matter, if Creon is right, favors Creon's notion of the multiplicity of killers. Jocasta indeed explains later that the alleged witness to Laios' death publicly declared that the former king was attacked by several men.

Teiresias' declaration, then, conflicts with what most people at Thebes believe. But it does not necessarily conflict with what Oedipus believes. For Oedipus, we have noted, oscillates between accepting that plurality of killers and the possibility that it was just one— although he has not yet explained why he oscillates. We have not yet been told that Oedipus remembers having killed an old man at a crossroads. We have yet to grasp that he is worried by a fear still not clearly enunciated: that he himself may be the killer(s) he seeks.

For the present, let us simply note that Oedipus does not protest his innocence. He reacts with sufficient nonchalance that Teiresias seems almost dissatisfied with the results of his statements (364–65):

Teiresias: Should I speak on to fan your temper more?
Oedipus: As much as you feel need. You're wasting words.

Teiresias now openly admits that he intends to anger Oedipus, confirming our previous suspicion that such may have been his intention all along. But the positions have changed. Now Oedipus tells Teiresias he is wasting time trying to provoke him further. Earlier, Teiresias claimed Oedipus could not compel him to speak.

Teiresias cunningly recaptures the initiative in three steps. First he returns to his protests of truthfulness—where he must reestablish his credentials. Then he intimates that Oedipus is guilty of some family sexual crime, possibly incest, which, as we will discover, Oedipus greatly fears he may commit (or has committed). Finally the blind prophet opens up for Oedipus an obvious path along which to counterattack. He accuses his ruler of blindness to the real truth of the situation (366–69):

Tieresias: The truth eludes (*leLÊTHEnai*) you; you associate
              in vile sin with those dearest to you
              yet don't see where you are in evil's grasp.
Oedipus: Do you have the illusion you can talk
              this way for ever with impunity?
Teiresias: If truth's (*aLÊTHEias*) strength is not illusory.

Teiresias uses an etymologizing wordplay to reinforce his point, much as Plato later suggests the "truth" of Er's vision at the end of the *Republic* (10.621A–D). There Socrates reports that Er wandered in the divine world of disembodied souls who are about to be reincarnated. He journeys with them to the plain of the *LÊTHÊ*, "forgetfulness" and camps beside the river of indifference. A person who drinks (*PiONTA*) from this river forgets everything (*PANTÔn LAnTHAnesthai*). But Er is prevented from drinking and therefore remembers everything. Since knowledge, to the Platonic Socrates, is recollection, it would also be in a sense nonforgetfulness, that is to say, *A-LÊTHE-ia*: the truth.[11] Plato gives us, in short, an etymologizing assurance of the truth. And Socrates suggests it will be useful to remember Er's message when we come to cross the *LÊTHÊ* too.

Similarly Teiresias, by suggesting that knowledge has eluded (*le-LÊTHEnai*) Oedipus, is undermining in his listeners the possibility that Oedipus could know the truth.

The etymologizing force of Socrates'—and Teiresias'—suggestion finds interesting confirmation in Plato's *Cratylus* 421B, where Socrates defines truth, *ALÊTHEIA,* as *THEIA . . . ALÊ*: "heavenly wandering," which is no more than an anagram of *ALÊ THEIA* and an interesting reinforcement of the ideas that Er's journey is a heavenly wandering toward the truth. We must give this ancient etymologizing careful attention in Sophocles' *Oedipus,* no matter how bizarre or even silly it may sound to modern ears. For Oedipus himself will go on to accept an etymologized identity for himself, derived from the assertion that his name, Oedipus, means "swollen foot."

The Prophecy of Blindness

The bait to which Oedipus rises, however, is not the issue of the truth itself. It is Teiresias' boast that, though blind, he has special sight. Blindness, one might—and Oedipus does—suggest, could be an obstacle to discerning the truth (370–77):

> *Oedipus*: It's strong, but not in you. In you it's dead.
> Your ears and mind are sightless as your eyes.
> *Teiresias*: You are pathetic, taunting me the way
> that soon the whole world will be taunting you.
> *Oedipus*: Child of unbroken darkness, never could you
> harm me or anyone who sees life's light.
> *Teiresias*: Fate does not set your downfall by my hands.
> Apollo wants to finish this himself.

We see again the success of Teiresias' tactics: he provokes Oedipus' insults and accusations, then turns them against him. In this instance we find Teiresias' only prophetic statement in the play. It immediately prompts the question that should always arise when prophecies are addressed to believers in prophecy: is prophecy in such cases proof of the seer's foreknowledge of subsequent actions, or is it the *cause* of what follows? Let us remind ourselves that there is *nothing* in Apollo's oracle, even as reported by Creon, that said anything about the killer blinding himself. And there is nothing in what Oedipus subsequently reveals about his own visit to Delphi to suggest that he will blind himself. The statement that he will do so comes from a blind prophet whose blindness and prophetic powers Oedipus has insulted.

Here we gain a glimpse of what ought to be a central issue in the discussion of Sophocles' *Oedipus*. Yet it has not been, for the simple reason that readers and critics themselves make a curious act of faith: that Teiresias is actually speaking the truth. The reasoning that precedes the act of faith is quite straightforward. Because Oedipus ultimately blinds himself, Teiresias must be a purely objective clairvoyant. How else would he know that Oedipus will take such drastic action against himself?

The counterexplanation is not particularly hard to grasp: that Oedipus' behavior, based on prior observation, is predictable. He will respond to a given stimulus in a given and predictable way. It is not only the biologist but the witchdoctor and the psychologist who understand this principle. We see from the beginning of the play that there is an element in Oedipus that makes him take prophecy seriously. Thus he risks allowing prophetic utterances to control his life, whether he acquiesces in his "doom" or tries to avoid fulfilling it.

The danger is that if he is convinced one prophecy is correct, he will accept other prophecies as similarly binding. If he concludes that he has killed his father and married his mother, as he fears he will, because Apollo prophesied that he would, Oedipus may go on to blind himself, in the belief that he is not only fulfilling his doom but justly punishing himself. We are dealing with the huge power of suggestion that is often wielded over the superstitious, in this case by a blind prophet whose trade and whose blindness Oedipus has just insulted. Here is the difference between Teiresias and an attorney in court: Teiresias is trying to persuade *the accused* of his guilt, not the jury.

The same vagueness in Oedipus' thinking that makes him assimilate Creon's explanation to the oracle reported makes him assimilate what Teiresias says to the prophecy of matricide and incest. It thus makes little sense to argue that Oedipus can accept the efficacy of Apollo's prophetic powers without believing in those of Teiresias. We have seen how readily Oedipus accepts not just Apollo's word but whatever is reported as Apollo's word. Hence the force of Teiresias' attribution of the fulfillment of Oedipus' destruction to the prophetic god whose oracles Oedipus fears and respects: Apollo.

The Theory of Conspiracy

Oedipus is not, however, so hopelessly naive as immediately to accept at face value Teiresias' insinuation of Apollo into the argument. The moment Apollo is mentioned, in fact, he sees a link between Creon and Teiresias. There is a plot: Creon is in league with Teiresias. Oedipus asks (378): "Creon or who came up with these findings?"

Oedipus realizes he may have been trapped by his dependence on religious sources, by his use of Creon to consult Apollo, and by calling Teiresias. To make things worse, he has conducted his investigation in public. The people of Thebes have heard Creon speak; they have witnessed the accusations of Teiresias. Oedipus is in deep rhetorical and political trouble. Teiresias tries to turn Oedipus back on himself again with the immediate retort (379): "Creon is not your problem, you are your own." This time, Teiresias fails. Oedipus explodes into a denunciation of Creon and Teiresias (380–89):

> Riches, tyranny, and skillfulness
> surpassing others' skill makes for a life
> much coveted. The envy that stands guard
> upon you is so great! I did not ask
> the city to put in my hands the power
> to be first lord. The city gave it me,
> this power for which Creon, a trusted man,
> a friend from my first days of lordly rule,
> now yearns to throw me out. He secretly
> creeps on me from behind, quietly works in
> a plot-weaving, king-making charlatan,
> a treacherous liar who sees personal gain
> but was born sightless in the trade he plies.

There is no overwhelming reason to suspect, on the basis of what has been said thus far in the play, that Creon has been plotting with Teiresias against Oedipus to take over Oedipus' *tyrannis*, his position as tyrant (380). We, of course, do not have access to any prior "knowledge" such as Oedipus might have to support such charges in his own mind. True, we have noticed that Creon is curiously reticent in reporting the oracle, blurring the lines between what the oracle may have said and his own interpretation of it. The motive Oedipus attributes to Creon, envy, is not impossible, given Creon's reasonable expectation that he might have become ruler after Laios' death—as he does in some versions of the myth.

Indeed, envy could also explain Teiresias' hostility toward Oedipus. For Oedipus' strongest single claim to superiority over Teiresias is that he, not Teiresias, solved the riddle of the Sphinx. He now knows he must publicly match his credentials in riddle solving against Teiresias'. He abruptly adopts the skeptic's position on oracles and divination, then turns on Teiresias with the haughtiness of God to Job: where were you when I solved the riddle of the Sphinx? Here is his attack (390–403):

> Come on now, prove your clear prophetic powers.
> When the riddle-singing bitch was here,
> how was it you said nothing to release
> these fellow citizens of yours? Here was
> a riddle needing power of prophecy,
> not an accidental passerby to solve.
> But you did not come forward with your birds
> or words of god to make it known. Then I,
> Oedipus, no wit at all (*mêden eidôs Oidipous*), passed by.
> And I defeated her, not by learning
> from birds, but by using my intellect.
>
> This is the man you now try to turn out,
> thinking you'll stand up close to Creon's throne.
> But I think you will weep, both you and he
> who organized all this. Did I not think
> that you were old, you would have learned by now
> what your reasoning power had brought you to.

Oedipus here offers his strongest possible evidence that he is intellectually superior to Teiresias and casts in his teeth Teiresias' claims to "reasoning power." He might well have gone on to reestablish his own credentials as savior of the state, had he pursued further the matter of the Sphinx and its riddle. The question is indeed interesting. If Teiresias is the "only human in whom truth is born," and if he has great reasoning power, why was he unable (or unwilling) to solve the riddle? Oedipus, however, mixes up the issue of Teiresias' professional competence with accusations of political plotting. And his explosion of anger provokes the chorus to intervene, censuring both men and asking them both to return to the central issue (404–7):

> The words he spoke seem shaped in temper and
> yours too, Oedipus. That's what we think.
> The situation does not call for this.
> Rather one must look for the best way
> to break down, answer the god's prophecies.

Teiresias, however, has been let off the hook and has no intention of returning to it. He takes advantage of Oedipus' political accusations to reply in astonishing political kind. He does not engage Oedipus on the latter's strong ground—his solution of the Sphinx's riddle. Nor does he deny involvement in a conspiracy. Instead he focuses on Oedipus himself, on the nature of his power, and on the personal insults Oedipus has directed toward him, especially the insult to his blindness. And he picks up on two political words Oedipus has used.

The first word is *tyrannis,* which Oedipus used in reference to Laios' power in lines 128–29 and again, in Teiresias' presence, in line 380. Oedipus, himself a tyrant, understandably has no sense that *tyrannis* is a politically "negative" word. But Teiresias is not so naive. He uses Oedipus' general description of absolute power as a means of accusing Oedipus of behaving tyrannically. Teiresias is in fact, the first person in the play to describe Oedipus' rule as tyrannical (*tyrannein*) in an overtly negative sense (408). Tyrants, proverbially, are the enemies of free speech. So with rhetorical aplomb, Teiresias demands the right to reply, which no one has denied him. Indeed, the problem earlier was precisely Teiresias' *refusal* to speak (408–9):

> Though you're the tyrant, still, equality
> must be allowed at least in equal time
> to make reply. In this I too have power.

The second word is *prostatês,* "sponsor, champion," a word Oedipus had used flatteringly of Teiresias himself in line 303 as the seer was entering: "only you can be her [Thebes'] savior, sponsor (*prostatês*), and spokesman." This is how Teiresias picks up and uses the term (409–11):

> I live as Apollo's slave, not yours,
> so don't enroll me as an alien
> with Creon as my sponsor (*prostatou*) and spokesman.

The last line cited carries some extraordinary undertones which smack of fifth-century Athens rather than mythic Thebes, and which I am quite sure would have jolted Sophocles' audience. So we must digress briefly to discuss some of them here.

Creon as Champion

The word *prostatês* ("sponsor, champion") and its associated adjective *prostatêrios* ("protecting, championing") are often used by Sophocles of divine rather than human patrons.[12] In fact, when Oedipus calls upon Teiresias as sole *prostatês* and savior in the plague (303), he is using language that, as Dawe observes on that line, "can be used unaltered of a god."[13] More often, however, *prostatês* carries political resonances. The word came, Victor Ehrenberg observes, to denote "the political leader of the people," though the first clear use of the term in that sense does not occur until Aristophanes' *Peace* 684, some time after the production of *Oedipus*.[14] We saw in Chapter 1 how such a champion of the people can be a threat to democracy and lead to the imposition of tyranny. A comment by Orestes, in Euripides' *Orestes* 772, shows that the *prostatês* can be a demagogue in tragedy as well as in Plato: "The populace is a formidable entity when it has mischievous champions (*prostatas*)."

The earliest and most common political use of the word, however, is that exemplified in Aeschylus' *Suppliants* 963, where king Pelasgus is described as "sponsor of the future metics [resident aliens]." And this is the particular sense of the word that Teiresias seems to have in mind here.

Jebb paraphrases Teiresias' sentiments (cited above) as follows:

> You charge me with being the tool of Creon's treason. I have a right to plead my own case when I am accused. I am not like a resident alien, who can plead before a civic tribunal only by the mouth of that patron under whom he has been registered.

"Every *metoikos* [resident alien] at Athens," Jebb continues, "was required *epigraphesthai prostatên*, i.e. to have the name of a citizen, as patron, inscribed over his own." The allusion to the need for resident aliens in the Athens of Sophocles' own day to speak "through" a citizen patron is fascinating in many ways.[15]

Sophocles' audience was composed not of literary scholars but of ordinary citizens who understood political issues most readily in terms of their own experience of government. The same Athenian citizens, gathered in the Assembly, were the city's legislative body, and gathered in the various courts, the judiciary. As Ehrenberg observed, the Greek tragedian was not "a private person writing beautiful poetry in an ivory tower," and tragedy itself was "an event of public life in which the trends of people's minds were reflected, discussed, and displayed."[16] Sophocles himself had taken a prominent part in Athenian public life, and almost certainly served as general with Pericles in 441/40.[17] He was not simply a professional writer who observed politics from a distance, but a man at the very hub of political activity, and in political contact with those most active in government.

We must then look once more at the role of Creon as *prostatês* and F. J. Parsons's note on Aristotle's *Rhetoric* 3.8 (1408B) makes a good starting point:

> Emancipated slaves, like the *metoikoi* [resident aliens], seldom arrived at the dignity of Citizens, or were allowed to manage business in their own names; but were obliged to select some one of the Citizens as their "Patron," (*prostatên, epitropon,*) under whose name to be enrolled, and to whose care and protection to be committed. Compare Sophocles' *Oedipus Tyrannus*, 411 [Teiresias' remark about Creon, cited above]. . . . The popularity of the demagogue Cleon, of course, caused many to solicit his "Patronage," indeed so many, that the boys in the street anticipated the close of the Crier's proclamation on these occasions [i.e., when the Crier asked who would speak on someone's behalf] by calling out "Kleona."[18]

Creon's role as *prostatês,* as intermediary and spokesman for the ordinary person, combined with his overt "popularizing" could hardly fail to evoke thoughts of the Athenian demagogue Cleon, who was one of the major political forces in Athens in the years following Pericles' death—the very years during which Sophocles must have written *Oedipus*: 429–25 B.C. Cleon was bitterly hated by the historian Thucydides and mocked again and again by Aristophanes in his comedies where Cleon's control over the Athenian people is savagely satirized.[19]

Thucydides saw him as the main driving force of the prolonged and ultimately disastrous war Athens waged against Sparta, as the agent of the most callous Athenian imperialism, who again and again prevented the conclusion of a just and advantageous peace by stirring up war fever in the gullible populace. It was he who used his power as a champion of the people to build the basis of a personal authority in the state which no one was able to challenge successfully until his death. Cleon paved the way for a succession of popular leaders who were able to wrest control of the state from more genteel and aristocratic leaders. In Aeschylus' day a *prostatês* may have been a kindly champion of the dispossessed. But this was no longer true in the later years of the fifth century, as we have seen from Orestes' comment in Euripides' *Orestes* 772: "the populace is a formidable entity when they have mischievous champions (*prostatês*)."

The passage in Aristotle (*Rhetoric* 3.8[1408B]) that drew Parsons's attention to Teiresias' remark about Creon deserves, then, our special attention:

> The form of one's prose style should not be either metrical or un-rhythmical. If it is metrical it is unpersuasive because it appears contrived. It is at the same time distracting because it prompts the audience to look out for when similar occurrences will again arise—the way the children do when they anticipate the answer when the heralds ask: "Who does the freedman choose as his patron?" "Cleon!" they say.

Cleon had been dead for more than fifty years when Aristotle wrote. Yet Cleon's popularity as champion of resident aliens was still proverbial, as it was for Aristophanes in the *Frogs,* written twenty years after Cleon's death. A hostess who considers herself to have been wronged by Heracles calls upon Cleon as *prostatês* (*Frogs* 569): "Go and call Cleon to act as *prostatês* for me." How much more striking, then, must Teiresias' *metrical* reference to the need for a *prostatês* have been in Sophocles' *Oedipus,* written when Cleon was at the pinnacle of his career, and when there were fears that he, like the *prostatês* of Plato's *Republic,* might make himself a tyrant.

Creon and Cleon

The names Cleon and Creon are not far apart upon the Athenian aristocratic tongue. The letters *r* and *l* were readily confused by the Greeks, and their confusion is even the subject of a famous epigram by Palladas (*Anthology* 11.323): "Rho and Lambda are the only things separating ravenous crows (*korakas*) from craven flatterers (*kolakas*). So the raven and the craven would both rob a shrine. Be on your guard, good friend, against this creature, knowing that among the living, cravens are as ravens." In Aristophanes' *Wasps*, a play focused on Cleon and produced in the year of Cleon's death (422 B.C.), this confusion of *l* and *r* emerges prominently in the opening scene. Sosias describes a dream in which he saw the politician Theorus with a crow's head (*kefalên korakas* [*Wasps* 42]). As the dream continues, Alcibiades, a young aristocrat and nephew of Pericles, came up to him and said (*Wasps* 45): "*olas. Theôlos tên kephalên kolakos echei.*"[20] Alcibiades lisped, in Greek fashion, substituting *l* for *r*: instead of *oras*, "you see," he said *olas*, which means (more or less) "you destroy." The name Theorus, which suggests a pilgrim, "one who goes to see god (*theos*)," becomes Theolus, "destroyer of god." His head becomes that of a flattering craven (*kolakos*), not a raven (*korakos*). With the Greek *r*'s the line means: "You see? Pilgrim Theorus has a raven's head." With the Greek *l*'s, the changed meaning is something like: "You destroy? Pogrom Theorus has a craven's head."

It should be noted that the Theorus mentioned by Aristophanes is one of Cleon's friends. At the end of the *Wasps,* in fact, when Philocleon and his son Bdelycleon are imagining themselves at a drinking party among Cleon's entourage, Bdelycleon gives us the image of Theorus lying at Cleon's feet (*pros podôn*), holding his right hand and singing (1236–37).[21]

The same speech impediment that makes Theorus Theolus makes Creon Cleon; it also has a name most appropriate to the tale of Thebes: Labdacism (*labdakismos*). Labdacism, Quintilian says (*Instructing the Orator* 1.5.32), along with iotacism, solecism, and so forth, are mistakes that "happen through sounds, and which cannot be shown in writing because they are errors of speech and of the tongue" (*per sonos accidunt, quae demonstrari scripto non possunt, vitia oris et linguae*). I mention Quintilian's use of the Greek term to demonstrate that "la(m)bdacism" was used in antiquity to describe this particular speech problem. It is not just a modern coinage used by speech therapists.[22]

Laios, the son of Labdacus, then, was killed while leaving his native people to consult the oracle: *theôros . . . ekdemôn*, as Creon reports. And through Labdacism and Labdacus, a link is forged between the myth of Oedipus and Sophocles' contemporary Athens. For a fleeting instant, Creon and Cleon, mythic Thebes and fifth-century Athens, merge in Teiresias' words.

Curiously, another way Creon resembles Cleon is in his role as intermediary between Oedipus and the sources of oracular wisdom.

He is Oedipus' envoy to Delphi; he prompts Oedipus to consult Teiresias; finally he suggests that Oedipus himself go to Delphi to check out the validity of the report he has brought. Similarly, in Aristophanes' *Knights* 61, a complaint is made that the Paphlagonian slave (sometimes identified as Cleon) bewilders Dêmos (i.e., the people) by chanting oracles (*aidei de chrêsmous*). In fact the speaker suggests to his fellow-slave that they steal the Paphlagonian's oracles while he is asleep (1109–10). As Fontenrose observes: "Kleon is in effect a chresmologue who possesses a collection of Bakis' oracles, which help him to keep Demos under his control (*Knights* 109–143, 195–210, 960–1096)."[23]

It is in his role as purveyor of oracles that Creon influences Oedipus' actions in Sophocles' play: an inquiry which will lead Oedipus to the conclusion that he is, as Teiresias suggests, a native-born son of Thebes (*engenês Thebaios*), not a resident alien (*xenos . . . metoikos*) (452–53). Oedipus, then, owes his citizen status to the oracle Creon brings from Delphi.

I am not trying to suggest that Sophocles' Creon *is* Cleon, but rather that Sophocles uses the suggestive resonances of Cleon in the play to color his presentation of Creon. He might thus, and reasonably, expect his audience to react more skeptically to Creon's rhetoric than many modern critics do, when they choose to see in him an honest and detatched observer, fulfilling his citizen duty in a forthright way. In a world where Cratylan etymologies are taken seriously, we must not just privilege the etymology of Oedipus' name in this play. After all, Creon's own name is nothing more than the adjective *kreôn*, "the ruler."

Parents and Defeat

Let us return now to the exchanges between Oedipus and Teiresias. After contemptuously dismissing the possibility that he is conspiring with Creon (though with words, as we have seen, that might arouse rather than quell our suspicions), Teiresias resumes the theme of his (and Oedipus') blindness (412–28):

> You taunt my blindness. Therefore I shall speak.
> You don't see where you are in evil's grasp,
> though you have eyes, or where you make your home,

> or who you share it with.
>   Who gave you birth?
> Do you know this?
>   Does it elude you that
> you are an enemy to relatives
> both buried and alive upon the earth?
> And yet the curse of mother and father,
> moving its inexorable feet,
> will strike a double blow, some day drive you
> out of this land. Now you can see well,
> then you'll see darkness. Oh what place, what place
> will not give harbor to your scream that day?
> Will Cithaeron not quickly sing with you
> when finally you understand the tune
> of your own wedding hymn with which you sailed,
> with what smooth sailing, straight into a home
> that had no proper berth for your vessel?
> There is a host of other evils too
> which you don't grasp but which will make of you
> an equal to your very own children.
>
> Counter that by throwing mud at Creon
> and at my own face! There is no mortal
> who will ever appear more vile than you
> when the veneer is some day scraped away.

The allusions are much more explicit in this third announcement of
Oedipus' "crimes." But there is now no reference to their more public
nature. Teiresias focuses on the pollution Oedipus has been within
his own family. Then, after these accusations of incest, he returns to
a more political tone and, with consummate rhetorical bravado, re-
bukes *Oedipus* for mudslinging (425–26).

At this point Oedipus' rhetorical defeat begins to become a rout.
He understandably, but feebly, protests (429–31):

> Must I hear these insufferable slurs
> from this man? Go to hell! Turn round and back
> and get out of this his house. And make it quick!

But Teiresias turns the very dismissal against him (432): "I'd not have
come. But then you summoned me." Oedipus tries bravely to retort,
hoping, perhaps, that he can get Teiresias to respond to one insult
with another, and thus shift the focus away from himself. But Teiresias, ignoring the taunt, intensifies the focus on Oedipus (433–36):

> *Oedipus*: I did not know you'd talk such idiocy,
>   or I'd have waited before asking you.
> *Teiresias*: We are what we were born. Idiots, you think.
>   Those who begat you thought me rational.

Teiresias is not simply making a point of his superior age and experience when he says he was respected as a prophet by Oedipus' parents. He is implying that he knew Oedipus' parents and they him.

Teiresias has baited a rhetorical trap for Oedipus and, as we will see from Oedipus' response, obviously starts to walk off the stage. His answers, like those of Euripides' Dionysus, are designed to make his questioner curious. There has been no indication up to this point that Oedipus is uncertain about his parents' identity. And there is no reason to assume that the chorus was previously concerned with the issue.

The audience, however, familiar with the Oedipus myth in other forms, is certainly ready to pounce on Teiresias' words. So too, it happens, is Oedipus (437):

> "Who were they?
>   Stay!
>   Who is my real father?"

By calling Teiresias back to consult him at this moment, Oedipus loses any rhetorical momentum he has gained and ruins his contention that Teiresias is a fool. He again approaches the seer as an oracular authority with true answers, implying that Teiresias may know the secret answer to a riddle about his own existence. Oedipus has instantly and publicly rebuilt Teiresias' credentials as a prophetic authority. He has also, in effect, conceded Teiresias' truthfulness.

Teiresias' oracular response sets up the rhetorical coup de grace for Oedipus (438–40):

> *Teiresias*: This day will start your life. Destroy it too.
> *Oedipus*: Your words are all too riddling and obscure.
> *Teiresias*: Weren't you born best at finding riddles out?

Teiresias' enigmatic utterance elicits an objection from Oedipus that he is baffled. Teiresias leaps on the error. Any momentary success that Oedipus' mention of his triumph over the Sphinx may have registered a few lines earlier has been neutralized.

Oedipus, sensing his blunder, does not pursue the question of his birth. He only retorts, pitifully (441): "Keep taunting me with this! You'll find me great." To which Teiresias responds (442): "It was just luck, and now it's ruined you." Teiresias claims total victory and voices the professional's view of amateur success, a view that finds some vindication in the play. If intelligence and skill enabled Oedipus to destroy the Sphinx, why doesn't he even try to repeat that success, relying on his own wits instead of on the established sources of religious and political power which rarely have any love for the interloper? Perhaps it was just "beginner's luck." Indeed, as we have seen in the Introduction, there are traditions that have Oedipus find the solution to the riddle in a prophetic dream rather than by his own intellectual force. Oedipus himself seems to adopt Teiresias' view later when he claims to be the "child of Luck," or "child of Fortune."

However much Oedipus may be an amateur in Teiresias' world, he is not so unaware of his humiliation as is sometimes suggested. Oedipus now accepts the possibility that he is, as Teiresias suggests, destroyed and declares that it was all worthwhile (443): "Well if it's saved this city, I don't care." Satisfied, Teiresias prepares, yet again, to leave. But Oedipus tries one parting shot (444–46):

> *Teiresias*: I'm going then. Come, boy, you take me out!
> *Oedipus*: Yes, take him out! When here you're under foot,
>   stir trouble. When gone, you can cause no more pain.

Go, Oedipus is saying, you cannot make things worse for me. Thus challenged, Teiresias does makes things worse. He modifies his assertion that he is leaving by setting forth his charges in all their details in a speech that opens with these words (447–49):

> I'm going once I've said what I came here
> to say. I'm not afraid of your facade.
> You do not have the power to destroy me.
> So I speak.

Teiresias claimed that he intended to say nothing and could not be forced to say anything when he first came on stage. Was that disclaimer no more than a pretext, the bait for the cruel hook, the red rag to Oedipal bullishness? We may recall, as we reflect on this brilliant scene between Oedipus and Teiresias, part of what Quintilian says of persuasive speech in court, cited in the Introduction in our discussion of ancient *emphasis (Instructing the Orator* 9.2.71–72):

> Use of the emotions helps a lot. It's good to break the flow of your speech with silence, to hesitate. Then you may be sure the judge will search out that certain something which he probably would not believe if he heard it actually stated. You may be sure he will believe what he thinks he himself has discovered. . . . In sum: *the judge is most likely to believe what is figured in our speech if he thinks we are unwilling to say it.*

In Quintilian's words we see the power of Teiresias' hesitation, and we remember that the chorus called Teiresias "the cross-questioner," "the refuter." But we also see the vulnerability of the judge to the suggestions implanted by the speaker. Oedipus does not appear to believe what Teiresias says when the charges of his guilt are made overtly. But Teiresias knows the seed of the idea is planted as he moves into his peroration where he spells everything out again, then orders Oedipus inside to think over what has been said (449–62):

> This man you've lately sought,
> threatened and publicly outlawed: this man,
> this Laian killer, is here with us now.
> Word is that he's a foreign resident.
> But he'll become a Theban, native born,
> though this turn of events will not please him.
> Now he sees, but then he will be blind,
> now rich, a beggar then, groping his way
> upon a staff into a foreign land.
> He'll become brother as well as father
> to his children in his house, both son
> and husband to the woman who bore him,
> he'll sow his semen where his father sowed,
> and kill his father.
>   Go inside your home.
> Figure it out. And if you catch me lying,
> claim I'm devoid of mantic reasoning.

This time Oedipus musters no response at all. He leaves, dismissed by the prophet he himself summoned, then sought to dismiss.

The professional seer has triumphed over the man who once triumphed over him by solving the riddle of the Sphinx—perhaps by sheer luck rather than reasoning. Indeed, when Teiresias first entered, he seemed depressed that reasoning seemed to count for so little at Thebes (316–18):

> Alas: reason's power! How formidable (*deinon*)
> when reason does not pay. I know this well.
> But I forgot it, or I'd not have come.

Perhaps these were the reflections of a man who had had to take second place to a *parvenu* ever since that *parvenu* solved the riddle of the Sphinx by a stroke of luck, which he certainly was able to make pay. But now, at the end of the scene, his power of reasoning seems vindicated. The word *phronein,* "reasoning," is the last as well as the first word Teiresias speaks. He has used his rhetorical skill to refute Oedipus as utterly as Oedipus had refuted the Sphinx. Indeed, Teiresias has made Oedipus the new Sphinx plaguing Thebes. And he, like the Sphinx of Old, will be destroyed by words. Proceeding inexorably from the top of the social scale to the bottom, his interlocutors will cause his undoing: Creon, his presumed rival and future ruler; Teiresias, the prophet smarting from his defeat in solving the Sphinx's riddle; Jocasta, his queen; an anonymous Corinthian of uncertain status who solves a riddle of feet; finally a slave. But it is Teiresias who most clearly sets Oedipus on the road to self-destruction in this play.

Teiresias' power of refutation is "formidable." Like a curious variant of Socratic *elenchos,* it is designed to win, and wins, an admission of defeat, either overt or tacit, from the baffled interlocutor. Oedipus presents no evidence to support his charge of conspiracy against Teiresias. But neither does Teiresias present evidence of Oedipus' guilt. It is all a matter of rhetoric and psychology. Teiresias' words expose a raw nerve in Oedipus: his doubts about his father's identity—doubts as old as Greek literature. Homer's Telemachus tells Athena that although his mother claims he is Odysseus' son: "I don't know. No one ever really knows in himself who his father is" (*Odyssey* 1.215-b). The reader, "knowing" the Oedipus myth, is confident Teiresias is right about Oedipus' parents. Oedipus fears Teiresias is right. Yet the chorus members, innocent of myth and fear, incline to see a feud at the root of this confrontation. The "great refuter" has *not* convinced *them.* Indeed, they now begin to doubt his mastery of truth.

4. CREON, OEDIPUS, AND JOCASTA

Although there is no evidence to substantiate Oedipus' assumption that Teiresias is plotting with Creon against him, it is at least worth noting that the distribution of characters among the three actors used by Sophocles in this play would mean that the tritagonist, the third actor, would play the roles of both Creon and Teiresias. Theatrical conventions may limit a playwright in some respects but can prove an important dramatic resource in others. In Shakespeare's *As You Like It,* for example, the use of male actors to play women's roles allows him to generate a scene with some curious, forbidden, homosexual overtones. Rosalind, played by a boy, disguises herself as a boy, and explains to Orlando how he should woo Rosalind. And to remind his audience of the convention, Shakespeare has Rosalind remark, in the epilogue: "If I were a woman." Too little has been done by critics on this subject of the creative use of such theatrical convention.[1]

In *Oedipus,* then, Teiresias' voice *is* Creon's in the sense that their *personae* are given life by the same actor, as they rarely are in modern productions. Not only might the audience, under these circumstances, come to share a little of Oedipus' suspicion, but its uneasiness would be heightened by the reaction of the chorus to Teiresias' words.

Teiresias' denunciation of Oedipus shocks the Thebans deeply. Despite their earlier, and obviously greater, deference to Teiresias, they seem much less convinced than Oedipus that Teiresias was telling the truth (498–501):

> Zeus and Apollo both understand,
> know what mortals do and did.
> But when it comes down to men:
> Does a seer fare better than I do?
> There's no unelusive (*alathes*) way to judge.

Their stated faith that Teiresias is the only human in whom truth (*alêtheia*) is born seems somewhat eroded. They realize that there is no unelusive, "true," way to judge the correctness of Teiresias' charges. Instead, they assume there must be some hitherto undetected political vendetta underlying the charges made by Teiresias against Oedipus (487–91):

> I for one have not learned
> what basis for dispute existed ever in the past,
> or up to today,
> on the Labdacid side,
> on Polybus' son's side.

Since Teiresias was not himself a member of the house of Labdacus, but Creon was, the chorus seems to be giving at least passing credence to Oedipus' suggestions of a plot.[2] Although they do not reject out of hand the possibility that Oedipus may be guilty of the terrible evildoings Teiresias declares, they do proclaim their unwillingness to accept the accusations without proof.

There are now, then, two sets of unsubstantiated charges at work in the play: Teiresias' accusations against Oedipus, and Oedipus' against Creon and Teiresias.

The Populist

As the chorus tries to analyze what has passed, Creon reenters, declaring he has heard (from whom, it is not clear) that he is accused of treason (513–22):

> Gentlemen, citizens (*andres politai*), I've learned that I
> have been most seriously accused

by our own tyrant Oedipus. I'm here
since my position is unbearable.
If he thinks he has suffered through my fault—
by what I've said or done—in the present
disastrous crisis, then I've no desire
to prolong my life. The punishment
I suffer for his words is not simply
a trivial matter between him and me,
it's very large—if I am to be called
evil in the city here, and worse,
called evil by yourself and by my friends.

Creon adopts a very different *persona* from the one we saw as he returned from Delphi, when he was terse, enigmatic, even secretive, when he wondered whether he should discuss the oracle in private with Oedipus, inside the house. Now he seems intent on contrasting himself with Oedipus in several ways.

First, Creon plays the populist, the demagogue, much as Oedipus plays the benevolent, paternal dictator (as he would see it), the tyrant (as Teiresias suggests). Creon's opening words, *andres politai* ("gentlemen citizens," [512]), are not a common formula in surviving Athenian literature, since orators in Athens take it for granted that they are addressing citizens. Demosthenes, Lysias, or Isocrates use, rather, *andres Athenaioi* ("gentlemen of Athens"). In the fifty or so instances where the phrase is found in Greek literature (mostly in writers of the Roman imperial period), it normally occurs in or as the opening words of a public, political pronouncement to a citizen body in a moment of very special crisis. In Xenophon's *Hellenica* 2.4.13, these words are the opening of Thrasybulus' speech to his exiled and disenfranchised Athenian democrats before their victorious battle against the thirty tyrants in 404 B.C., reminding them of the citizen rights they have lost. The formula is used again by Cleocritus, herald of the Eleusinian initiates, after same battle, as the beginning of his appeal not to be driven into exile from the city, a reminder to his audience that he is their fellow-citizen (*Hellenica* 2.4.20).

In tragedy, *andres politai* occurs only three times. In Aeschylus' *Agamemnon* 855 the phrase is used, with magnificent irony, by a *woman*, Clytemnestra as the opening of her response to the speech Agamemnon makes on his return to Argos. She calls on the people to bear witness to the love she has for her husband while readying the tapestries over which he will walk to his death. In *Oedipus at*

Colonus 1579, it is used by the herald announcing Oedipus' death. Finally, it is used here by Creon. He too is announcing the beginning of a momentous struggle for power between himself and Oedipus. He speaks, with a politician's touch, as Clytemnestra does, to the chorus, which in both *Agamemnon* and *Oedipus* is the citizen body. There is a similar politician's touch in the final words of Creon's opening statement, when he addresses the chorus in the second-person singular and links it with his circle of friends—even though nothing in the chorus's reaction indicates that it regards Creon as an intimate associate.

The second point is this. Creon poses as the loyal subject who would rather die than endure the shame brought by false charges. Oedipus, in contrast, has made no such declaration of death before dishonor and takes little overt account of Teiresias' terrible accusations. It soon becomes obvious, however, that Creon is engaging in shallow bravado: he quickly tries to negotiate for banishment when he thinks Oedipus will really have him put to death.

Third, Creon makes no allusion whatever to the substance of the accusations made against Oedipus by Teiresias, other than to imply they are lies. He behaves as if only he himself has been wronged.

The chorus, following up the mood of its choral song before Creon's entrance, senses that it must handle Creon carefully. Although admitting Creon was insulted, the chorus clearly does not want to get involved in a struggle between him and Oedipus. In fact, the chorus succeeds remarkably well in avoiding Creon's hints that Oedipus may have been not just angry but insane when he made the charges—a theme that will recur as the two men meet— (523–31):

> *Chorus*: This insult was more probably forced out
> by anger than by reasoning and thought.
> *Creon*: It was, then, actually voiced aloud
> that this seer was persuaded by reasons
> I adduced to speak words that were lies?
> *Chorus*: Words were uttered to the effect. But I
> don't know what reason they were based upon.
> *Creon*: Did he keep his eyes straight, was his mind straight
> when he accused me of this criminal charge?
> *Chorus*: I don't know. I don't see what rulers do.
> But notice that he's come outside himself.

In referring to the charges Teiresias made, Creon very carefully uses indirect speech with the optative mood—a rhetorical device that will be discussed in more detail in Chapter 8. It does not commit him to saying that the seer lied: it could simply be the opinion of those reporting to him that the seer lied. But his statement is vague enough to suggest that he does not vouch for the truth of what Teiresias said (525–26). He thus dissociates himself from both the report of the seer's words and the words themselves. By leaving open the possibility that Teiresias lied, he subverts Oedipus' claim that he has conspired with Teiresias.

No less important, Creon suggests, as he does frequently in the coming scene, that Oedipus is not really rational. As Teiresias undermines Oedipus' credentials as an interrogator, so Creon—and later Jocasta—will do much to subvert the chorus's opinion of Oedipus' sanity. Creon will also, by playing the populist, highlight Oedipus' tyrannical tendencies.

Oedipus Accuses

The chorus is careful to keep its distance from Creon and is relieved when Oedipus enters and assumes the initiative. Oedipus, however, does not aid his own cause by remaining calm in the face of his suspected foe. He was, understandably, under serious provocation by Teiresias when he accused Creon in absentia. Now, in his second encounter with Creon, he puts himself at great rhetorical disadvantage by emerging still angry into a fresh scene and into fresh rhetorical circumstances in which his interlocutor already has several factors working for him. Most obviously, Creon has talked, however obliquely, of Teiresias' accusations as lies. And this apparent concession weakens Oedipus' charge that Creon is in collusion with the prophet. More important, Creon presents himself as calm, composed, and politically courteous, as apparently sane as Oedipus is apparently irrational. The theme of reasoning and rationality, so important to the Teiresias scene, takes on a new flavor. Thus, when Oedipus bursts in, speaking in an overbearing, overstated, illogical, and unjust manner, his demeanour adds plausibility to Creon's intimations of insanity. Has Creon seen Oedipus like this before?

Oedipus addresses Creon with the arrogance of a master addressing a slave (532–42):

> You there! Why are you here? Do you put on
> so great a mask of boldness as to come
> into my very house? You murderer—
> that's certain—of this man before you now.
> How obviously you lay in wait, you thief,
> for my power as tyrant (*tyrannidos*).
>   Tell me, by god,
> what lack of nerve, what sheer stupidity
> you saw in me that made you plot like this?
> Did you assume that I would not observe
> your treacherous snaking up on me or that
> I'd see it, but lack power to ward it off?
> And isn't the stupidity your own,
> attempting to pull off a coup, without
> riches and a clique of friends? The goal
> you hunt is snared by cash and mass support.

Oedipus' talk of *tyrannis,* his tyranny, and how one becomes a tyrant, recalls Herodotus' accounts of coups in the sixth century B.C. and Plato's descriptions, discussed in Chapter 1 of the present volume. Is this how Oedipus himself came to power in Thebes?[3] The answer is probably negative. Although Sophocles does not explain precisely how Oedipus came to the throne, he never suggests a coup d'état. Oedipus' accession is rather described as a reward for his solution of the Sphinx's riddle, not as a prize for political or military savoir faire.

Oedipus' remark about one's need for friends to carry out a coup recalls, then, not his own accession to power but the odd, even ingratiating, way Creon courts power. Creon identifies the chorus, the "gentlemen citizens," *andres politai,* of Thebes as his "friends," just as certainly as he seeks to alienate them from Oedipus (who was a foreigner) with his insinuations of the latter's insanity. Is he, in fact, seeking the support of the chorus, the people, as "friends" in an attempt to gain power? After all, he will be the new ruler of Thebes before the tragedy ends.

Oedipus' overbearing manner allows Creon to play the democrat. Creon demands, as Teiresias had done, and as a contemporary Athenian might, a chance to speak in his own defense and reasserts his claim that Oedipus was not in his right mind when he made his accusations of treason. Indeed, the suggestion of Oedipus' insanity becomes a leitmotif in these and later interchanges (543–54):

Creon: You know what you should do? You've said your say.
Give me fair time to answer. Take your turn
at listening, then judge when you have learned.

Oedipus: You're formidable at speaking (*legein sy deinos*). But I
am bad at learning things from you. I've found
you ill-disposed and burdensome to me.

Creon: This you must let me speak to. Listen now!

Oedipus: This you must not tell me: that you're not bad.

Creon: If you reckon that mindless stubbornness
is worth the having, you're not reasoning straight.

Oedipus: If you reckon a kinsman can do harm
and escape justice, you're not reasoning.

Creon: There is justice, I grant, in what you say.
But teach me now the deed you say I've done.

Oedipus is as wary of Creon's skill with words as he is of Teiresias'. He considers Creon, as Socrates' accusers considered him, *deinos legein*: formidable at speaking, having the skill of making the lesser argument appear stronger. Creon's opening *andres politai* certainly establishes him as a political, oratorical presence. Yet how curious that Oedipus, who solved the riddle of the Sphinx, should again be viewed as rhetorically inferior to an interlocutor. The chorus thought Teiresias, rather than Oedipus, would be the man to refute Laios' killer. This time the negative judgment is passed by Oedipus himself.

Oedipus begins his interrogation by arguing that Creon (the formidable speaker) used his persuasive powers to have him send for Teiresias (555–57):

Oedipus: Did you persuade, or not persuade me, then,
to send someone for that prophetic seer?

Creon: Yes. I still stand by that advice of mine.

Creon's determination to stand by his original advice seems odd, considering his claim to have heard reports that Teiresias was lying. By maintaining his support of Teiresias, instead of conceding the possibility that he erred in suggesting the consultation, Creon has put himself in a position of opposition to Oedipus. Oedipus, of course, does not know of Creon's ambiguity about Teiresias' truthfulness, since he was not on stage when the ambiguous remark was made. But he should not have missed the next point on which Creon leaves himself vulnerable (558–67):

> *Oedipus*: How much time has passed since Laios...
>   *Creon*: Did what? I do not understand your point.
> *Oedipus*: Was mortally wounded by hand unknown?
>   *Creon*: Years deeply layered could be measured back.
> *Oedipus*: Then was our seer in practice in those days?
>   *Creon*: Yes: wise and just as honored as today.
> *Oedipus*: Then did he mention me during that time?
>   *Creon*: Not when I was in eye or earshot: no.
> *Oedipus*: You people did not search for the killer?
>   *Creon*: Why yes! We searched and we heard nothing then.

Creon interrupts before Oedipus can complete his first line with a verb, but does not yet throw his questioner off track. And when Creon does answer the completed question, he is much vaguer than he was in his previous meeting with Oedipus. Then he dated Laios' death to the time of Oedipus' arrival in Thebes and of Theban problems with the Sphinx. At their first meeting, Creon told Oedipus the presence of the Sphinx prevented full inquiry from being made (130–31). Now he says only that they heard no answers. And we note that he does not say absolutely that Teiresias made no comment about Oedipus then, only that Teiresias made no comment in *his* presence.

Oedipus does not follow up with the most obvious question: "Why did you not question Teiresias at that time, since you clearly prize his advice?" Instead, he asks—and gets no helpful answer—why Teiresias said nothing, thereby allowing Creon an easy escape (568–69):

> *Oedipus*: Why then did our wise man not speak as now?
>   *Creon*: I don't know—and when uniformed don't speak.

Seers in antiquity had no obligation to volunteer information. Thus, Oedipus has missed his opportunity to inquire why Creon did not consult Teiresias. He enables Creon to evade the resonances of his line of questioning by proclaiming unwillingness to speak without knowledge. When Oedipus insists that there are areas in which Creon must have knowledge, Creon again interrupts before Oedipus can finish (570–73):

> *Oedipus*: This much you know and are informed about...
>
>   *Creon*: What things? I'll not deny them if I know.
>
> *Oedipus*: It follows that if he'd not met with you
>   he'd never have blamed me for Laios' death.

Oedipus' contention is logical. If Teiresias did not blame Oedipus for Laios' death at the time, why is he doing so now? Someone must have suggested the idea to him, most probably Creon.

Creon's retort simply avoids the substance of the issue altogether. It addresses only the question whether Teiresias actually blamed Oedipus for Laios' death (574): "You're the one who knows if he said this." Creon now claims (or feigns) ignorance of the charges brought by Teiresias against Oedipus. He has fallen back on the ambiguity of his statement about Teiresias' lies—as if his informant had said: "Oedipus accuses you of having persuaded Teiresias to bring (unspecified) false charges against him." The audience and the chorus know as well as Oedipus does that Teiresias made precisely such an accusation. And Oedipus, given an instant to reflect, might have asked the chorus to substantiate the matter. But he, unlike Creon, does not know how to use the chorus to his advantage.

If Oedipus had turned to the chorus at this moment, he could have explained more fully why he thought it logical that Creon suggested to Teiresias that Oedipus killed Laios. More important still, he could have outlined the charges and challenged Creon to state whether he himself considered them true. As it is, the opportunity is wasted. Creon evades the question and distracts Oedipus with great cunning before the latter can respond (574–76):

> *Creon*: I think I have the right to learn from you,
>   just as you've now been learning things from me.
>
> *Oedipus*: Learn all! I'll not be proved a murderer.

Oedipus' last remark here reminds us that, outward appearances to the contrary, he considers himself, rather than Creon, the man on trial. He now abandons his questions even though he has learned little from Creon. Yet Creon wickedly gives the impression that Oedipus (who has just said he was "bad at learning" from Creon) has in fact been learning things from him. It is now time for Creon to become "the learner." Oedipus has lost the rhetorical initiative.

The Reluctant Tyrant

Oedipus is so drawn off the scent by Creon's flattering deceit that he abandons his line of questioning before it is even properly under way. And, as we will see, Creon has no serious intention of "learning" anything from Oedipus. On the contrary, he begins by feeding him a set of statements phrased as questions to which the answers are self-evident or noncontroversial (577–83). (This ploy is common in modern courts of law too, when the interrogating attorney seeks to establish a pattern of agreement between himself and a "hostile" witness. The object is to subvert the witness' credibility when he or she finally disagrees with one of the statements phrased as questions.)

> *Creon:* So then. You are married to my sister?
> *Oedipus:* There's no denying what you say on this.
> *Creon:* You rule this land with her quite equally?
> *Oedipus:* She gets anything she wants from me.
> *Creon:* And am I not an equal with you two?
> *Oedipus:* That's what shows you for an evil friend.
> *Creon:* No. Not if you'd reason with yourself
>   as I reason.

Here Creon, not Oedipus, acts as the interrogating attorney—as the instructor, that is. Oedipus has accepted all Creon's statements in the interrogative. Creon continues (584–68):

> First, then, consider this:
> Do you think anyone will choose the fears
> that come with rulership rather than
> the carefree sleep that he can have if he
> has the same power without it?

The question is of course rhetorical, but nastily put, since it is addressed to a man who has the very kind of official position (with accompanying paranoia) that Creon claims he would not want. Thus, when Creon answers his own question, as lawyers often do, he does so not only overtly and positively for himself but covertly and negatively for Oedipus. He also hints, as Teiresias hinted earlier, that he is more intelligent than Oedipus, perhaps as a retort to Oedipus' almost pathetic claim in 536ff. that he is no fool (587–95):

                         Personally,
I have no deep yearning to be tyrant
rather than to act as tyrants do,
and nor has anyone in his right mind.
Thanks to you, I have it all without
the fear. But if I ruled all by myself,
I'd be doing much I'd rather not.
How could being tyrant be of itself
sweeter to me than painless control,
than pure power and influence?
I'm not so self-deceived that I would want
more than high standing and rich benefits.

Here is "formidable" speaking indeed! Creon has already suggested several times that Oedipus is not in his right mind. Now he suggests that anyone who prefers the title of tyrant to the powers of tyranny (as, presumably, Oedipus does) must be mad and self-deceived. But Creon cleverly blunts the insulting edge of his *emphasis,* his innuendo, by doffing a courtier's hat to Oedipus: "Thanks to you, sire, I don't have to make that choice."

Creon's ostensible purpose in making the statement cited above is to allay Oedipus' suspicions that he is plotting a coup d'état. And the audience may sympathize with him. Oedipus, after all, has concluded that a conspiracy is afoot without any supporting evidence. He is prepared to condemn Creon without trial. Frustration and anger have unleashed the tyrant in him. This is the scene in which he becomes "Oedipus the Tyrant." Provoked by unsupported charges, Oedipus draws savage, unsupported conclusions. And he moves quickly to threats of violence. No democratic jury would convict Creon on the charges Oedipus brings against him, especially now that Oedipus has been characterized as a tyrant by a man playing the democrat before the people.

Although Oedipus' accusations are based only on suspicion, some doubts about Creon may well sneak up on us as Creon mounts his defense. Cedric Whitman observes that he "defends himself with the ready-made arguments on the undesirability of power, arguments which were already well known in Athens, and already under suspicion."[4] The most obvious comparison in tragedy is with Hippolytus' response to Theseus' charges of incestuous rape in Euripides' *Hippolytus* 1013–20. And the close mythic association of Oedipus and

Theseus, greatly advanced by Sophocles himself in his later *Oedipus at Colonus,* encourages us to view the plays together.

So striking are the similarities in diction between parts of the *Oedipus* and the *Hippolytus* that T. Zielinski suggested Euripides must have derived his lines from Sophocles' *Oedipus.*[5] He therefore dates *Oedipus* to 429 B.C. and *Hippolytus* to 428. In the broadest terms, these dates are approximately right. Both plays, it is generally agreed, seem to respond to the great plague in Athens (430–28 B.C.). The question of which play actually came first, however, is not at all clear. Scholars generally assume that *Oedipus* precedes *Hippolytus.* It is, however, quite plausible that Sophocles is drawing on Euripides rather than vice versa.[6] *All* the Euripidean passages Zielinski cites as echoes of the Sophoclean Creon occur in one passage in *Hippolytus,* the famous encounter between Theseus and Hippolytus.

The disputes between Creon and Oedipus, Theseus and Hippolytus, seem curiously interdependent since they not only resemble each other in a significant way but differ significantly too. Theseus wrongly finds Hippolytus guilty and sentences him, without trial, to banishment and, in effect, death. His only evidence for Hippolytus' wrongdoing is Phaedra's accusatory written statement—which is in fact false. Oedipus, on the other hand, suspects Creon is guilty and sentences him, without any tangible evidence and without trial, to banishment, or rather death. For reasons we will examine in due course, however, he does not actually carry out his threat but bows to the pleas of Jocasta and the chorus, and drops the matter altogether.

Hippolytus' contention that he does not desire kingship probably seemed believable enough to the audience no less than to the chorus.[7] For the audience saw onstage the enactment of Phaedra's guilty love and Hippolytus' innocence. Unfortunately for Hippolytus, however, it is Theseus, not the audience, whom he must convince. And his statement that he does not wish to be king is part—and only part— of his effort to establish that he is not the sort of person Theseus now assumes him to be. Indeed, in Hippolytus' principal defense speech, which runs from 983 to 1035, the disavowal of kingly ambition takes up no more than eleven lines in all (*Hippolytus* 1011–20):

> Did I hope to gain control of your
> place, seize and inherit power through
> the bedroom? I'd be a fool and nowhere near
> my wits. But is not a tyrant's power

sweet to those sound of wit? No, not at all,
unless desire to rule alone has killed
the hearts of mortals who delight in it.
I'd like to be the first power in our Greek
athletic contests. But within the state
I'd like to keep to second place, enjoy
the constant blessing of the noblest friends.
This is the good life. And danger's absence
gives greater joy than does tyrannic power.

Is Creon's disavowal similarly believable for the ancient audience in *Oedipus*? First, let us note that the undesirability of being tyrant is Creon's *only* line of defense. Nor does Creon explain, as Hippolytus does, that his real ambitions lie outside politics. Creon does not deny his interest in exercising tyrannical power. He just denies, as we have seen, that he wants to *be* a tyrant (587–88):

> Personally,
> I have no deep yearning to be tyrant
> rather than to act as tyrants do,
> and nor has anyone in his right mind.

Indeed, Creon makes much of his present political role as a kind of intermediary between Oedipus and the people (596–602):

> I get on with all people, they all
> love me, and they call on me to help
> whenever they need anything from you.
> Their hope of getting what they want resides
> wholly in me. How could I give up this
> to grasp at that? A mind that reasons well
> cannot become evil. I was not born
> to court this kind of power, nor would I be
> so rash as to help someone else, who was.

Creon casts himself as a mediator between populace and ruler, a champion and spokesman for the disenfranchised: what the Greeks called a *prostatês*. At the same time he makes negative implications about Oedipus' exercise of power: Oedipus is inaccessible. To assume the kind of position Oedipus holds is to change from rationality to evil. Again, the Platonic tyrant lurks in the background.

Creon is not alone in thinking he is the intermediary between individual citizen and ruler in this play. Teiresias, we will recall, implies that people see Creon this way when he addresses Oedipus as tyrant and yet claims that he does not need Creon's services as *prostatês* (408–11):

> Though you're a tyrant, still, equality
> must be allowed at least in equal time
> to make reply. In this I too have power.
> *I* live as Apollo's slave, not yours,
> so don't enroll me as an alien
> with Creon as my sponsor (*prostatou*) and spokesman.

Thus Creon's Hippolytan defense serves only to heighten suspicion that he has political power as a *prostatês,* as Cleon and Pericles (who was also called *prostatês*) had. One man's popular champion is another man's tyrant.

The Kingly Name

Ironically, of course, monarchy is already in Creon's *name* just as surely as, to the ancient etymologist, Hippolytus' destruction by horses is in his name.

Socrates notes in Plato's *Cratylus* (394C) that there are many names meaning "king." One of these is Creon (*Kreôn* in Greek), which patently means "ruler, king," occurring as such in *Odyssey* 11.269 in the Homeric form *kreiôn*. As a participial form, *kreiôn* or *kreôn,* "ruling one," does not simply refer to any ruler but, most frequently in Homer, to the one who holds supreme power: Agamemnon in *Iliad* 1.130 is described as *kreiôn* when he speaks to Achilles, proposing to compensate himself for the loss of Chryseis by taking some other king's girl.[8] And if Agamemnon is *kreiôn* to men, Zeus is "highest of *kreiontôn*" as Athena hails him before the assembled gods in *Iliad* 8.31. That Sophocles' contemporaries would be aware of the governing power in Creon's name is evident not only from Plato but from Euripides. In *Electra* 1262 the divine twins, the Dioscouri, are called "twin children of the ruling (*kreontos*) sea." Similarly, in *Hippolytus* 1168 the messenger announcing Hippolytus' death calls Theseus' father Poseidon "your father of the ruling (*kreontos*) sea." So when someone named Creon denies that he wishes to have absolute power, as Creon in the *Oedipus* does, his very name gives the lie to his disclaimer. As Pietro Pucci points out: "from the *Cratylos* and other texts it is clear that the slightest phonetic resemblance allowed the Greeks to make derivations or etymologies."[9] In this case, the etymology is beyond even scholarly doubt.

Creon, of course, does become ruler of Thebes before Sophocles' *Oedipus* is over, and we have already noted that other versions of the Oedipus myth make Creon ruler of Thebes in the interval between Laios' death and Oedipus' arrival (Apollodorus 3.5.8). So the potential for monarchy in his name is speedily actualized, and with it the potential for abusing power. Indeed, throughout Greek and Roman literature rulers named Creon, notably the Theban Creon of the Oedipus cycle and the Corinthian Creon familiar from the myth of Medea at Corinth, are synonymous with monarchical power and tyrannical behavior. In Plato's second *Epistle* (310E–311B) Creon is set in opposition to Teiresias as Pericles is to Anaxagoras, as Croesus is to Solon, as Periander is to Thales, and as Agamemnon is to Nestor. Even in Sophocles' *Oedipus,* our awareness of his kingly power is triggered when Oedipus greets him as *anax,* "king, lord," (86). In Sophocles' earlier *Antigone* and later *Oedipus at Colonus,* the Theban Creon is a caricature of brutal and offensive government. The *Antigone* was produced perhaps around 441 B.C., more than a decade earlier than the *Oedipus,* which belongs to some time after 429 B.C. In *Antigone* Creon is the tyrannical ruler of Thebes who forbids burial of the Argive dead in the war of the Seven against Thebes, in violation of all normal ancient conventions of war. Elsewhere, as in *Medea* and *Oedipus at Colonus,* he is usually banishing someone.

Nonetheless, in *Oedipus* Creon says that only someone who does not understand what wisdom is would want to rule, would want to be the leader, the first man of the state, when he could be second or even third (577–95). Both Oedipus and Sophocles' audience might feel disconcerted by this argument if Creon's name is the clue to his identity. His name makes him suspect of monarchical ambition, as Oedipus' name seems to indicate that he is the man who "knows the feet"—or the child whose feet were pinned together: "Swollen Foot." For *Oedipus* is a play in which etymologies are of far more than casual significance. And we will discuss the etymologies of Oedipus' name in more detail in Chapter 6.[10] Creon, then, whose name means "king," and who wants to act as a tyrant, claims he does not desire the *title* of ruler. It is little surprise that Oedipus does not believe him. It is more surprising that we, as readers, do. For who *is* the ruler of Thebes at the play's end if not the reluctant Creon?

In this respect the dispute between Oedipus and Creon in *Oedipus* recalls not only Euripides' *Hippolytus* but, with a kind of ironic reversal of roles for Creon, Euripides' *Medea*. In *Medea* 271–409 Creon of Corinth holds the royal power of death or banishment over Medea: the Corinthian Creon suspects Medea of plotting to destroy him, and his failure to kill Medea or banish her instantly, results in the annihilation of himself, his daughter, and the children of Jason and Medea. Oedipus, like the Corinthian Creon, has an uneasy sense of foreboding, suspecting that the chorus and Jocasta, when they later intercede successfully on Creon's behalf, have not merely saved Creon's life but sentenced *him,* Oedipus, to death or banishment (658–59):

> Then understand, as you beg this for him:
> you beg my death of exile from this land.

Creon's Last Line of Defense

Creon's final appeal in his own defense in Sophocles' *Oedipus* is that Oedipus should check the truth of his report of Apollo's oracle by traveling to Delphi himself (603–8):

> As proof of this, go to the Pythian seer:
> you'll find if I reported her response,
> its pith and substance. Then, if you catch me,
> find I've been hatching plots with our expert
> on prodigies, take me, kill me, not
> on the basis of your single vote,
> but with a double vote—both mine and yours.
> Don't damn me without evidence, and on your own.

Creon, who at the opening of this scene (513–14) had "no desire for life" if under suspicion, now wants some vindication. And that vindication, he suggests, should come from another consultation of Delphi. Creon has logically assumed that if Oedipus suspects him of conspiracy, he must therefore doubt the authenticity of his report from Delphi. Yet the accuracy of the oracle as reported by Creon is an issue Oedipus never touches on even after Creon himself raises the subject.

We have asked before why Oedipus, if he had previous suspicions of Creon, entrusted him with the mission to Delphi and accepted his report so unquestioningly. Now we need to append a further question. Why does Oedipus, even as he comes to accuse Creon of conspiracy, still express no doubt about the essential correctness of the oracle as reported by Creon? Under such circumstances there would be good reason to assume the oracle had been tampered with. And such oracular tampering was familiar enough to Sophocles' Athenian audience from recent experiences with Spartan attempts to discredit Pericles by manipulating Delphi.

It is perhaps understandable that Oedipus does not act on Creon's suggestion of going to Delphi himself. He would be unwise to leave Thebes at this moment if he really thinks Creon is planning a coup. The surprise is that he does not react to Creon's suggestion at all: that he is uninterested in questioning the substance of Creon's report from Delphi.

There is thus a special irony in Creon's final appeal to Oedipus that he not pass judgment and convict hurriedly and without evidence: Oedipus will ultimately convict himself of murder and incest without evidence. There will be no one to argue in his defense when that time comes. Creon's parting words, then, are prophetic. Playing on the proverbial wisdom that a friend is another self (*allos autos*), Creon likens the discarding of a friend to an act of self-destruction (609–15):

> It is not just so whimsically to judge
> bad men as honest, honest men as bad.
> To cast off a good and concerned friend
> is like, I think, casting away one's life—
> something that most concerns us. But you'll know,
> you won't be fooled about this if you take
> your time. For it takes time and nothing else
> to show who's just. Yes, you could recognize
> a bad man in the span of just one day.

Creon's observation about the need of time for the just man to be recognized recalls Hippolytus' request in Euripides' play that Theseus let time make his innocence clear (1051–52):

> Oh me! What will you do? You'll banish me,
> you won't accept the evidence of time
> on my behalf, you'll drive me from the land?

Phaedra's apparent dishonor and death are recent. Hippolytus might well expect the truth to surface in time. But before we adduce this parallel as corroboration for Creon's maxim, we should remember that Hippolytus has, at the moment he speaks, already convinced the chorus of his innocence (1036–37). Before the play is over, Artemis will have convinced even Theseus. It doesn't necessarily take a long time for the good man to be vindicated.

We could, I suppose, find an interestingly ironic vindication of Creon's cliché in Euripides' *Medea,* if we see Medea and her actions as wicked. Medea asks the Corinthian Creon for exactly one day to plan her exile (*Medea* 340). But it is not necessarily true even within the conventions of Greek tragedy that a wicked man (or woman) will be discovered in a day. In *Oedipus* it has taken many years to get on the track of—much less find—the man who killed Laios. And how "wicked" was Laios' killer? Does killing a tyrant, even unintentionally and unknowingly, make the perpetrator evil? And was the killing of Laios *really* the cause of the plague in Thebes as Creon suggests?[11]

Creon is probably alluding to Oedipus rather than to himself, Teiresias, or persons unnamed when he claims that Oedipus is judging bad men as honest. He further implies that he has himself in mind as the exemplar of the opposite. But how good or bad is Creon, and how wicked is Oedipus?

At this point Sophocles' chorus puts in its own maxim about the inadvisability of haste (616–17):

> That's good advice for men who'd watch their steps,
> my lord. Think hurriedly and trip.

But Oedipus has a retort to validate his instinct for quick action— one that Euripides' Creon in *Medea* would have been well advised to take (618–21):

> When someone hurries with his secret plans
> I must plan hurriedly to counter him.
> But if I take it easy and just wait,
> his plans succeed and mine will miss the mark.

His point is well illustrated in Thucydides' description of the civil strife in Corcyra (also, incidentally, accompanied by a plague), where quick, spontaneous reaction was more effective than prudence or rational caution.[12]

There seems to be little Creon can do now to counteract Oedipus' resolve. So he tries to guide Oedipus toward what he presumably regards as the lesser of the two possible punishments: banishment, rather than death. He has made a complete volte-face from his earlier declaration that loss of honor makes him ready for death (622–25):

> *Creon:* What do you feel you must do? Exile me?
> *Oedipus:* No! I want to see you dying, not banished.
> *Creon:* Your words show you won't trust me or pull back...
> *Oedipus:* No, since you exemplify envy.[13]

Again, the contrast with Euripides' *Hippolytus* is interesting. For Theseus contemplates the alternatives of death or banishment for Hippolytus, first asking Poseidon to destroy his son (*Hippolytus* 887–90), then suggesting that exile might be more appropriate and bitter (895–98). Hippolytus, however, after his defense-speech, declares that were he in Theseus' position he would kill, not banish, his son if that son had laid hands on his wife (*Hippolytus* 1042–44):

> I am surprised at you, father, in this:
> if I were your father, and you my son,
> I would have killed you, not just exiled you,
> if you'd seen fit to tamper with my wife

Hippolytus' apparent preference for death confirms Theseus in his desire to have his son banished: he does not wish to give Hippolytus a punishment of his own choosing (1045–50).

In *Oedipus* Creon reverts to attacking Oedipus' mental competence once Oedipus makes clear that he wants him dead. Creon sees, from the chorus' last remark, that he has some popular support in this exchange with Oedipus and presumably wants to use it to his advantage (627–30):

> *Creon:* Your reason's failing...
> *Oedipus:*   Failing you not me.

> *Creon*: They should serve both.
> *Oedipus*:   You were born bad.
> *Creon*: Yet if you grasp nothing . . .
> *Oedipus*:   I still must rule.
> *Creon*: Not if you rule badly.
> *Oedipus*:   Oh, my city!
> *Creon*: This city is mine too. It's not just yours.

Oedipus' "Oh, my city!" (*ô polis, polis*) echoes Theseus' similar cry of kingly anxiety for the state in *Hippolytus* 884: *iô polis* ("alas, my city!"). But Creon does not simply acquiesce in Oedipus' judgment as Hippolytus does in Theseus'.

More curiously, Oedipus makes no move (as Theseus does) to have the accused physically removed by his attendants. On the contrary, the chorus sees the situation more as a family quarrel that must and can be settled, and pointedly addresses them both as *anaktes*, "lords, kings." (631–33):

> Stop it, my lords! I see Jocasta now
> coming outside, and just in time for you.
> Settle this quarrel with her help. You must!

We see, perhaps to our surprise, that there really is a kind of ruling triumvirate at Thebes. And the decisive force may well be neither Creon nor Oedipus, but Jocasta.

Jocasta's Intervention

Jocasta sweeps in energetically and authoritatively. She sees the struggle between Oedipus and Creon more as the prelude to civil disorder than as a matter of kingly justice, however crude and tyrannical. She has no hesitation in ordering both men off the scene, as if she were a queen breaking up a fight between unruly young princes. Although neither leaves immediately, each defers to her (634–43):

> *Jocasta*: You fools! Why use your tongues to stir senseless
>   civic unrest? Aren't you ashamed to rouse

> private enmities now the whole land
> is sick? You, go inside! You too, Creon!
> Won't you stop turning prickles into wounds?
> *Creon*: Sister of my own blood, your husband thinks
> it just to punish me grimly, ruling
> that I must suffer one of two bad fates:
> exile from homeland, or arrest and death.
> *Oedipus*: Agreed. Good wife, I've caught him in the act
> of doing evil with his evil craft
> against my personal safety and my life.

Oedipus and Creon immediately identify Jocasta in terms of their personal relationships to her. Creon identifies himself as her blood relative—a relationship of old and deep importance in Greek culture—and simultaneously distances Oedipus by calling him her husband. We think, perhaps, of the famous passage in Sophocles' earlier *Antigone,* where Antigone defends her decision to give last rites to Polyneices, her brother, in defiance of Creon's law. Such an action, she suggests, she would not do for a husband, only for an irreplaceable brother (*Antigone* 904–15).

While drawing such distinctions in kinship may be just Creon's attempt to remind his sister of their closer ritual bond, it also dissociates him from Teiresias' allegations that Jocasta is incestuously married to Oedipus, in which case Oedipus would be a blood relative too.

Creon either does not know Teiresias has accused Oedipus of incest or, if he does know, wishes to give Oedipus and the chorus, by this oblique rhetorical touch, the impression he does not know—or at least believe—what Teiresias has said. It is hard to assess Creon's innocence in this matter, though scholars, in presuming Oedipus' guilt, have tended to assume that Creon is telling the truth. But this does not necessarily follow. Creon is evasive, or at least not entirely truthful, in other remarks during this scene. He tells Jocasta, for instance, that Oedipus will either banish him or have him killed for his alleged wrongdoing. But Oedipus has just said Creon will be killed rather than banished. Creon adjusts what Oedipus has said, perhaps to reintroduce the possibility of the lesser sentence now that Jocasta has entered as a potential arbiter. In this adjustment is the difference between life and death. As Orestes observes to Pylades:

"Life or death. Short words of long significance" (Euripides, *Orestes* 758).

Scholars tend to miss Creon's "adjustment" in his report of what has just passed. They know, as Creon probably cannot know for certain at this point, that Oedipus will not try to carry out his threats of death. Yet Oedipus, surprisingly, does not reaffirm his decision to have Creon killed. Far from noting that Creon has misrepresented their recent interchanges, Oedipus promptly states his agreement with Creon's summary, as if conceding he has not yet decided between death and banishment.

Creon now swears he has not committed the crimes he is charged with (644–45):

> May I lose all pleasure in life and be
> accursed and destroyed if I have done
> any of the things you blame me for.

A contrast with Hippolytus' oath is instructive here (Euripides, *Hippolytus* 1025–31):

> I swear to you by Zeus, guardian of oaths,
> and by the earth we walk that I've not touched
> your wife, or wanted to, or thought of it.
> If I have been an evil man, may I
> wander the earth in exile, be destroyed
> without honor, name, city, or home!
> And when I die, may neither sea nor land
> receive my flesh!

Hippolytus attempts to validate his oath by an appeal to Zeus the guardian of oaths and to the earth, and makes himself liable to the effects of his curse in a very general way: "If I have been an evil man." Joseph Plescia points out in his study of Greek oaths and perjury that "the degree of solemnity and sacredness of the oath was . . . determined by the latitude and gravity of the curse."[14] Greek oaths—like Hippolytus', cited above—normally contained three elements: a declaration of the statement's truth, an invocation of the god(s), and a religious sanction upon the oath-taker if he proves false to his word.[15]

Although it is true that Hesiod maintains (*Theogony* 231) that Oath is itself a god, the fact is that Creon invokes no deity, makes no claim to general innocence, and avoids even the mention of the word *horkos*, "oath." In the *Rhetoric to Alexander,* attributed wrongly to Aristotle, an oath (*horkos*) is defined as follows: "An oath is an unproved declaration based on an appeal to the gods" (1432A). Thus Creon's oath has a much lesser degree of solemnity than Hippolytus'. Perhaps he has something in common with Homer's Autolycus, praised in *Odyssey* 19.396 because he surpassed other men in the making of deceitful oaths, or shares the cynicism of Plutarch's Lysander, who suggested that humans toy with oaths as children toy with dice (*Lysander* 8.3). After all in Athenian rhetoric and law oaths are a final resort for the speaker, after appeals to laws, witnesses, contracts, and evidence given under torture, according to Aristotle (*Rhetoric* 1.1377A–B).

But if the oath convinces, it does its rhetorical job and indeed puts one's rhetorical opponent in something of a bind. For he has, unless he can offer some counteroath, an obligation to accept the sworn testimony. In both plays the chorus, functioning as a kind of jury, takes the oath as proof of its maker's innocence. In *Hippolytus* the chorus observes (1036–37):

> You've said enough to turn away all blame,
> You've sworn by gods, no small persuasive proof.

The chorus in *Hippolytus,* admittedly, *knows* that Hippolytus is innocent. Unfortunately, it has been tricked by Phaedra into taking an oath of its own to Artemis not to speak of what it hears to anyone (*Hippolytus* 713–14):

> I swear by holy Artemis, daughter
> of Zeus that I will never bring to light
> any of your evils.

By "evils" (*kakôn*) the chorus means, at the time of speaking, evils that Phaedra has suffered—most obviously her unrequited love for Hippolytus. The members of the chorus do not realize, at the time of swearing, that they will also be bound not to speak of any evil deeds she has done. Had they exercised more caution in the phrasing of their oath, they would not have been bound by its literal meaning. As it is, their failure to break their oath—and Hippolytus' failure to break his similar oath of silence to the nurse—lead to a suppression of testimony that could corroborate Hippolytus' claim to innocence.

Theseus, of course, is not convinced by Hippolytus' oath. He thinks it is all verbal trickery. And he is wrong. The verbal trickery is Phaedra's: in writing the false deposition against Hippolytus and in duping the chorus into taking its critical oath of silence.

In *Oedipus,* Jocasta's acceptance of Creon's truthfulness precedes even the chorus's approval. And, curiously, her first words provide the gods that were missing from Creon's oath (646–54):

> *Jocasta*: By the gods, I urge you, trust him in this,
> Oedipus. First you should respect an oath
> sworn by the gods. Second, you should respect
> both me and these men who are with you now.
> *Chorus*: Be willing, think, my lord! Obey, I beg!
> *Oedipus*: What will you have me say I'll do?
> *Chorus*: Respect this man. He was no childlike simpleton
> before. His oath now gives him great stature.

Jocasta and the chorus either have failed to notice that Creon did not really swear by the gods or choose to represent his oath as if it were made "by the gods." Since Jocasta's own appeal to Oedipus is made "by the gods," she perhaps assumes that Creon's oath must be too. There is also the possibility that she moves in so quickly to supply the missing gods because she wishes to help Creon out of his difficulty. Her apparent oversight is important, because an oath, unless sworn by some divine power, is not creditable legal testimony in most ancient legal systems, including that of Athens, because it is not binding upon its maker.

The Costs of Clemency

Oedipus' reaction to the chorus's and Jocasta's appeal is remarkable. It shows that his thought is proceeding along altogether different lines from those pursued by the chorus and Jocasta (655–59):

> *Oedipus*: You know what you're asking?
> *Chorus*:   I know.

Oedipus: State it!
  Chorus: Don't use words and logic so unclear
            to damn a friend whose own oath curses him,
            if he is false. Don't shame and banish him.
Oedipus: Then understand, as you beg this for him,
            you beg my death or exile from this land.

The chorus, surprised by Oedipus' suggestions of the consequences to his own person of clemency toward Creon, reacts as if Oedipus were accusing it of complicity in the imagined plot and vehemently protests its innocence (660–67):

> No! By the foremost god of all the gods,
> the Sun, I hope to die most hideously
> without god, without friends, if ever I
> had any such intention in my thoughts.
> I'm suffering, my land is perishing.
> It all wears down my soul, if I must add
> the rift between you two to old sorrows.

Oedipus responds (699–72):

> Then let him go, even if I must die
> or be thrown out by violence from this land.
> I'm moved to pity by your words, not his.
> He will be hated wherever he may be.

The chorus's oath by the "foremost god of all the gods" resembles that of Euripides' *Hippolytus* rather than the "godless" imprecation of Sophocles' Creon.

Oedipus, of course, need not be reacting as paranoically as the chorus assumes. In suggesting that such intercession for Creon means his own banishment, he is pointing to what he considers the inevitable, rather than the planned, consequences of its appeal. His observation is prophetic and correct. At the end of the play when Creon is ruler of Thebes, Oedipus will be asking to go into exile. And Creon will earn himself an unenviable place in myth as one of the most villainous of tyrants.

Perhaps, indeed, the pardon given Creon at this moment really is an antecedent cause of Oedipus' overthrow. Oedipus will soon proceed, if I may rephrase the chorus's observation, "to use words and logic so unclear to damn" not "a friend" but himself. For he has placed himself under a curse if he shelters the killer of Laios, whether that killer be himself or someone else—*such as Creon.*

As Creon has said (611–12): "To cast off a good and concerned friend is like, I think, casting away one's life." If a friend is another self, as the proverb suggests, then this man who attacks a friend may easily attack himself when the attack on the friend is warded off. Teiresias has already observed Oedipus' potential danger to himself (379): "Creon is not your problem, you are your own." And Creon will soon reinforce this notion (673–77):

> Creon: You're full of hate when clement, oppressive
> when enraged. But then, natures like yours
> are hardest on themselves. And rightly so.
>
> Oedipus: Won't you let me alone and go away?
>
> Creon: I'm on my way—a mystery to you (*sou*),
> but in their view equal (*isou*) to you and just.

Perhaps I am overstressing the play in line 677 between *sou* ("you")—the nominative of which is *sos*—and *isos* ("just, equal"). But Creon's sense of angry vindication, his declaration of equality, stands in sharp contrast to his earlier insistence that he was content to play second fiddle to Oedipus. We are left with the sense that there will be no goodwill in the future between the two men, regardless of what happened—or did not happen—in the past.

The stage is now left to Oedipus, the chorus, and Jocasta.

Inopportune Silence

The chorus, in a surprisingly patronizing manner, urges Jocasta to carry or convey (*komizein*) Oedipus inside, and is calculatedly vague in its response to her request for further information (679–86):

> Chorus: My lady, why not have him taken in?
>
> Jocasta: I will once I've found out what has occurred.

Chorus: An uninformed and specious argument
intruded. Then injustice took its toll.
Jocasta: Are both to blame?
Chorus: Yes.
Jocasta: And their argument?
Chorus: I think enough's been said. Best let things stand
right where they are. The land has suffered enough.

The chorus is taking all three of its "lords" to task for neglecting the
public interest. But its refusal to give details as it rebuffs Jocasta's
request deprives her of an opportunity to confront the charges of
incest as well as of homicide that underlie Teiresias' accusations which
Oedipus has alleged were prompted by Creon. Thus she does not
now learn that she too has been maligned in the seer's accusations.
How she would have reacted if the chorus had told her this, we can
never know. The chorus surely grasps that if Oedipus thinks Creon
the author of the slanderous charges Teiresias has leveled against him,
he will probably go on to mention the accusation of incest.

Before Jocasta can protest the chorus's reticence, Oedipus interrupts, taking the chorus to task once more for interceding on Creon's
behalf (687–88):

I know you meant well. But don't you now see
where you've brought us by diverting my wrath?

Not only is Oedipus acknowledging the embarrassing need to tell—
or avoid telling—Jocasta all that has been said. He is pointing out the
altered relationships in the power structure of the state. Creon has
left contemptuously defiant, saved from peril—and from further investigation—by the intercession of the chorus and of Jocasta. When
he next enters, he will be ruler of Thebes.

The chorus does not answer Oedipus' question directly but merely
offers an assurance of its continued, though conditional, confidence.
The meaning of the passage is not completely clear and has been
subject to much scholarly debate. It runs as follows (689–96):

My lord, I've said this not just once:
know that I would be shown as

> lost to reason, unable to find my way
> to reason,
> if I put you apart from me.
> For you set my own country
> on a straight course
> when it was mad
> with suffering.
> Now send a favorable breeze,
> if you can.

Oedipus does not respond immediately. The chorus's refusal to discuss the situation with Jocasta, and its polite but oblique response to
Oedipus, leave the two characters to resolve what they can in discussion between themselves. Jocasta appeals to Oedipus (696–97):

> I beg you, by the gods! Explain to me
> what has been done to plant such wrath in you!

Oedipus must now choose between the chorus's suggestion that it
would be best to say no more about the matter and Jocasta's urgent
plea that he tell her what he knows. He could, one supposes, fall back
on the old male position that it is none of the woman's business. But
instead, he pointedly and unhesitatingly prefers to accede to what the
woman requests in order, perhaps, to put down quite icily the chorus
whose obliqueness he has not missed (700–701):

> I will. Dear woman, I respect you more
> than them. It's Creon's plotting against me.

His contemptuous slight upon the chorus silences it for 134 lines.
Teiresias and Creon are already alienated. Oedipus is now alienating
the more sympathetic citizens of Thebes.

Oedipus does not grasp that people have individual motives for
their actions: professional prestige for Teiresias, power for Creon,
protection from the powerful for the chorus. His egocentric paranoia
translates disparate motives into conspiracy, his tyranny empowers
him to act willfully. His willfulness allows others to assimilate him
to the negative, tyrannical paradigm, yet his own self-doubts make
him an indecisive tyrant. With or without a conspiracy, then, the
outcome is the same: a coup d'etat.

5. JOCASTA

Jocasta was played in *Oedipus* by the deuteragonist, the second of the three actors used by Greek tragedians to cover all the *dramatis personae*. The deuteragonist also played the priest, the palace messenger, and the servant (or rather slave) of Laios. The third actor, the tritagonist, played Creon, Teiresias, and the Corinthian. Only the protagonist was assigned a single part: that of Oedipus.[1] This division of roles may be significant not only in terms of the allocation of stage space and time—Creon and Teiresias cannot be on stage together, for example—but because the same voice, however modulated, speaks through the different masks. The tritagonist's voice, for example, is more obviously threatening to Oedipus than is the deuteragonist's. Jocasta, the priest, the slave, and the palace messenger seem not quite so overtly involved in the power plays as Creon and Teiresias—or even the man from Corinth, who sees himself as kind of king maker.

The Intermediary and Judge

Jocasta asserts herself with confidence the moment she steps on stage. It may seem at first that she separates Creon and Oedipus as a mother calms an outburst of sibling rivalry. But her language and her au-

thoritative tone suggest rather a judge or magistrate. Note her exchange with Oedipus (698–706):

> *Jocasta*: Speak—if you'll say precisely on what grounds
> you charge him with beginning this quarrel.
> *Oedipus*: He claims I'm guilty, I'm Laios' killer.
> *Jocasta*: He really knows this for himself? Or has he just
> learned about it all from someone else?
> *Oedipus*: He sent a seer to do his dirty work
> and keeps his own mouth free from all offense.

Jocasta treats the quarrel between Oedipus and Creon as if it were a
lawsuit. She carefully distinguishes at the outset between knowledge
based on personal familiarity with an incident and information acquired from others, what we would call "hearsay," which was of no
account in an Athenian court. At the same time her rhetorical attention
is focused not on whether Creon actually said what Oedipus alleges
that he said, but on whether Creon was *correct* in the substance of the
charges.

Jocasta's questioning is not at all naive. She is leading Oedipus
away from any examination of Creon's possible guilt, not exploring
it. Indeed, she has already, in a matter of seconds, secured the re-
mission of Oedipus' sentence of death upon her brother. It will not
occur to Oedipus again that Creon was (or is) plotting against him.

Jocasta addresses Oedipus as if the real issue were not Creon and
conspiracy but Oedipus' personal anxiety that he may be guilty of
Laios' murder. And, of course, in a large sense she proves right. She
knows Oedipus from years of close familiarity. So too, presumably,
do Creon and Teiresias. We, the audience, are just discovering him.
We realize in the course of this scene, as we suspected from occasional
earlier remarks, that Oedipus is not excluding the possibility that he
himself might be the pollution upon the city. Teiresias has, of course,
said that the force weighing down on Oedipus is not Creon but
Oedipus himself. Jocasta states the matter in legal rather than religious
terms: Oedipus is prosecuting himself. She says (707–10):

> Well now, acquit yourself of what you've been
> saying. Hear me and learn—you should—the proof
> that nothing mortal has prophetic skill.
> I'll right now reveal signs that show I'm right.

Jocasta in fact pointedly parodies the famous adage about Delphi: that the god neither speaks nor hides but gives signs. She herself usurps the oracle's mysticism. And oracular utterances have a special hold on Oedipus' attention.

Jocasta takes it for granted that Oedipus is dissembling when he claims Teiresias was merely Creon's mouthpiece. She assumes her husband is frightened by what Teiresias, a prophet, has said. How much she knows of what the seer proclaimed during his confrontation with Oedipus we cannot tell, since she was not on stage at the time. Report may have reached her of what had passed, as it apparently reached Creon. Has she heard, for instance, that Teiresias proclaimed Oedipus would discover that he was living incestuously? Sophocles has drawn an impenetrable curtain here. Rather than speculate, let us simply take the minimalist position, assume she has heard nothing, and pay close attention to her subsequent remarks.

Jocasta's Oracle

Jocasta illustrates her argument with an oracle that, she says, demonstrates Apollo's (or his human interpreters') inability to bring things to accomplishment. The oracle is not drawn at random. It pertains to Laios, the very man, as Jocasta knows, that Oedipus worries he may have killed. Jocasta softens this reintroduction of Laios in a somewhat different capacity with an aside reaffirming her skeptical pose and maintaining her initial distinction between actual report and hearsay, between what the god, as opposed to his ministers, might have said. Her rhetorical caution here shows us that even within this play, the failure to distinguish critically between direct and reported statements is not as characteristic of everyone else as it is of Oedipus (711–12):

> An oracle once came to Laios—well,
> I won't say it was from Phoebus himself,
> but from his ministers.

Laios is reintroduced by Jocasta not as a killer's victim but as the recipient of an oracle (713–16):

> It said that fate
> would visit him as death at his child's hand—

> a child, that is, born of himself and me.
> Report, however, says that Laios died,
> waylaid by foreign bandits (*lêistai*) at a place
> where three roads meet.

Her statement of Laios' death at the hands of *foreign* bandits at a crossroads not only obliquely supports Creon's claim to innocence but also makes it clear that Creon was not telling as much as was even popularly known in his response to Oedipus' questions.

The report of Laios' death, Jocasta also points out, is based on a report that is itself rumor. If the oracle is possibly secondhand and unreliable, so too is the report of Laios' death.

Jocasta continues (717–25):

> The child did not survive
> birth even by three days. For Laios pinned
> his feet, cast, but with others' (*allôn*) hands, the child
> away upon a trackless mountain-peak.
> Apollo, then, did not cause him to be
> his father's killer or cause Laios
> to die the formidable death he feared
> through his son's actions. Such was the chart
> of life prophetic utterances made.
> Don't turn a hair at them. The things that god
> has need (*chreia*) to answer and track down, he will
> quite easily reveal all by himself.[2]

She does not give much detail about the prophecy to Laios. Other versions of her child's birth suggest Laios assaulted her while he was drunk.[3] But Jocasta makes no allusion to this episode. The motif of drunkenness will soon appear, but in Oedipus' narrative, not Jocasta's, and in a rather different context.

Jocasta, so keen to distinguish direct observation from hearsay, first makes, then modifies, a statement that Laios personally bound and exposed the child. He exposed the child—but used the hands of other people to do it. She thus specifically leaves open the age-old mythic scenario of the rescue of the cast-off child. Further, Jocasta's plural, "others'," implies that more than one individual was involved in exposing the infant. The detail may seem trivial; but *Oedipus* focuses as insistently as an ancient philosopher on distinctions between singularity and plurality, just as Jocasta distinguishes between observation and hearsay.

Jocasta's Account of Laios' Death

We might anticipate that Oedipus will react to the larger text of Jocasta's new narrative, which pertains to the prophecy Laios received. He pays overt attention, however, to only a tiny segment of what is said (726–28):

> *Oedipus*: My soul is cut adrift, my mind astir,
>   on hearing, dear wife, what you said just now.
> *Jocasta*: What troubling thought spun you, made you say this?

Oedipus does not yet indicate that he sees any chance Laios may be his father. He is determined, for the moment, to pursue the issue of Laios' death; he ignores the vagueness about, and reliability of, the report and fixes on the precise details it involves (729–37). We might then assume that everything else Jocasta said went unheeded—though it really did not, as we will see in due course.

> *Oedipus*: I thought I heard you say this Laios
>   was cut down at a place where three roads meet.
> *Jocasta*: Such was the rumor (*êudato . . . tade*) that has not yet
>   stopped.
> *Oedipus*: Where is this place the incident occurred?
> *Jocasta*: The region's called Phocis, the road, Split Road.
>   It leads there from Delphi and Daulia.
> *Oedipus*: How many years have passed since this happened?
> *Jocasta*: It was announced in town a bit before
>   you showed up and took over this country.

Jocasta again supports an important detail in Creon's first conversation with Oedipus: the association of Laios' death with the time of Oedipus' arrival at Thebes. She now adds precise details of place, the famous *Schistê Odos,* pointed out by Pausanias (10.5.4) as the site of Laios' death (see Introduction, above). And since she omits any allusion to the Sphinx, she makes a shorter and more direct bridge of time and narrative between Laios' death and Oedipus' assumption of power than even Creon did. Laios and Oedipus are now traveling in opposite directions on the same road at the same time. True, we may argue, Jocasta does not necessarily know that Oedipus was himself journeying from Delphi when he arrived in Thebes. But even if he had been arriving from Corinth, he would probably have been on that fatal road.

Oedipus now makes a major change of mental direction. His notion of conspiracy remains. But in his mind now it is not Creon and Teiresias who are plotting against him, but the gods (738): "O Zeus, what have you plotted to have done with me?" He is on the verge of concluding that he is Laios' killer. Jocasta prods him forward (739–49):

> Jocasta: What is it, Oedipus, upsets you so?
> Oedipus: Don't ask me yet. Laios' nature, tell me,
>   What was he like? Also, how young was he?
> Jocasta: A dark man,[4] his hair newly streaked with gray.
>   In shape, not so much different from yourself.
> Oedipus: I'm lost! I think that I've, unknowingly,
>   been calling hideous curses on myself!
> Jocasta: What's this? I shrink (oknô) with fear as I observe you,
>   lord.
> Oedipus: I'm terribly concerned our seer can see.
>   But tell me one thing to make matters clear.
> Jocasta: I shrink (oknô) from it, but I'll tell what I know.

Jocasta's suggestion that Oedipus looks like Laios, together with her account of the oracle about Laios and the subsequent exposure of their child, might seem enough to trigger a more overt reaction from Oedipus than they do. Indeed, Jocasta seems to anticipate a stronger response, to judge by her use of the verb oknô in lines 746 and 749. Oknô—meaning "I shy (in fear) from," "I shrink from," "I hesitate"—and the related noun oknos and the adjective oknêros occur eight times in Oedipus between here and line 1,175. There are just twenty other instances of these words in all the remaining plays. Their introduction here marks the beginning of an extensive obtrusion of words denoting fear—a topic we will examine in the next chapter.

It is important that Jocasta, rather than Oedipus, introduces the motif of fear. Oedipus' disturbed, but less specific, language of anxiety here suggests that he has not yet consciously grasped the larger possibility that, if he accepts Jocasta's account as true, he may also have to accept that he is Laios' son as well as Laios' killer. After all,

Teiresias has marked out Oedipus not just as killer of Laios but as incestuous mate of his own mother. For the moment, Oedipus keeps the second element of Teiresias' prophecy out of his speech, if not of his mind.

Oedipus' next remarks show the importance of his earlier confusion about the number of Laios' killers. From the moment Creon first talked of Laios' death, Oedipus must have considered the possibility he himself was the killer. He asks Jocasta about Laios and his entourage (750–55):

> *Oedipus*: Was he lightly escorted, or had he
> many retainers, as a ruler would?
> *Jocasta*: Five was the total (*xympantes*). Of these, one was just
> a herald. Laios rode the only coach.
> *Oedipus*: Now it's coming clear. But who on earth,
> dear wife, told you what you're telling me?
> *Jocasta*: A houseboy, the sole survivor who came back.
> *Oedipus*: Does he happen to be inside right now?

Numbers matter. Oedipus is told that Laios' entourage was an un-kingly (but very Delphic) five, of whom one was herald and another an *oikeus,* a houseboy—unless herald and houseboy are intended to be one and the same.[5] This alleged sole survivor is an *oikeus,* a house-hold slave, who, curiously, serves as a kind of herald of the news of Laios' death and seems to have a place in other versions of the myth, notably, as we have seen, in Pausanias 10.5.4, where an *oiketês,* "household slave," is commemorated as having *died* with Laios at the Split Road.

Since the survivor is an *oikeus,* the quite logical assumption is that the man might be available in the palace at the moment of this con-versation with Jocasta. But he is not. Jocasta explains that when the houseboy returned, saw Oedipus in power and Laios dead, he begged to be sent as far out of sight of the city as possible (758–62), to be *apoptos* (either "not to be seen" or "not to be able to see"):

> No. The moment he came back from there
> and saw you holding power and Laios dead,
> he grasped my hand, begged me to send him to
> the countryside to look after the flocks
> so he might be well out of sight (*apoptos*) of this

> city. So I sent him. A worthy man,
> although a slave, and he deserved to get
> this act of kindness—and much more than this.

Her account is confused and, in an odd way, directed toward and against Oedipus. She implies that the man recognized Oedipus, ran in fear, and did not wish to cause trouble by being close to town. Again, her report accords with Creon's. We cannot therefore argue that the witness must have been wounded and left for dead. Creon says the survivor ran away, through fear (118).

In line 758 there is a baffling inconsistency. Jocasta implies, as Dawe points out, not only that the witness saw Oedipus as ruler of Thebes before he realized Laios was dead, but also that he did not get back to Thebes until after Oedipus had solved the riddle of the Sphinx and succeeded to the vacant throne. Dawe comments: "there are no other places [in Greek tragedy] where temporal relativity receives such arbitrary treatment. More serious perhaps than the offence against real life logic is the offence against dramatic likelihood."[6]

Dawe sees the enormity of the inconsistency, which Jebb, in his commentary a century ago, tried to minimize: "The poet has neglected clearness on a minor point . . . and had overlooked the inconsistency."[7] It is not a minor point; Dawe is right. But we should try other explanations before saying that Sophocles made a serious dramatic blunder, thereby attributing our perplexity to a monumental authorial error. There is so much conflicting testimony in this play that it is more just to the poet to assume the dramatic force lies precisely in that conflict of evidence, as does the drama of a court trial.

If Jocasta is correctly reporting the alleged survivor's behavior, we have to assume either that this man was lying or that he ran away from the scene of the attack without realizing Laios had been killed, and stayed away from Thebes for quite some time, until Oedipus became tyrant after solving the Sphinx's riddle. But the conflict runs deeper still. Between the death of Laios and Oedipus' tyranny at Thebes there is the riddle of the Sphinx. Jocasta omits, for the second time in this scene, any mention of Oedipus' solution of the Sphinx's riddle as part of the sequence of events leading to his assumption of power. Jocasta draws us to the conclusion that her slave's hurried request to be sent from Thebes the instant he returns is made because Oedipus is the ruler. Is that what she intends to communicate?

Oedipus and the Old Man at the Crossroads

Oedipus again fails to observe conflicting or improbable elements in what his interlocutors say. The houseboy, as Jocasta recounts her interview with him, cannot possibly have witnessed Laios' death. And this slave must have given a false account of Laios' death if we are to conclude that Oedipus really was Laios killer. For we will recall from what Creon said earlier, and from what Jocasta goes on to reaffirm, that the survivor insisted Laios' assailants were numerous. Nonetheless, Oedipus now tells Jocasta that he killed an old man and his entourage at a crossroads, and fears this old man might have been Laios. Yet Oedipus' account makes it clear that he acted alone and that *there were no survivors* (800–813):

> I'll tell you the whole truth, my dear wife.
> As I traveled (*hodoiporôn*) eagerly close to this place
> of three crossroads, a herald and a man
> in a horse-drawn coach encountered me,
> coming the opposite way, just as you state.
> The leader and the older man drove straight
> toward me, violently. Angered, I hit
> the driver as he runs me off the road.
> Then the older man, seeing me walk
> right past the wheels, aimed at the middle of
> my head and hit me with a two-lashed whip.
> I did not simply match him. Instantly,
> struck by the staff held in this very hand,
> he toppled back and out although he was
> in the middle of his coach. And then,
> I kill every one of them (*xympantas*).

Although Oedipus notes a conflict between the alleged witness's account of what happened and his own recollection of killing an old man and his entourage, he does not even allude to the most obvious discrepancy: in his encounter, no one survived to be a witness. We might also note that although Jocasta gives five as the total number of travelers with Laios, Oedipus mentions the killing of only three, even though he says he killed the entire group. For future reference, we should also observe that Oedipus says he killed the old man with a blow to the head, not with a sword or a spear.

Dawe comments (on line 813) that Oedipus "never goes on to use the argument that therefore these two events must be unrelated."[8]

Oedipus questions the numbers of assailants in the surviving witness's report but never questions whether there could have been a witness to make the report. He thus never raises the possibility that the man was lying. Oedipus is still fixated on the issue raised by his earlier conversation with Creon: whether Laios' assailants were one or many. He tells Jocasta that if this man maintains Laios was killed by a solitary assailant, he, Oedipus, is Laios' killer. He assumes, that is, that the alleged witness will tell the truth, and wants to interrogate him further (842–46):

> You said he reported that robbers,
> men, waylaid and killed him. If he still
> maintains the plural number I did not
> do this killing. For one just could not
> be equivalent to his many. However,
> if he says one man, traveling alone,
> clearly the evidence weighs against me.

Oedipus distinguishes between one and many, but not between five and three, or between one and zero. He also echoes, without specially noting it, the chorus's observation from line 292 that Laios was killed by travelers rather than bandits. He recalls being a lone traveler (*ho-doiporôn*) when he killed an old man at the crossroads. In assuming that the testimony of this alleged witness might outweigh his own memory of what happened and thus establish his guilt, Oedipus shows an extraordinary lack of confidence in the reliability of his own perceptions. As a result, he makes a disastrously wrong assumption that this alleged witness was telling and will tell the truth. For if Jocasta and Creon have accurately reported his announcement after Laios' death, the houseboy-slave was, without a doubt, lying. And, to judge by Jocasta's comment at line 850, this report was general knowledge at Thebes: "The city," she says, "heard him [the witness] say this, not just me" (850).

Sandor Goodhart, in an extremely important article about the witness's testimony, has pointed out that if the witness was telling the truth when he reported the incident at the crossroads, Oedipus was not Laios' killer.[9] To reverse matters: if Oedipus was Laios' killer, the witness was not telling the truth about Laios' death. Since he made his report publicly, he cannot retract it without admitting that he lied—and such an admission would make his further testimony highly suspect. Thus it is very important that Oedipus examine the witness on the subject of Laios' death. Recognizing this point at least, he requests that Jocasta summon him (859–60).

On the basis of the testimony of this dubious survivor and that of an anonymous Corinthian, Oedipus will conclude that he has killed his father and married his mother. Yet, most curious of all, the person who most solidly keeps Oedipus on the road to his conclusion that he was the murderer of Laios, and that Laios was his father, is Jocasta—to whom we must now return.

What the Houseboy Saw

Let us look again at Jocasta's words as she mentions the houseboy to Oedipus (763–64):

> A worthy man,
> although a slave, and he deserved to get
> this act of kindness—and much more than this.

Jocasta's concluding aside invites a further question. What made this slave so special to her? Oedipus does not ask. He simply wishes the man could be brought to him (765–66):

> *Oedipus*: I wish he could come back to us quickly!
> *Jocasta*: He can. But why do you command this?

Jocasta quickly turns Oedipus' wish into an order. The slave who will make the fateful connection is to be summoned. Oedipus responds to the "why" rather than the "command" (767–68):

> I fear myself, dear wife, that I said
> many things in excess (*mê poll' agân*). It's these words
> that make me want to take a look at him.

Now Oedipus talks of himself in Delphic terms, not ironically, as did Jocasta, but self-deprecatingly. The Apollonian motto in Delphi is *mêden agân*, "nothing in excess." But Oedipus suggests that he has foolishly exceeded Apollonian wisdom. It is he, not Jocasta, who now resorts to the vocabulary of fear. Her reply is remarkably authoritative and calm (769–70):

> Well, he'll be here. But I am worthy too,
> I think, to find out what it is in you
> that makes you so greatly upset, my lord.

Her comment suggests that the merits of her slave are still on her mind as she speaks. He deserved consideration from her. She deserves no less from Oedipus.

The Drunk at the Party

We have already discussed that part of Oedipus' ensuing narrative where he explains how he killed an old man who may have been Laios. But the narrative is set amid an extraordinary autobiographical sketch which needs some comment of its own (771–78):

> You will not be deprived, since I have come
> so far in my anticipations now.
> Who should I tell them to rather than you
> as I go through the lot fortune gives me?
> My father was Corinthian—Polybus.
> My mother, Merope the Dorian.
> And I was thought the biggest man in town
> until fortune assailed me in this way.
> It's worthy an astonished glance, if not
> worthy the serious thought that I give it.

Oedipus continues in a self-deprecating manner as he assesses the worth of the story he's about to tell, recognizing that no one but himself would probably pay any attention to it. Remarkably, he addresses Jocasta as if he were explaining his lineage for the first time. He also says that Polybus *was,* rather than *is,* his father. As he speaks, he has no reason to believe that Polybus is dead. The "was" suggests rather that Oedipus no longer really accepts that Polybus is his father—a suspicion speedily confirmed by the story that Oedipus tells (779–85):

> There was a man, at dinner, flying high
> on drink. And in his cups he calls me, said
> I was a spurious child who'd been passed off
> on my father (*plastos . . . patri*). I was deeply angered.
> That whole day I restrained myself, but then,

the next, I went right up and cross-questioned
mother and father. They were greatly upset
at the gross slander and the drunkard who
had let it fly. Then I was pleased by what
they both said.

Stephen Berg and Diskin Clay recognize that the word that hurt
Oedipus was *plastos*. But a *plastos* is not just a "bastard" or, in an
artistic sense, a "fabrication," as they suggest.[10]

A *plastos . . . patri* is an infant imported by the mother and "passed
off on his father." In other words, the insult is that Oedipus is the
kind of supposititious child Euripides' Jocasta says he was. Merope,
she states "persuades her husband she has given [Oedipus] birth"
(*Phoenician Women* 31). We may also compare Euripides' *Ion,* where
the pedagogue does not believe that the temple-boy recently named
Ion by King Xuthus is really the king's newly discovered son: he
thinks him rather an illegitimate child "planted" by Xuthus at the
temple of Apollo for Queen Creusa to "find." So he observes (*Ion*
830–31): "This is a new name fabricated (*pePLASmenon*) to suit the
date: Ion 'because he met him as he went (*IONti*) out.' " The gist of
the pun could be rendered in English as: "because his *eye* fell *on* him
as he left."

The implication is that the child is "passed off" as legitimate by
one supposed parent on the other, in Ion's case on Creusa, in Oedipus'
on Polybus. The detail is important. Soon a Corinthian will arrive
and claim that he gave the infant Oedipus to *Polybus,* i.e., to Oedipus'
Corinthian *father,* with his own hands. This Corinthian, then, will
not be confirming what the drunk at the banquet said: that Oedipus
was a child his *mother* had passed off on his father. Hence there is, a
fundamental contradiction between the drunk's statement and the
Corinthian's.

Oedipus describes the insolent drunk as a man *hyperplêstheis methêi,*
which I rendered as "flying high on drink," or, more literally in the
most grammatical sense, "overfilled with drink" (779). Oedipus then
tells how he mentioned the incident to Polybus and Merope, who
took the insult badly and were angry with the man who had "let it
fly (*methenti*)" (784). Oedipus is playing on the similarity in sound
between *methês* ("drink") and *methenti* ("let . . . go"), as if he wished
to suggest "said, while in his cups."

Oedipus' own anger is directed not against the man who insulted him but against Polybus and Merope who denied vehemently that Oedipus really was a supposititious child. His first reaction to their strong denials, he says, was happiness: "then I was pleased by what they both said" (785). But in the following lines he admits that doubts kept nagging at him (785–88):

> Nonetheless, this rankled me
> constantly: the tale took hold, got round.
> So, with no word to mother or father,
> I travel to consult the Delphic shrine.

Oedipus simultaneously believes and disbelieves the reassurances Polybus and Merope offer about his legitimacy. But disbelief is stronger. He accepts the word of an anonymous drunk over that of his parents and travels to Delphi.

Why does Oedipus believe the drunk? There may be something lurking in the wordplay on *methenti,* noted above: Aristotle (*fragment* 102 [Rose]), cited by Athenaeus in *Deipnosophists* 2.40D, derives *methyein* ("to be drunk") from *meta to thyein* ("after the act of sacrifice"). Another passage from Athenaeus offers further light (*Deipnosophists* 2.37E–F):

> Philochorus says that people when drinking not only make clear who they themselves are, but they reveal others too as they indulge in their free speech. Hence the sayings "wine is also truth" [Alcaeus, *fragment* 57] and "wine shows a man's mind." And the victory prize at the festival of Dionysus is a tripod, for when we use the expression "those speaking from the tripod (*ek tripodos legein*)," we mean those who tell the truth. One must grasp that the mixing bowl is the tripod of Dionysus. In antiquity there were two types of tripod, both of which came to be called cauldrons. The one called *loêtrochoos* (pitcher for washing) could stand over a fire. The other was called a mixing bowl.

In vino veritas, the explanation seems to be. Oedipus thus proceeds from the drunk speaking from the tripod of Dionysus to the tripod of the Pythian priestess at Delphi.

Although Oedipus does not tell Jocasta (or us) what he asked the oracle, it is fair to presume his question was "Who are my parents?"— the same question he asks Teiresias, with disastrous rhetorical consequences, earlier in the play. The oracle is less precise in its answer. Oedipus reports (788–99):

Phoebus sent me away, not honoring
the questions I had come to ask, saying
other terrifying miseries, actions
appalling: I must mate with my mother,
show mankind a brood they could not bear
to see and become killer of the man
who'd fathered me. On hearing this I went
into exile from Corinth, measuring
its land from then on not by strides upon
the ground, but by the stars above. I went
to where I'd never see the gross slander
of what was prophesied for me come true.
I travel on. I reach these regions here
where you say this tyrant of yours died.

As Oedipus recalls his consultation of Delphi, we see once more his characteristic behavior. He asks, it seems: "Who are my parents?" and receives not an answer but a declaration: "You will kill your father and marry your mother." Instead of realizing that to avoid killing his father he must first know who his father is, he responds as if Polybus were in fact his father and Merope his mother—although it was uncertainty on this point that first sent him to Delphi.

The Text Unspoken

Jocasta's reaction to Oedipus' narrative about the drunk is surprisingly calm. We might expect his story to stir in her some verbal response to show that she recalls how she conceived the child she herself exposed. Her husband Laios, though warned not to have children by Jocasta, assaulted her when he was drunk, according to most versions of the myth. Yet Sophocles' Jocasta does not mention the incident.[11] Is she deliberately withholding mention of a sorrowful experience, or does Sophocles suppose his audience will not know—or suppress its knowledge of—that widespread tradition? We cannot answer with certainty. But characters often withhold information from each other—either pointedly, as Teiresias does, or more subtly, as in Creon's case—depending on whether the speaker's purpose is to draw attention to or to gloss over the omission.

In *Oedipus*, connections we would anticipate are frequently not made or lie dormant for substantial portions of the play. Jocasta, for

instance, remains calm even when Oedipus mentions that he killed
an old man at, perhaps, the very crossroads where Laios was killed.
Neither Oedipus nor Jocasta ties together, at least overtly, the com-
plementary strands of their stories: the prophecies of patricide and
the killing at the crossroads. Why not? In Oedipus' case, the explanation is, superficially, simpler. Nothing in Jocasta's report of Laios'
oracle suggests that her child and Laios' will marry his mother. There
is nothing to trigger, that is, his own oracular anxieties—except for
one detail. Jocasta says her child's feet were pinned together when he
was exposed. Oedipus, as we will see, was self-conscious about his
own swollen feet.

Sometimes a single word alerts us that an idea is present in a character's mind even if it is not overtly expressed. In Oedipus' long
speech to Jocasta we have a fleeting sense he might be wondering
about his relationship to Laios when he uses the word *syngenes*, "related in birth." Let us set the scene by briefly reviewing Oedipus'
account of his killing of the old man (810–26):

> I did not simply match him. Instantly,
> struck by the staff held in this very hand,
> he toppled back and out although he was
> in the middle of his coach. And then,
> I kill every one of them.
> > Yet if
> there is some kind of kinship (*ti syngenes*) then between
> the stranger (*xenôi*) and Laios, what man
> is more pitiable than the one
> who stands before you (*toud' andros*), and what man ever
> could be more divinely cursed than he?
> No one, citizen or stranger, is
> allowed to take him home or speak to him,
> rather, they must drive him from their house.
> And nobody (*outis*) but I imposed all this:
> I set these very curses on myself.
> Then with my own two hands, the very hands
> by which he died I stain the dead man's bed.
> Was I conceived evil, and am I not
> wholly a thing unclean, if to be banished
> is my fate, and when banished not to be
> allowed to see my family or walk
> my native soil, if it is sealed that I
> must marry with my mother and couple
> with her and murder my own father...

The word *syngenês* is generally used by Sophocles to indicate someone related by blood or, less frequently, marriage. In *Oedipus* 551, Oedipus during an angry interchange refers to Creon with a nice touch of dramatic irony as *syngenês*, a "kinsman." In *Oedipus at Colonus* 771, in another interchange with Creon, Oedipus charges the latter with neglecting *to syngenes*, "the [ties of] kinship." In the same play, Theseus describes Polyneices to Oedipus as a kinsman (*syngenê*) but not a fellow-citizen (*Oedipus at Colonus* 1157).

Oedipus is clearly aware that he has in a way become the agent of his own downfall by unleashing a curse that may fall upon himself. Thus, although he can see himself as the victim of the curse, or the gods, of external powers, he is aware, when he chooses to be, that these external forces are to a large extent of his own creation. In much the same way he varies between treating his own person as "self" and "other." His reference to himself in the third person as *toud' andros*, "the one who stands before you," allows a nice moment of confusion between himself and the stranger (*xenos*) who, he thinks, could have some kind of kinship with Laios. We may recall Teiresias' words at lines 452–53 of this play, where he describes Laios' killer as a stranger (*xenos*) who will prove to be a "native Theban" (*engenês Thêbaios*).

On the other hand, Oedipus' rhetorical and psychological distancing allows him to talk in very impersonal terms about his marriage to Jocasta. He does not say: "After killing Laios, I then came to Thebes and married you, his widow, Jocasta." Instead, he states: "with my own two hands, the very hands by which he died, I stain the dead man's bed" as if he were talking to someone other than Jocasta herself. This critical distancing enables him to avoid admitting that Laios and Jocasta might be his father and mother at the end of his narrative by firmly asserting something we know he doubts: that Polybus *is* his father (825–27):

> . . . if it is sealed that I
> must marry with my mother and couple
> with her and murder my own father,
> Polybus, who sired me and who raised me.

The question he himself asked during this very scene still lurks unanswered. His insistence that Polybus was his biological parent contrasts oddly with the uncertainty he felt as the anonymous drunk's insults sent him on the way to Delphi, wondering who his parents were, and with his eagerness to have the hostile Teiresias tell him who his parents are. It is almost as if Oedipus were saying here: "My father—it must have been Polybus, he must have begotten me, he did raise me."

Again he returns to the theme of conspiracy against him by the supernatural, but with an undertone of self-incrimination (828–29):

> If someone said that these things came upon
> this man before you (*andri tôid'*) from raw force, divine (*daimonos*)
> and self-assertive, who would set him straight?

Oedipus gains distance once more by referring to himself as "this man" rather than "I." It is as if he were treating himself as "other." And that is why his choice of *daimôn* to describe the persecuting force is particularly appropriate. Sophocles is of course a contemporary of Socrates, whose *daimôn*, often rendered "divine sign," is on the borderline (if there is such a border) between the internal and the external. It is the philosopher's conscience and his god. As Oedipus oscillates between describing himself in the first and the third person, between self and other, so he employs a word for god that suggests the power within as well as the power outside, a word that makes god self as well as other. And Sophocles sets his verse astride the gap between self and other with a delicate play on words. The phrase I have rendered "raw force divine and self-assertive" is in Greek *ap' ômou . . . diamonos*.

Wilhelm Dindorf noted in his *Lexicon Sophocleum* that this use of *ômos* is not "proper," since the word means "raw," and the apparent meaning Sophocles has in mind is "cruel."[12] I suspect the poet had something more in mind. He had used *ômos*, "raw," to describe Antigone in her confrontation with Creon and her readiness to accept death. The chorus declares that she is the "raw born daughter of a raw (*ômou*) father" (*Antigone* 471–72). She is, then, a child worthy of Oedipus' self-destructive determination, his "rawness." In *Oedipus* too, Sophocles may be stretching the meaning of *ômos* for special effect, using the closeness in sound of *ap' ômou*, "from raw," to *apo (e)mou*, "from me," to enhance that sense of self-destructiveness which permeates the play. Hence my "stretched" translation: "raw self-assertive."

At the conscious level, Oedipus declares himself the victim of divine power, but at the level of dramatic irony, which often seems coextensive with what one might call Oedipus' subconscious, he is partially aware that the divine force trapping him is himself. He now calls not on the gods but on man's sense of reverence for the gods to prevent him from seeing the day he kills his father and marries his mother (830–34):

> See, see to it, holy reverence for the gods,
> that I may never see this day. Let me
> vanish from mortal sight before I see
> the stain of such horror come upon me.

Like the alleged survivor of the slaughter at the meeting of three roads, Oedipus wishes neither to be seen nor to see. Exile will be the path to one wish, self-blinding to the other.

The Summing Up

The chorus, a silent observer for 150 lines, throughout the interchanges between Jocasta and Oedipus, now intrudes, reminding Oedipus that he has not yet established his guilt, and prompting Jocasta to ask what it is Oedipus wishes to learn (834–38):

> *Chorus*: Well, these are things we'd shrink from too, my lord.
>   Until, however, you get *him* right here
>   and question him in person, cling to hope.
> *Oedipus*: Such is the greatness of my hope today!
>   To await a man, a shepherd. That's all.
> *Jocasta*: What is it you want said when he appears?

The chorus takes for granted that the alleged witness has the answer to the question of Oedipus' guilt. And Oedipus now refers to that man not as a herald (*kêrux*) or houseboy (*oikeus*) but as a herdsman (*botêr*). His perceptions seem to be in a turmoil of confusion. Jocasta, however, reiterates her question from line 766 ("Why do you command this?" i.e., the survivor's return). Has nothing Oedipus says from line 771 onward registered with her? Or has she already noticed that Oedipus *wants to believe the worst*?

Oedipus for his part assumes Jocasta is being naive. This piques him and moves him from anguished theatricality to a condescendingly didactic tone (839–47):

> Oedipus: I'll teach you what it is. If he were found
> agreeing with you, I myself would stand
> acquitted, free from any suffering.
> Jocasta: What did you hear me say that seemed special?
> Oedipus: You said he reported that robbers,
> men, waylaid and killed him. If then he
> still maintains the plural number I
> did not kill Laios. For one could not be
> equivalent to his many. However,
> if he says one man, traveling alone,
> clearly the evidence weighs against me.

Oedipus reacts to something he has already been told by Creon: that the killers were many, not one. Jocasta's additions, about the prophecy to Laios, are brushed aside.

Jocasta now responds forcefully, reintroducing these overlooked elements in her response to Oedipus. Her reply (848–58) falls into five sections which I mark (a), (b), (c), (d), and (e):

> (a) Then understand that this is what he said
> in public. It is not possible
> that he could now back down upon this score.
> The city heard it. It was not just me.

> (b) And, if he were to change some small detail
> of what he said before, he'll never prove
> that is was done just as forecast, my lord,
> this killing of Laios (*ton ge Laiou phonon*).

> (c)   Apollo Loxias
> clearly said that Laios had to die
> at my child's hands.

> (d)   Yet that poor thing never
> killed Laios, but himself died long before.

> (e) So I would never give another glance,
> myself, this way or that, at prophesy.

The logic of Jocasta's statement is baffling if one assumes, as critics do, that her intent is to assure Oedipus he is not Laios' killer. Such an assumption would seem well and good if she had cut her statement

short at the end of (a). But in (b) she allows the possibility that the
alleged witness might change a detail here and there (the number of
assailants, for instance). It might not, then, be such a good idea to
send for him. His statement is on record, as it were, and he might
get away with a few dangerous changes if he actually appeared. Jocasta
does not deny that Oedipus could be Laios' killer. On the contrary,
she talks of Oedipus as if he *could be* Laios' killer in everything except
prophetic nicety.

In terms of prophetic nicety, Jocasta continues in (c), the killer of
Laios *has to be* her son by Laios, who it cannot be (d) because he died
as an infant. Since Laios is, it appears, dead, but not in accordance
with prophecy, the religious offense, in terms of the fulfillment of
the oracle, is nonexistent even if Oedipus killed Laios. Hence her
conclusion (e) is, that oracles in general are meaningless—the very
point she was attempting to establish in Oedipus' mind at the beginning of their dialogue here.

Yet there is an alternative conclusion missing from her calculations:
that her child did not really die after all. If Oedipus were both her
son and the killer of Laios, the prophecies would be intact, but the
testimony of the alleged survivor/houseboy/herdsman would be
proven false. Oedipus' determination to show the efficacy of oracles,
however, will leave him no rhetorical choice but to conclude that he
is Jocasta's son, long presumed dead. What is hard to assess is whether
Jocasta knows this and is deliberately setting this choice before him,
and if deliberately, why. To destroy him, or to warn him that he
will destroy himself?

Oedipus approves her reasoning, whether he understands it or not,
and they take their leave for a short choral moment (859–62):

Oedipus: Good reasoning. Send someone, nonetheless,
      to bring this worker here. Don't let it slip.
 Jocasta: I'll send for him quickly. But let's go in.
      I wouldn't do something you wouldn't like.

Oedipus' first comment calls attention to the fact that Jocasta has not
yet sent for the alleged survivor despite her apparent willingness to
do so. And she does not actually send for him now. Rather she says
she *will* send for him very soon. Her principal concern is to get
Oedipus inside. Although her concluding comment is generally taken

as little more than a dramatic excuse to clear the stage for the chorus, we should recall that often in this play the house is where people go (or consider going) to discuss matters away from the public eye. Jocasta is suggesting the need for such a private conversation here, perhaps before actually sending for the supposed survivor. But it is certainly worth noting that Oedipus has already been, in effect, ordered into the house by Teiresias, the chorus, and Jocasta even before this last, and gentlest, suggestion by his wife. His tyrannical presence, then, seems surprisingly unintimidating to the Thebans.

There seems little doubt that, when offstage, Oedipus and Jocasta do converse—though what passes between them we are never specifically told. For the Jocasta who emerges after the choral song is very different and gives all appearance of being panicked by her husband's behavior. And, ironically, it is she who summons Oedipus back on stage for his fateful meeting with a man from Corinth.

6. AN ANONYMOUS NAMER

The chorus, alienated from (and having alienated) Jocasta and Oedipus, offers a stinging meditation on tyranny and irreverence when the two of them leave the stage. Although the chorus does not criticize Oedipus and his wife directly and personally, its tone of contempt and disdain is unmistakable, climaxing in the famous and withering comment: "Uncontrolled arrogance (*hybris*) begets the tyrant, arrogance (*hybris*), if it is overfilled with many things, and all to no purpose" (*hybris phyteuei tyrannon, hybris, ei pollôn hyperplêsthei matân* [872–73]).[1] Underlying this remark is the conventional tragic and Herodotean paradigm: too much of a good thing (*koros*) leads to *hybris,* then to *atê* (a kind of blindness to reason, or destruction), and finally to a restoration of the balance that was disturbed (*nemesis*). Tyrannical conduct, not only its inception, was primarily associated with *hybris,* both physical and political. The stories about the historical tyrants of Greece are full of acts of *hybris* against men and women.

The use of the traditional formula is itself ominous; the chorus has begun to see Oedipus as an exemplar of the tragic paradigm. It is not just money and a clique of powerful friends that make a man a tyrant, as Oedipus suggested when he attacked Creon; it is his way of looking at, and treating, the world about him. Oedipus' tyrannical anger, his preparedness to condemn without trial, his haughty dismissal of the chorus, which represents the people of Thebes, and Jocasta's slighting remarks about Apollo and prophecy prompt the chorus to conclude that Oedipus' regime is tyrannous in the most classically negative sense. Since tyranny, as we have seen in Chapter 1, is a *nosos*, a disease, which undermines the *isonomia*, the "balance of power," in the body of the state, the chorus has made a major step toward accepting, on these grounds alone, that Oedipus is the pollution upon the state—regardless of whether or not he killed Laios.

Something else lurks in the observation of the chorus. When it was silenced but listening, Oedipus described to Jocasta the drunk who claimed Polybus was not really Oedipus' father: Oedipus called him *hyperplêstheis methei,* "overfilled with drink" (779)—an intoxication which, in Oedipus' opinion, accounts in part for the outrageous insult. So when the chorus now declares that "uncontrolled arrogance (*hybris*) begets (*phyteuei*) the tyrant, arrogance, if it is overfilled (*hyperplêsthei*) with many things," it picks up the drinking imagery and uses the opportunity of Oedipus' absence to talk freely of the tyrant and his insolence, his *hybris*. This is in fact the first time the chorus has been left alone on stage since Creon entered and quarreled violently with Oedipus. Its words, then, color the description of tyranny with the language of drunkenness.

The anonymous drunk's insolence, his *hybris,* set Oedipus on the road to Thebes, tyranny, and a search for who it was that begat him. He went, *lathrâi de mêtros kai patros,* "unbeknown to his mother and father," to consult the oracle of Apollo at Delphi (787–88). Although he says he did not heed Polybus and Merope who insisted that he really was their child, he quite deliberately calls Polybus not only his father but "the father who begat me and who nurtured me" (*patera . . . hos exephyse kaxethrepse me*) when talking of him to Jocasta (826–27). There is clearly a rift in Oedipus' mind between what he outwardly accepts as truth and what he inwardly fears may be true.

We glimpse, then, the raw force and curious irony of the chorus's words. A drunken act of *someone else*'s insolence sent Oedipus off on the path that led him to Delphi and to Thebes, and consequently "begat" Oedipus' tyranny and his high-handed treatment of Creon. In similar vein, Apollodorus (*Library* 3.5.7) states Laios was drunk (*oinôtheis*) when he violently overpowered Jocasta and begat Oedipus. Euripides' Jocasta in *The Phoenician Women* 21–22 says the same. "*Hybris* begets the tyrant," then, takes on a literal as well as a metaphorical force. Oedipus' own curious intoxication makes him tyrannous now and makes him susceptible to the suggestion that he is not only the *nosos*, the sickness upon Thebes, but the child of Laios and Jocasta, the very product of that wine-induced violence. He had been susceptible to such suggestions at a drunken party many years before.

The Episode of Fear

When Jocasta reemerges, her amazing calm and touches of religious skepticism have yielded to a panic-stricken return to the religious fold. She addresses the chorus members in terms consonant with their concern for the gods, and as if they, rather than Oedipus, Creon, or Teiresias, were the lords or kings (*anaktes*) of the land. Her description of herself as a garlanded suppliant concerned about the foundering ship of state exactly recalls the approach made to Oedipus by the priest at the very beginning of the play (14–25). She also reechoes Creon's earlier and persistent suggestions that Oedipus is no longer rational (911–23):

> Lords (*anaktes*) of the land, I thought it right to come
> as suppliant to the gods, their temple naves (*naous*),
> taking in my two hands these garlands, this incense.
> How I have begged him. I can do no more.
> For Oedipus upsets himself too much
> whenever stressed or pained. He turns not where
> (*oud' hopoi*) the rational man turns, to evaluate
> the new against his past experience.
> *No: he's owned by any man who speaks to him,*
> *provided that man says things that stir fears (phobous).*
> To you, Apollo Lycaeos, since you
> are closest, I do now present myself
> as suppliant, with these offerings and prayers,
> so you may find some way to free us now
> and leave us undefiled. For all of us
> shrink back (*oknoumen*) in horror as we watch him stunned,
> this naval helmsman of our holy ship (*neôs*).

The wordplay here between *naous* ("temples") and *neôs* ("ship"), reinforcing the metaphor of the ship of state, is curiously underscored by the variant forms Sophocles selects. In Attic Greek, *neôs* is usual for "temple" and *naus* for "ship." The absence of leadership in the state prompts an appeal to the gods' shrines for leadership. No less important is Jocasta's psychological analysis of Oedipus, which we discussed in the Introduction: he is controlled by his anxieties about the future rather than by his knowledge based on the past. And, as Lucian shows in *Alexander* 8, there were those in antiquity who understood that "human life was tyrannized (*tyrannoumenon*) by these two very great forces, hope (*elpidos*) and fear (*phobou*), and that a man who could use both to his advantage could get rich very quickly."

Fear is the leitmotif of this scene. At no point in Sophocles' surviving plays do *phobos* and words from the base *phob* occur so densely. Of the fifty-three instances in Sophocles' seven surviving plays (there are another eleven in the fragments), seventeen, around a third, occur in *Oedipus*. Of the seventeen, over half, nine, occur in this episode, grouped between lines 917 and 1013. In a little over a hundred lines of *Oedipus*, then, there are as many words expressing fear as there are in the whole of *Oedipus at Colonus*, and more than in any other Sophoclean play. The usual frequency is between five and eight words based on *phob* per play, as is also the case in Euripides. In all Greek tragedy, only Euripides' *Orestes* has more such words than *Oedipus*: twenty-one. And only *Rhesus*, of disputed authorship, has as many. This episode is, then, the episode of fear in a tragedy of fear. And no one manipulates Oedipus' fears more effectively than an anonymous newcomer who enters either immediately after, or even while, Jocasta makes her statement about fear.

I'm from Corinth

Oedipus is easily distracted. He errs and loses the initiative not only when cross-questioning obviously "formidable," potentially threatening opponents such as Teiresias and Creon but also when examining socially "insignificant persons" who are not, by virtue of their power and status, in the least intimidating. Indeed, they are better able to play on Oedipus' innermost fears precisely because they are not themselves objects of fear. Thus it is not surprising that Oedipus' name and identity should be defined for him in this play not by an oracle or by Teiresias, but by two men who are given only the most imprecise identity themselves. One of them is the newcomer whose arrival robs the chorus of the chance to respond to Jocasta's appearance as suppliant. The newcomer is usually presented in translations as a messenger—though "free-lance reporter" would convey a better idea of his role. For the term messenger suggests someone commissioned and *sent* by one person to another. As we will see, the newcomer

seems to be operating on his own. He lacks even the most characteristic mark of the messenger in Greek tragedy: a messenger speech.
So we will call him simply "the Corinthian," since that is how he
identifies himself.

The Corinthian asks the chorus where he can find Oedipus' palace
and Oedipus himself. Here are his opening words, in Bernard Knox's
translation, with the Greek phrases transliterated to illustrate the
points Knox wishes to establish (924–26):

> Strangers, from you might I *learn where* (*mathOIm' hoPOU*)
> is the palace of the *tyrannos OIDiPOUS,*
> best of all, where he himself is, if you *know where* (*katOIsth' oPOU*).

"These," as Knox comments, are "violent puns, suggesting a fantas-
conjugation of the verb 'to know where' formed from the name
of the hero who, as Teiresias told him, does not know where he
is."[2]

OIDa in Greek means "I know," and *POU* means "where." The
echo of the syllable *POU* at the end of each of the messenger's first
three lines emphasizes a play on OIDiPOUs' name. And how fascinating it is that the Corinthian should be the one to produce it here
as he enters; for he will convince Oedipus not only that he knows
where Oedipus comes from but that he can interpret Oedipus' name
on the basis of another etymology: that of *OIDI,* "swollen," and
POUS, "foot," which appears here for the first time in surviving
Greek literature.

This is an important issue. Simon Goldhill points out:

> It was Oedipus who could solve the riddling language of the sphinx,
> the answer to whose question was the nature of the questioned (man
> Oedipus)—as will be the answer to the investigative process here in-
> stigated in order to free the city from this trouble. Indeed as his name
> *Oidipous* [*dipous* = two-foot] echoes the riddle, it was an answer that
> he found for himself.[3]

The reader who relies on a translation, of course, will have no idea
that such wordplay is in progress. To illustrate my point, I cite these
lines in Bernard Knox's own, earlier translation of the play:

> *Corinthian*: Stranger, can one of you tell me—where is the palace
> of King Oedipus? Better still, if you know, where is
> the king himself?[4]

The reader in English (or other modern languages) is deprived of this crucial wordplay even by those who think it fundamental to the play's meaning for two reasons. First, the translator would have to devise a comparable wordplay to encompass the various possibilities in Oedipus' name: to change his name or at least append to it an epithet containing the wordplays. Second, modern scholars associate puns and wordplays with comedy not with tragedy, and someone who substituted a punning name or epithet for Oedipus would immediately be accused of "ruining" the tragic grandeur of the original. Shelley's parody, "Swellfoot the Tyrant," is a powerful deterrent. But if we are to get the idea of how language itself functions in this play, we *must* find at least an approximation. For Sophocles is here exploring and uncovering the forces of the irrational and demonstrating how those forces operate through language—including puns and other wordplays.

I therefore adopt a compromise course. Instead of giving Oedipus a different name from which the wordplays may develop, I provide him, from this point on, epithets in which at least some of the many Greek wordplays may be imitated: Oedipus, "Undefeated," "Nowhere defeated," and so forth. Thus the Corinthian's opening words and the chorus' response might appear as follows (924–28):

> *Corinthian*: Could I ask, friends, if you know where Oedipus
> your nowhere defeated tyrant lives?
> And better, say where *he* is if you know.
> *Chorus*: Here is his home, my friend, and he's inside.
> This is his children's mother and his wife.

The wordplaying Corinthian is, from the outset, both courteous and considerate. When the chorus introduces him to Jocasta, he prays for a blessing upon her and says how lucky her husband must be (929–30):

> Then may she prosper, may she always live
> amid prosperity, a perfect wife for him.

His blessing, Dawe notes, "is a *captatio benevolentiae* from a lower member of society to his betters."[5] There is no reason, however, to apply elitist overtones. The Corinthian is courteous and flattering as even a gentleman can be if he needs to establish himself in someone else's graces. Jocasta clearly appreciates his compliments, as her charming (and charmed) reply shows. Yet although she returns the compliment, she apparently detects from his tone that he may be after something for himself (931–33):

> Greetings in kind, my friend. So you deserve
> for all your courtesy. But tell me why
> you've come. What do you need, or want to say?

She asks him what he needs (*chrêizei*) or what he wants to say. We will discuss more fully in Chapter 10 the force of this verb *chrêizei* in *Oedipus*; suffice it now to note that Jocasta's use of this word shows her awareness that the newcomer may be using flattery as an overture to a request for some help or benefit. He is not *obviously* a messenger.

The newcomer ignores the first part of Jocasta's instructions. He says nothing about what he needs but immediately indicates that he has news good for both Jocasta and her husband (934): "Good news, my lady, for your home and spouse." Jocasta now, unwisely, floats two questions at the same moment (935): "What sort of news? And who have you come from?" Her second question is a good one, and one not generally posed to messengers in Greek tragedy. For it is usually assumed that the bearer of news is qualified to make the report. But Jocasta seems not sure that he *is* a messenger, and she tends to be an alert and quick-minded person, a keen observer of things and people. The Corinthian responds to her second question first (935–36):

> From Corinth. And the word you soon will learn
> could please—how not?—perhaps upset you too.

His answer is not entirely satisfactory on two counts.

First: Jocasta is asking *who* has sent him, not *where* he is from. Translators deal with the problem in some curious ways. Luci Berkowitz and Theodore Brunner, and Robert Fagles dispose of it before it reaches us. Here are, respectively, their versions of 935–36. First Berkowitz and Brunner:

> *Jocasta*: Where do you come from?
> *Messenger*: From Corinth . . . [6]

Now Fagles:

> *Jocasta*: Who sent you?
> *Messenger*: Corinth . . . [7]

Berkowitz and Brunner adapt Jocasta's question to the answer she receives. Fagles implies that the Corinthian has been sent by the city of Corinth. Nor is this the only instance in this scene where translators glide over major problems in the text.

Second: although the Corinthian introduces himself as the bearer of good tidings, he has gone on to suggest that his news is more ambiguous: it could be pleasing or upsetting. This is precisely the same approach taken by Creon when reporting the oracle to Oedipus (85–88):

> *Oedipus*: My lord and kinsman, Menoeceus' son,
>   what statement (*phêmên*) do you bring us from the god?
> *Creon*: A good one. For I say things that are hard
>   to bear could all turn out quite happily
>   if they ultimately turn out straight.

It is worth reminding ourselves that in the original production of *Oedipus,* the same actor, the tritagonist, played Creon and the Corinthian. Such an approach, then, might be Sophocles' way of using a dramatic stage convention to rhetorical advantage: the same voice introducing itself with similar words.

Let us look again at 936—37:

> *Corinthian:* From Corinth. And the word you soon will learn
>   could please—how not?—perhaps upset you too.

Jocasta fails to pursue, or perhaps even notice, the imprecise—or is it evasive?—reply to her question about who sent the Corinthian. Why, if she is normally so quickwitted? Perhaps because the newcomer immediately focuses on her first question in a rather disturbing way. Although he introduced himself as bearer of good news, he now stresses the ambiguous nature of what he has to report: it could be pleasing or upsetting. Predictably, the clarification Jocasta now seeks is about the ambiguous tone of what he says, not about his unclear identity (938): "What is it? And what is its double force?" Here is the Corinthian's reply (939–44):

> Corinthian: He'll be the tyrant. The Corinthians
> will give him power. So it is rumored there.
> Jocasta: How so? Does not old Polybus still rule?
> Corinthian: No more. For death now has him in the grave.
> Jocasta: Are you then saying Polybus is dead?
> Corinthian: If I don't speak the truth, *I* risk dying.

Jocasta is so distracted (and apparently delighted) by the news of Polybus' death that she fails to notice how odd the first part of the report is. The newcomer does not say Oedipus *has been* appointed tyrant of Corinth, but that Oedipus *will be* appointed tyrant, if *rumor* is correct.[8]

Several translators nonetheless confer official status on man and message. Kenneth Cavander has the messenger say:

> The people of Corinth—it was already announced
> there—will make Oedipus their king.[9]

Berkowitz and Brunner render the passage as:

> Your husband now is ruler of the Isthmus![10]

These translators' changes prevent us from grasping that we are dealing not with fact but with hearsay, and hearsay that is at least doubly removed, since the evasive Corinthian is reporting rumor. Dawe comments on line 940 that it shows he is "not an official representative, but one hoping to earn a reward on his own account by enterprisingly informing Oedipus of local gossip."[11] His comment about Oedipus' rumored, pending appointment as tyrant of Corinth does, then, provide a negative clue about the newcomer's identity. He is not an official ambassador from Corinth. He seems to have picked up some rumors that were circulating and hurried to Thebes with them.

Readers are often no more interested in the identity of the Corinthian and his credentials than is Jocasta or, for that matter, Oedipus. We often approach Sophocles' play on the assumption that everyone is speaking the truth—which, as we have already seen, cannot possibly be the case. So we attribute the Corinthian's evasiveness and obliqueness to sloppy writing rather than authorial intent. We have been careless in our listening, as Jocasta has been in her questioning. We are hearing what we expect to hear. She is hearing what she wants to hear.

Jocasta is not always so incautious. When she asks Oedipus, for instance, on what basis Creon is accusing Oedipus of murdering Laios, she knows how important it is to distinguish between knowing something oneself and picking it up from someone else (704):

> He really knows this for himself? Or has he just
> learned about it all from someone else?

Ironically, Jocasta is fully aware of the difference between knowledge and hearsay. But her concern for that distinction seems to obtrude only when she is deeply interested in the issue under discussion. And Jocasta is not interested in what the Corinthian thinks is his good news. Her delight is in his *bad* news (945–49):

> Maid! won't you go as quickly as you can
> and tell your master?
>   Where are you, prophecies
> from heaven? This is the man that Oedipus
> has long been running from, fearing he might
> kill him. But now this man (*hode*) has been destroyed
> by Luck's (*Tychê*) hand, not by this man (*toud'*) who's now here.[12]

Jocasta gloats over the failure of divine prophecy. But now her skepticism appears more blasphemous, since she approached the gods only moments before as a suppliant with prayers and incense. Further, she is not justified in assuming that Polybus was simply the victim of Luck or Fortune, the divine name attributed to the nonevident causal forces operating within the world. The Corinthian has not yet explained how Polybus died.

Oedipus' entrance during Jocasta's final sentence intensifies the dramatic irony by endowing her words with a multiplicity of reference that probably lies beyond her intent. In conventional tragic diction, the demonstrative *hode* (genitive *toude*) may mean: "this person just mentioned," "this person here," or "this person speaking, that is, myself." Because of the distinction in gender, the last possibility does not really apply in this instance, since the speaker is a woman. But two meanings do emerge here. There is the meaning intended by Jocasta: Polybus was not killed by Oedipus; and another: "*hode* (this man, Oedipus) has been destroyed by Luck's (*Tychê*) hand, not by *toud'* (this man, the Corinthian) who's now here." The second meaning has an ironic ring. For the Corinthian will destroy Oedipus.

Given Jocasta's preamble about Oedipus' psychological condition at the opening of this scene, we might expect Oedipus, as he reenters, to show some immediate sign of stress. His conversation offstage with Jocasta seems certainly to have disturbed her profoundly. But he does not show any public signs of anxiety. He addresses Jocasta with great courtesy in the following exchange (950–54):

> Oedipus: Wise, dearest head of Jocasta, my wife,
>   Why have you sent for me to come outside?
> Jocasta: Hear this man (*toude*)! Think, while you listen, where
>   the holy prophecies from heaven have gone.
> Oedipus: Who is this person? What's his news for me?

Oedipus not only reverses the order of Jocasta's two questions to the Corinthian but directs them to his wife, not to the newcomer. For a second time, the question arises as to the newcomer's identity, and there is absolutely no doubt that the questioner wants to know *who* he is, not just *where* he is from.

We also notice that Oedipus seems eager to acquire information secondhand, even when he could obtain it directly by his own questioning. Nor is this approach unusual for him in the play. He did, after all, send Creon to Delphi and did not go himself. Such reliance on indirect questioning seems characteristic of monarchic behavior in ancient writers.

Jocasta, instead of saying "Ask him yourself," answers (955–56):

> From Corinth. He'll announce that your father
> lives no longer. Polybus is dead!

She simply echoes verbatim the newcomer's vague statement that he is from Corinth, and reports his "bad" news. She omits the "good" news altogether. Oedipus is never told about the rumor that he will be tyrant of Corinth. The Corinthian is piqued by the lack of interest in his "good" news (957–59):

> *Oedipus*: What's your word, stranger? Tell me this yourself!
> *Messenger*: If I must first say this part of my news,
>   know well that he has passed on through death's door.

Had the Corinthian tyranny interested Jocasta (or Oedipus himself), more acute questioning about the newcomer's credentials and certainty of information might have arisen. As it is, we are still no closer to knowing the trustworthiness of his news or the details of his identity. And we will learn no more. News of Polybus' death so preoccupies Oedipus and Jocasta that neither pursues the reporter's identity, much less asks when Oedipus will become tyrant of Corinth. Further, there emerges later another, more aristocratic reason why Oedipus is not deeply concerned about who the newcomer is: Oedipus' opinion that this is a person of no consequence. Yet this mysterious nobody will explain Oedipus' name to *Oedipus'* satisfaction and establish *Oedipus'* identity even though he remains tight-lipped about his own.

How Polybus Died

Oedipus, who still fears he may be responsible for his father's death, asks the Corinthian how Polybus died (960): "Was it conspiracy or some sickness (*nosou*)?" Here, surely, is the moment for the classical messenger speech of Greek tragedy. But we get nothing of the kind. The Corinthian simply replies in one line (961): "A small scale stroke (*rhopê*) tips old bodies to sleep." Dawe calls this "the most beautiful line in Sophocles."[13] He may be right. But the Corinthian's use of the present tense makes his statement a generalization about the tendency of old men to die easily rather than an explanation of how this particular old man actually died. The Greek *rhopê* indicates a medical "turn" for the better or worse (Hippocrates, *Epidemics* 1.26). Bernard Knox observes: "the Corinthian messenger answers like a Hippocratic physician: 'A small impulse brings aged bodies to their rest.' "[14] Yet Plato (*Republic* 8.556E–557A) uses that medical image as a simile of the state's vulnerability to radical political change: as the diseased body needs only a small stroke (*rhopês*) to tip the balance, so forces within the sick state need only a slight pretext to spawn factionalism and revolution. I translate *rhopê* as "stroke" (rather than, say, "turn") to catch the ambiguity, not to suggest that the ancients understood what we now call "strokes." The Corinthian rules out *neither* conspiracy *nor* medical ailment as the cause of death. His response, then, is not an adequate answer to Oedipus' question, much less an adequate explanation of how Polybus died.

Oedipus tentatively interprets the old man's expression in a medical sense. He does not ask any further details; he fills in the blanks himself (962): "The poor man succumbed to sickness (*nosois*) then, it seems." The Corinthian adds a further touch of the self-evident with non-committal helpfulness (963): "And he had measured out so many years." Having said this, he falls silent for the next twenty-five lines. Again some translators fall short. Fitts and Fitzgerald render the Corinthian's words and Oedipus' response thus:

> *Messenger*: A little thing brings old men to their rest.
> *Oedipus*: It was sickness then?[15]

Kenneth Cavander does much the same and even adds a touch of filial sympathy from Oedipus which is not in the original:

> *Messenger*:   A small
>   Touch on the balance sends old lives to sleep.
> *Oedipus*: So, my poor father, sickness murdered you.[16]

The medical imagery in the Corinthian's words is lost, leaving Oedipus' reaction incomprehensible.

Since neither Oedipus nor Jocasta appears particularly interested in the details of Polybus' death, we are left to speculate not only about the Corinthian's knowledge but about the reasons for Oedipus' disinterest and lack of sympathy. Not a word of grief escapes him when he hears of Polybus' death, only a sense of triumph over the oracle and a curious realization that Polybus might have died of grief and longing for him, a fleeting pang of anxiety that he is responsible in a remote sort of way for the old man's death (964–72):

Well, well, dear wife! Who now would give a glance
at Pythian prophecy or ominous birds
cawing above our heads? Allegedly
they showed that I'd kill my father. Now he's dead,
buried beneath the earth. And I, this man (*hode*),
am here and did not touch my sword. Unless—
unless he died because he missed me so,
so in that way I could have caused his death.
But still the prophecies in their strictest sense
have come to nothing. Polybus is dead
and took them to the underworld with him.

For an instant even Oedipus sees the possibility that he fulfilled the oracle in a figurative, Herodotean way: that he is the killer of *Polybus*. Oedipus also gives us a glimpse of how much Polybus cared for him and of his own curious combination of guilt and self-centeredness. But since he never presses the issue about how Polybus dies, neither he nor we ever learn whether this beautifully Delphic *ambages* provides a solution to the problem of the oracle. Suffice it to say that a child who reacts so callously and, later, joyously, to his father's death, when there is no suggestion of ill-feeling between them, should perhaps excite a little more severe comment than Oedipus has earned from critics, and remind us that there are more ways of killing one's father than striking him down at a crossroads. To Oedipus, Polybus' death means only his personal escape from fear—or so he thinks.

Speaking to Oedipus' Fears

Several issues and question, I suggest, should now be in our minds about the taciturn and anonymous Corinthian and his news. Why has he come to Thebes, as it appears, on his own initiative? Was Jocasta's first instinct right, that he needed something? Is it possible that he does not actually know how Polybus died—that he simply gathered from gossip that the king was dead, just as he apparently gathered from gossip that Oedipus would be appointed tyrant of Corinth? This newcomer himself is, we have suggested, an anomaly in Greek tragedy; a "messenger" without a speech who sidesteps questions. But he has an ear for gossip and uses what he learns. After his vague mention of Polybus' death, he leaves the talking to Jocasta and Oedipus, and listens.

He may also have been listening as he entered. For as he comes in, and before he first speaks, Jocasta makes the remark we have mentioned earlier: that her husband belongs to the person speaking to him, if that person voices fears (914–17). And fear, we have suggested, is the leitmotif of this scene. Let us now look at it in detail, beginning with Jocasta's reassurance to Oedipus that his fears of the oracle have proved groundless (973–88):

> *Jocasta*: Wasn't I predicting this to you for years (*palai*)?
> *Oedipus*: You said so. I was drawn off track by fear (*phobôi*).
> *Jocasta*: Don't let it go on gnawing at your heart.
> *Oedipus*: How can I *not* shrink (*oknein*) from my mother's bed?
> *Jocasta*: What should man be afraid of (*phoboit'*)? Luck (*Tychê*) controls
> his life, and no one has proven foresight.
> The most effective course is, I should think,
> to live to the very fullest of one's powers.
> Don't fear (*phobou*) this marriage with your own mother.
> Many a mortal before you has slept
> with mother in dream fantasies as well.
> He who sees no significance in them
> endures his life most easily, and best.
> *Oedipus*: You'd be correct in all of what you say
> if she who gave me birth were not alive.
> But since she is alive, I am compelled
> to shrink (*oknein*) from this, although you are correct.
> *Jocasta*: At least your father's death brightens your eye.
> *Oedipus*: A lot. I know. But she lives. I fear (*phobos*) her.

The sexual imagery of this famous passage has elicited much comment, notably that of Sigmund Freud in *The Interpretation of Dreams* which, "with its first public association between the names of Freud and Oedipus, marks the beginning of psychoanalysis."[17] Oedipus not only delights in his father's death but seems worried that his mother is not also dead, for fear he will fulfill what he thinks is his incestuous, oracular destiny. Yet, curiously, the Sophoclean Oedipus does not react as strongly as Seneca's at this point. To Seneca's Oedipus, his mother is now a widow (*vidua*) and thus available for marriage.[18]

Sophocles' Jocasta, interestingly enough, identifies Oedipus' fears of incest and parricide based on the oracle with incestuous dream fantasies. She recognizes that there is more than just a Delphic prophecy underlying the intensity of Oedipus' irrational behavior. For fears are, in Aristotelian terms, based on a disturbing fantasy: "Let fear (*phobos*) be some pain or disorder stemming from fantasy (*phantasia*) about a future evil which will cause pain or death" (*Rhetoric* 2.1382A). And Jocasta indicates that she and Oedipus have discussed his fears repeatedly over a long period (*palai*). Their dialogue on stage, then, is at least in part the reenactment of a familiar family scene. Hence, perhaps, Jocasta's earlier and puzzling calm. What was said was not as new to her as we may have thought.

Jocasta contends that what we now call Oedipal dreams are nothing unusual. As we saw earlier, in our discussion of Sophocles and Plato in Chapter 1, such dreams are commonly reported in ancient writers and discussed in detail by Artemidorus of Daldi in his own *Interpretation of Dreams (Oneirocritica* 1.79). Cesare Musatti observes in the introduction to his Italian translation of Artemidorus that "as regards the dream of incest between son and mother, Artemidorus talks about it as if he had known and divided up the ideas formulated by Freud on the Oedipus complex."[19] Indeed, as Musatti notes, Freud was familiar with Artemidorus from Theodor Gomperz's *Traumdeutung und Zauberei.*[20] Freud in a sense was rediscovering an idea well known in antiquity but later ignored (or repressed!), rather than formulating an idea hitherto unknown.

As we have seen in Chapter 1, Oedipal dreams in antiquity are generally mentioned in connection with the powerful, with Plato's "tyrannical" types: Julius Caesar (Plutarch, *Caesar* 32.6), and Hippias (Herodotus 6.107). Plato, to recap briefly, argues that man is brutalized by the dominance of the irrational, despotic elements of the soul over the rational and thus rendered tyrannical and unsuitable for the proper government of the state (*Republic* 9.571C–D).[21] The passage merits another glance here:

> "Those that awaken when we sleep," I said, "when one part of our soul is at rest—the part that approaches things reasonably and verbally, with gentle clarity, the part that rules the other element of the soul. That other element is like a wild and ferocious animal, gorged on food

and drink. It leaps up, pushes sleep away from it, and goes off on a lively search to satisfy the call of its particular nature. You know it is bold and stops at nothing at these times, for it is freed from—and unburdened by—morality and thought. Its lust, people think, does not shrink at intercourse with its mother or anything human, divine, or animal."

According to Jocasta, then, Oedipus allows his irrational dreams to superimpose themselves on reality. That, presumably, is why she told the chorus that Oedipus was no longer a capable helmsman of that state. Oedipus has abandoned reason for irrational fears, thus making "real" for himself grotesque desires and incestuous fantasies. Whereas other tyrannic dreamers, like Caesar or Hippias, apply the reasoning, verbal faculty to the incestuous dream, as they do to other dreams, when they wake up, Oedipus does not. He takes the fantasy literally; he fears the incestuous image, whereas they take it as a good sign. Oedipus assumes, as Sophocles' readers generally do, that the prophecy (which coincides with what Jocasta regards as common, incestuous dreams) has a literal force. In that sense he is both more "modern" and more primitive than the other characters of the play. For in his response to Jocasta, Oedipus admits that she is right but then instantly discounts his own recognition of her rightness. Logic cannot triumph over his fears. And standing by him, attentively listening to the dialogue, is our wordplaying Corinthian who will offer him an alternative way of interpreting his fears.

The Interpreter of Fears

When Alexander the Great, at the siege of Tyre, dreamed that a satyr was cavorting on his shield, his associate Antander interpreted the satyr as signifying his impending capture of Tyre. He did so by means of a wordplay: SATYROS = SA TYROS: "Tyre is yours" (*Oneirocritica* 4.26). "Dream activity," Musatti comments, "plays with words . . . wordplay is a great part of dream activity"—as Freud was equally well aware.[22] We should add, as the Alexander anecdote reveals, that wordplay is also a major part of dream interpretation, as it is of the interpretation of oracles. And it may be worth recalling that in one version of the Oedipus myth, Oedipus learns the solution to the (verbal) enigma of the Sphinx in a dream (Pausanias 9.26.4).

Like a dream interpreter or modern psychologist, the Corinthian inquires about Oedipus' object of fear (989–1003):

> Corinthian: Who is this woman you so greatly fear (*ekphobeisth'*)?
>
> Oedipus: Merope. Polybus lived with her, old sir.
>
> Corinthian: What is it about her you both so fear (*phobon*)?
>
> Oedipus: A formidable (*deinon*) prophecy of god, my friend.
>
> Corinthian: Can you say what it is, or is it wrong,
> a sacrilege if someone else should know?
>
> Oedipus: Of course. Apollo Loxias once said
> fate had determined I'd have intercourse
> with my own mother, and then said I
> would shed my father's blood with my own hands.
> Hence Corinth, my home, has long been kept
> away from me. Happily so, although
> it is pleasure supreme to look into
> the eyes of those who brought us into life.
>
> Corinthian: You shrank (*oknôn*) from this? This kept you from
> Corinth?
>
> Oedipus: I was determined not to kill father.
>
> Corinthian: Since I came in all good will, my lord,
> why have I not yet freed you from this fear (*phobou*)?

It is curious that Oedipus so readily accepts the anonymous stranger as confessor here. It is no less curious that when he says he cannot return to Corinth he reiterates not his fear of marrying his mother, but that of killing his father (who has just been reported dead). The Corinthian, of course, has already heard a lot. He arrives on stage as—or right after—Jocasta mentions Oedipus' fears to the chorus; he remains on stage to hear Oedipus' public conversation with Jocasta about his fears. He hears Oedipus and Jocasta ridicule oracles, and he hears Jocasta's famous comment that all men dream of sleeping with their mothers (980–83). He now rejoins the dialogue and addresses to Oedipus a series of precise questions, all of which deal with fear: Who is this woman you fear (*ekPHOBeisth'* [989])? What is your fear (*phobon*) about her (991)? Can you tell what the oracle said (993)? Is it your shrinking (*oknôn*) from this that kept you away from Corinth

(1000)? He learns, that is, exactly which fears to address. Oedipus will be putty in his hands.

The Corinthian's own knowledge appears to be minimal. He is aware that Oedipus' father is dead, but either does not know or will not say precisely how Polybus died. He knows there is speculation Oedipus will gain the throne, but evades the question as to who, if anyone, sent him to announce that possibility. His questions are so designed that he himself can give the appropriate answer: the answer he thinks Oedipus wants. It is here the Corinthian makes one crucial mistake: he offers to release Oedipus from his fears. What he does not understand, but we are beginning to understand, is that Oedipus really wants his fears confirmed, not set to rest. Like the Sphinx, Oedipus is challenging people to destroy him.

Again we must ask why this anonymous man has come to Thebes and why he is so eager to play Oedipus to the Sphinx of Oedipus' fears. He gives us and Oedipus a clear answer (1002–6):

> *Corinthian*: Since I came in all good will, my prince,
>   why have I not yet freed you from this fear (*phobou*)?
> *Oedipus*: And I'd (*kai mên*) reward you well if you still could.
> *Corinthian*: And I (*kai mên*) came here primarily for this:
>   the hope that I'd do well when you came home.

The Corinthian echoes Oedipus' words to show that a reward is exactly what he had in mind.

We might again compare some translations that subtly redirect the text of the last two lines. Dudley Fitts and Robert Fitzgerald make the messenger more courteously self-concerned:

> I had that in mind, I will confess: I thought
> I could count on you when you returned to Corinth.[23]

Kenneth Cavander also mutes the Corinthian's motivation:

> I had hoped for reward
> When you returned as king of your palace at Corinth.[24]

H. D. F. Kitto, Peter Arnott, and Robert Fagles all stay closer to the Greek. Here is Kitto's version:

> It was the chief cause of my coming here
> That your return might bring me some advantage.[25]

Jocasta's instinct that the newcomer wanted something was, it seems, correct. But in the excitement following his announcement, he and his "good" news about Oedipus' possible appointment as tyrant of Corinth are simply forgotten. Since Jocasta and Oedipus, after the initial announcement of Polybus' death, have continued as if he did not even exist, the Corinthian must wonder whether he has lost his opportunity for getting the expected reward for his good news. He presumed—and possibly still hopes—that Oedipus might return to Corinth. But he has assessed the situation wrongly. What he thought was his "bad" news is what interests Oedipus and Jocasta. His "good" news, as we have seen, never reaches Oedipus at all. When Jocasta passes on his words to Oedipus, she does not mention that "rumor has it he will be made tyrant" at Corinth. Perhaps she does not consider this important information. Perhaps she does not want to leave Thebes for Corinth. The Corinthian, we noted, seems irritated when Oedipus demands the news about Polybus' death. Here is Oedipus' question and his response in lines 957–59:

> *Oedipus*: What's your word, stranger? Tell me this yourself!
> *Corinthian*: If I must first say this part of my news,
>   know well that he has passed on through death's door.

Knox also catches the mood in his translation:

> If that's what you want to hear first, here it is,
> a plain statement: Polybus is dead and gone.[26]

"What would the messenger have mentioned second?" Dawe asks. He, and we, can only speculate. A reasonable assumption is that it would pertain to Oedipus' possible future as tyrant of Corinth: what the Corinthian thought was his "good" news. "In any event," Dawe adds, "he seems nettled at the insistence of his betters that he give priority to the less attractive side of his message."[27]

The Corinthian must get Oedipus' attention again. He must persuade Oedipus if not to return to Corinth, at least to provide some tangible token of gratitude. He has given his news, and no one has even thanked him for it. What other resources has he?

Instead of slinking away, then, the Corinthian waits for an opportunity to draw attention to himself again. As he listens to the conversation between Oedipus and Jocasta, he finds such a moment. And he carefully pursues his questions so he can determine precisely what news he must deliver to achieve the results he wants. He gathers, as he listens, that to persuade Oedipus, he must first dispel Oedipus' fear of marrying his mother, who lives at Corinth. He is possibly aware of the old accusation of the drunk at the banquet suggesting that Oedipus is a supposititious child. Hence his eagerness to establish which woman Oedipus fears, even though he seems to know Merope is Polybus' wife. But he also faces a rather deeper problem: that Jocasta seems uninterested in going to Corinth, and Oedipus never asks the logical question: "Do I become tyrant of Corinth now that Polybus is dead?"

The Corinthian therefore does not raise the matter of the tyranny again. It is irrelevant until other obstacles are removed. He has heard Jocasta fail to convince Oedipus that fears of marrying his mother are irrational. The only viable alternative he has is to persuade Oedipus that Merope is not his mother. He will thereby neutralize Oedipus' fear of returning to Corinth. But more is needed. To gain his reward he must induce Oedipus to leave Thebes—a thought that does not seem to have crossed Oedipus' mind. The obvious means is to reverse the magnetic poles of Oedipus' fear: to establish a Theban identity for Oedipus that will drive him, in fear, from Theban parents. The strategy may not work. But as he develops it, he may find a way of putting Oedipus in his debt.

Oedipus becomes, in the Corinthian's dialectic, a foundling child, and he that child's savior, who discovers the foundling and gives him to Polybus, ruler of Corinth, and a royal destiny. Oedipus' fears make the Corinthian's prospects on getting home rosier than he could have hoped when he set out. The self-seeking Corinthian and the inquisitive Oedipus are moving down different pathways to their tragic intersection. As Oedipus is trying to establish his birth, his interlocutor is trying to establish his own position as Oedipus' savior—and indeed surrogate father (whom Oedipus would want to protect from harm).

The scene proceeds (1007–26):

Oedipus: I'll never go where my begetters live.

Corinthian: My child, you clearly don't know what you do . . .

Oedipus: (*interrupting*)
What, old man? Then, by the gods, teach me.

Corinthian: . . . if they are why you run from coming home.

Oedipus: Phoebus. His words scare me. They may come true.

Corinthian: Worried you'll violate those who gave you life?

Oedipus: You're wise, old man. It's my eternal fear.

Corinthian: So you don't know there's no just cause for fright?

Oedipus: Why not, if I was really born their child?

Corinthian: Polybus was nothing to you by birth.

Oedipus: Polybus did not father me, you say?

Corinthian: No more, no less, than this man standing here.

Oedipus: You're nothing to me. How could he equal you?

Corinthian: Well, he did not beget you, nor did I.

Oedipus: Why did he legally name (*ônomazeto*) me as his child?

Corinthian: You were a gift. He took you from my hands.

Oedipus: Got me from other hands, yet loved me so?

Corinthian: His previous childlessness persuaded him.

Oedipus: You gave me to him? You bought me, got me by chance?

Corinthian: I found you in the vales of Cithaeron.

The Corinthian begins by telling Oedipus that Polybus was his father "no more, no less, than this man standing here" (1018). He thus establishes two themes. First, and most obvious, he denies Polybus' paternity. He negates the importance, if you will, of the news he has just brought and in so doing reestablishes the fear he has just abolished. Oedipus, if he believes the Corinthian, must once again fear he may kill his father. Second, by saying Polybus was Oedipus' father "no more, no less, than this man standing here," he establishes himself on a curious, if negative, par with Polybus. It may seem just casual cheekiness, but it is a theme to which he returns shortly, as we will see. And it is (as usual) the second part of the double statement that catches Oedipus' attention.

Oedipus takes the restoration of fear with amazing calm. His calm, I submit, arises from his long-standing fear that Polybus was not his father. The Corinthian simply confirms what Oedipus already fears. What is, however, particularly odd is that Oedipus registers no verbal reaction to the place in which the Corinthian claims he found Oedipus: Cithaeron, the mountain wilderness around Thebes. For this assertion establishes an ominous connection between Oedipus and Thebes and ought, one would think, to make him worry about the possibility that Jocasta is his mother. But if that thought *does* arise in his mind, it finds no immediate overt expression. For here is his reaction (1027–29):

> *Oedipus*: Might I know why you traveled to this place?
> *Corinthian*: I used to watch my flocks there on the hills.
> *Oedipus*: You were a shepherd, a migrant, hired hand?

Again we see Oedipus' contempt for the Corinthian's lowly status, and with it the beginnings of a new fear that seems to sting Oedipus— or rather a fear he has not hitherto voiced: that he himself may be of ignoble origin. His fears cannot be lightened by the paternal tone the Corinthian now adopts toward him, as he claims to have been, more or less, his surrogate father (1030): "My son, I was your savior at that time." Oedipus' fear of being baseborn makes him later insist to Jocasta, with some bitterness, that he must investigate his birth, even though he may turn out to be of humble stock and thus socially "beneath" her (1062ff.).

Oedipus' immediate response to the Corinthian's disclosure is not, as we and the Corinthian might expect, renewed fear of marrying his mother or even of killing his father, but fear that his father may prove no more than the social equal of a peasant like the Corinthian. Oedipus asks haughtily: "You're (a) nothing (*mêdeni*) to me. How could he equal you?" (1019). The anonymous messenger neither takes offense at the insult nor backs off from the albeit negative parity he has ventured: "Well, he did not beget you, nor did I" (1020). Oedipus retorts: "Why did he legally name (*ônomazeto*) me as his child?" (1021).

Oedipus poses a good rhetorical counter-question. As Sophocles' audience no doubt knew, to name a child is to accept it as your legitimate offspring under Athenian law. Indeed, there is an interesting case in Athenian law where a legitimate child of Mantias, named Mantitheus, claims the exclusive right to his own name and takes his half-brother Boeotus to court for usurping the name for himself. Demosthenes, who wrote two speeches against Boeotus, observes (Demosthenes, *Against Boeotus* 1.22): "I think that none of you is unaware that no one would have celebrated the tenth-day festival [for a child] if he did not believe that child was genuinely his." This "tenth-day festival," also known as the Amphidromia, was the moment of a child's official acceptance into a family. And it was, as Hesychius notes in his Lexicon under *amphidromia,* the time when the parents *epetithesan autôi onoma,* "gave the child a name." A. R. W. Harrison observes:

> It is true that at its birth a child in Athens was so completely in its father's power that it rested with him whether or not he admitted it to membership of the family. He openly signified his intention to do this at the ceremony of the *amphidromia,* which took place on the fifth, seventh, or tenth day after birth. At this ceremony the child was also named. But the father had no duty, even towards a legitimate child, to take this step. He could, either of himself or by the agency of some other person, a slave for example, expose the child.[28]

Harrison cites a number of references to the *Amphidromia;* to these we may add Aristophanes, *Lysistrata* 757 (with the scholiast's explanatory comment) and fragments of the comic poets Euboulus and Ephippus.[29] The subject was as well known to the theatrical as to the judicial audience.

Giving someone a name, even when that person is an adult, also appears to have been an official way of acknowledging paternity, if Euripides' *Ion* is any guide; and acceptance of that given name is acceptance of paternity. Xuthus, believing the attendant at Apollo's shrine to be his son, declares (*Ion* 661–63):

> I name (*onomazô*) you Ion ("the one who goes"), as it seems to fit
> the circumstance: my *eye* fell *on* you first
> when I was going out (*exIONti*) of the god's shrine.

The Greek in line 662 runs, more literally: "you first crossed my path." But a "literal" translation loses the crucial wordplay.

I mention this matter at some length because Oedipus has responded to the Corinthian with an argument that would unquestionably have been upheld in an Athenian court of law. The only way one could normally pass off a supposititious child was if the mother tricked the father into thinking that the child was his when it was not: the kind of scenario Aristophanes offers in *Thesmophoriazusae* 502–16, where a woman pretends to be pregnant, buys a baby, has it imported with its mouth plugged up with wax into the birthing room in a *chytra,* an earthenware pot of the sort in which infants were exposed, where it is "born." This is the strategy Euripides' Jocasta says Polybus' wife, Merope, used when she was given the infant Oedipus: *posin peithei tekein* ("persuades her husband she has given it birth" [*Phoenician Women* 31]).

Let us return now to Sophocles' Oedipus and the Corinthian. How does the Corinthian respond to Oedipus' objection? To cite Dawe, "The messenger does not answer Oedipus' question precisely in the terms in which it is put."[30] In fact he does not answer it at all. He declares (1022): "You were a gift. He took you from my hands." Oedipus might well protest this statement for several reasons. It suggests the unlikely scenario that Polybus was the principal family member involved in accepting a foundling as his son, and further that *both* Polybus *and* Merope were lying when they insisted they were Oedipus' parents. A woman may be able to dupe her husband into thinking that he is the biological father of a supposititious child. But a woman can hardly be duped into thinking she has given birth to a child that someone had just presented to her husband. Further, as Harrison notes: "The finder of an exposed child might at his discretion treat it as slave or free, but he acquired no rights over it and he could not even adopt it, since adoption of a minor was a reciprocal transaction between the adopter and the adopted child's father or his representative."[31] It would have been very hard, certainly by Athenian law, to make a foundling one's heir. Pericles found it hard enough to get citizenship for his illegitimate son by Aspasia, as Plutarch points out (*Pericles* 32).

Yet Oedipus does not for a moment question the substance or plausibility of what the Corinthian says. Nor does he take further note of his increasingly personal and paternal pose. When the Corinthian said Polybus was no more Oedipus' father than he was, he used an almost conventional cliché of distancing. But now he is suggesting equality of *closeness* as well as equality of distance: *he* gave Oedipus to Polybus. Oedipus' shocked reaction, however, has already been spent on the first suggested parallel between Polybus and the Corinthian stranger. He already appears absolutely convinced he is not Polybus' child, although not a shred of evidence or even hearsay has been adduced to support the contention. An unknown man simply announces that he gave Oedipus to Polybus when Oedipus was a baby.

Oedipus does no more than venture a question about Polybus' motivation, addressed more to himself than to the Corinthian: "Got me from other hands, yet loved me so?" (1023). The Corinthian supplies the logical answer: Polybus had no children of his own (1024). But Oedipus' reaffirmation of the intensity of Polybus' love should remind us that he may well have died because he so missed his son, as Oedipus imagined, for a fleeting moment, at lines 969–70.

A Baby Found or Given?

The ease with which the anonymous newcomer convinces Oedipus that he is not Polybus' child and insinuates himself into a quasi-paternal role is explicable in terms of what Oedipus has already told Jocasta—and thus the audience—of his old, lingering doubts about his legitimacy. A similarly anonymous drunk once declared at a banquet that Oedipus was a supposititious child passed off on his father, a *plastos . . . patri* (780), an expression we have already discussed in Chapter 5. We see immediately, however, that the Corinthian does not confirm at all what the drunk at the banquet said. For the messenger says he gave the child to *Polybus,* not to Merope, with his own hands, whereas the drunk apparently told Oedipus he was a child his mother had passed off on his father. There is, then, a fundamental, but curiously unnoticed, contradiction between the two stories.

Oedipus, still governed by fear, not by reason, ignores the inconsistency and more readily believes an anonymous Corinthian than Jocasta, just as he more readily believed an anonymous drunk than Polybus and Merope. In both cases, he proves the correctness of Jocasta's observation that he believes the person who frightens him. He accepts, then, that he is a foundling with astonishing lack of resistance. He seeks no further assurance as to the Corinthian's identity or any corroboration of his claims. He simply asks how he obtained the child to give to Polybus (1025): "You gave me to him? You bought me, got me by chance?" This is a critical moment for both men. The Corinthian, no matter how keen to advance his own situation, cannot claim to be Oedipus' father since he has already said that Polybus is not Oedipus' father "any more than I." He also sees Oedipus' horror that he might be ignobly born and knows that in the event Oedipus accepted such an identity, he would not return to

Corinth for fear of killing his newly discovered father. So he says
(1026): "I found (*heurôn*) you in the vales of Cithaeron."

We must not be so distracted by this decisive location of the infant
Oedipus in Theban territory that we overlook the Corinthian's claim
to have *found* the child. A few lines later he will say the child was
given to him (1038–40):

> *Corinthian*: I don't know. But he who gave you to me will.
> *Oedipus*: You got me from someone, you didn't find me?
> *Corinthian*: No, a nomad shepherd gave you to me.

To find something and to be given something are not the same
thing. Sophocles' translators have recognized this. But some of their
responses have been amazing and rob the reader of the chance to see
the first step in a vital contradiction. Cavander shifts the lie away
from the Corinthian by not having him actually say he found the
child and by attributing the verb of "finding" to Oedipus:

> *Oedipus*: So you gave me to . . . Had you bought me for your
> slave
> Where did you find me?
> *Messenger*: You were lying beneath the trees
> In a glade upon Cithaeron.

Fitts and Fitzgerald use "came upon" instead of "found" in their
version, giving the impression the Corinthian is avoiding saying that
he found the child. Again the verb of "finding" is given to Oedipus.

> *Oedipus*: What of you? Did you buy me? Did you find me by
> chance?
> *Messenger*: I came upon you in the crooked pass of Kithairon.[32]

Robert Fagles, instead of "found," uses "stumbled on":

> *Oedipus*: And you, did you . . .
> buy me? find me by accident?
> *Messenger*:   I stumbled on you,
> down by the woody flanks of Mount Cithaeron.[33]

Dawe notes the problem and comments: "The messenger is not as
forthcoming as he might be, especially with *empôlesas* ["did you buy

me?"] in the line before, with its suggestion of things changing hands from one person to another."[34] Dawe is understating the problem. The Corinthian is lying either now when he says he found the child, or later, when he says he was given the child. He may also be lying when he identifies Oedipus as that foundling.

Etymologizing an Identity

It is not hard to suggest the Corinthian's motive for stressing his own role in saving the infant: the more he does to save the child, the more, he might suppose, he builds a debt of gratitude in Oedipus. So let us examine the interchanges preceding the change in the Corinthian's role from one who found the child to one who was given the child (1031–37):

> *Oedipus*: What ails me as you take me in your hands?
> *Corinthian*: The ankles of your feet should witness that!
> *Oedipus*: Dear me, why mention that old pain of mine?
> *Corinthian*: I know where the feet are pierced, untie the knot.
> *Oedipus*: Since childhood I've been cursed by that course
>   scourge.
> *Corinthian*: Hence your name, recording what occurred.
> *Oedipus*: By the gods!
>   By mother? father? Speak!

The messenger claims responsibility for unfastening Oedipus' feet, which, he says, were pinned together (1034)—something he is more likely to have done if he found the child than if the child was given him. More important, he etymologizes Oedipus' name as OIDi-POUS, "swollen foot" (1036), to substantiate his claim and to establish his own connection with the *naming* of the child. Oedipus replies, as Pietro Pucci has noted, with an anagram: *DEINOn g'ONEIDOs* (1035)—"a formidable slander," or, to catch the anagram, "a COURSE SCOURgE," as I translate it here.[35]

Oedipus' response may be an even more complex wordplay than I have suggested—a reply in kind to the eytmologizing Corinthian. Athenaeus (*Deipnosophists* 11.467D–F) shows us that *DEINOs* is a multiple pun in Greek, meaning a "spinning dance" (with a play on *DINOs*, "whirlwind") as well as a "pot"—and among the people of

Cyrene, a "vessel the feet are bathed in," *PODOniptera DEINOn*. Bathing and recognition: a motif as old as the *Odyssey*. And this pun on *deinos* occurs in tragedy. Athenaeus cites two lines from Strattis' *Medea*, as she speaks insultingly to Creon, king of Corinth:

> You know (*OISTH'*) what your head looks like, Creon?
> I know (*OIDa*): a DEINOs that's been turned upside down.

The Corinthian's etymology of Oedipus' name, however, is uniquely his. The play on *OIDein*, "swell," and *POUS*, "foot," now taken for granted, first occurs here. Jocasta in Euripides' *Phoenician Women* 21 reuses the "swollen foot" etymology for Oedipus' name, as does Apollodorus (3.5.7). So does Seneca's Corinthian messenger, who reproduces the name Oedipus from a Latin anagram (which my translation can only crudely approximate) as well as a translation of the Greek etymology (Seneca, *Oedipus* 811–13):

> *Oedipus*: Now say what distinguishing marks were on my body.
> *Old Man*: The trace of footprints pierced with steel:
> From the swelling you got your name and from your
> PITEOUS feet (*vitIO PEDUM*).

Similarly, modern commentators, almost without exception, also detect play on *OIDa*, "know," and *POUS*, "foot," in *OIDipous*.[36] Although it may still seem ridiculous to many of us that a man's fate is in his name, the idea of the *omen* within the *nomen* ("name")—or, as the Greeks put it, *onoma* ("name") is an *ornis* ("bird of omen")—is commonplace in antiquity.[37] Although Quintilian (*Instructing the Orator* 5.10) condemns the practice among orators, we find it taken much for granted not only by Plato but also by Aristotle, as, for example, in *Topics* 2.6.2. In *Rhetoric* 2.1400B it concludes Aristotle's discussion of the enthymeme—the figure of reasoning that is to rhetoric what the syllogism is to dialectic. And his first example of it is drawn from Sophocles' now lost play, *Tyro*:

> Another topic (*topos* of the enthymeme) is from names, as when Sophocles says: "You are obviously Steele (*Sidêro*); you have it as your name." People habitually do this sort of thing in praising the gods. Similarly Conon used to call Thrasybulus "rash (*thrasy*) in advising (*boulos*)," Herodicus used to say Thrasymachus was "always rash (*thrasy*) in fighting (*machos*)", and Polus "always horsing (*pôlos* = young

horse, colt) around." He said of the lawgiver Draco (= snake, dragon): "His laws are not human but dragonian" because they were severe. So too Euripides' Hecuba (*Trojan Women* 990) says of Aphrodite (born from the foam, *aphro*): "The goddess' name rightly begins with mindlessness (*aphrosynê*)." And Chaeremon: "Pentheus (*penthos*: suffering): a proper name (*epônymos*) for the catastrophe to come."

We can find the same phenomenon throughout extant Greek literature, with occurrences so numerous that as Sulzberger long ago pointed out, it is useless to list them all.[38] In fact Plato, like Aristotle, plays off Thrasymachus' name: Bold (*thrasy*) in fighting (*machos*). It is, after all, Thrasymachus who makes the case that might is right in the *Republic*. And the punning etymology of Pentheus' name is better known to us from Euripides' *Bacchae* 508, where Dionysus says: "You are fitted for suffering by your name." In Sophocles' *Ajax* 430–33, Ajax (Greek Aias) has no difficulty in finding his grief (*AIAi*) in his name (*AIAs*):

> Aiai! Who would ever have thought my name would be such a proper name (*epônymos*) and fit with my misfortunes! So now it's time for me to cry out aiai twice and yet a third time.

But note one difference between the etymologizing "name" puns of Ajax and Pentheus: Ajax is keenly aware of various possible etymologies of his name, and he makes the etymology himself.[39] In the *Bacchae*, it is Dionysus, not Pentheus, who offers the etymology; Pentheus himself has no conscious sense of the disaster in his name.

It is instructive to make a similar contrast between Seneca's and Sophocles' *Oedipus*. In Seneca, as we have seen from his *Oedipus* 811–13, Oedipus tests the old man's credibility by asking what bodily peculiarities the child had. And the Senecan Oedipus seems not in the least surprised by the etymologizing answer. He simply goes on to ask the old man to say who gave him the child—thus also bypassing the problem Sophocles' Corinthian poses by his contradictory answers as to how the infant came into his hands. In Sophocles' *Oedipus*, however, Oedipus seems not to have given any previous thought to the possibility that his "true" etymological name might be "swollen foot." For all the previous etymological plays on Oedipus' name up to this point in the play have been based on taking the *OID* element in his name as "know," not "swollen." For the first time Oedipus is confronted with an etymology of his name that explains something about him that would have been evident at his birth. The "knowing the feet" etymology, which encapsulates his verbal victory over the Sphinx, is an etymology suited to his *adult* life, not his existence as a child.

Oedipus' concern for the proper way in which the child was *named* (*ônomazeto*) by his parents we, and presumably the Corinthian, have already noted (1021). To accept the definition that a name gives is to accept the definition and indeed the destiny imposed by the namer. To name someone, then, is to set limits on, to define—even destroy— that person, not simply to accept him officially as one's child at the Amphidromia. But in *Oedipus* there is a still further significance in the notions of "name" and "naming," as we will see more plainly if we adduce Socrates' observations in *Cratylus* 421A: "The word *onoma* ("name") seems to be put together from a phrase, as if saying 'the *onoma* is the being for which the search occurs.' You could recognize it more clearly in the form *onomaston*, which clearly means *on hou masma estin*: 'the being for which the search is.' " In Sophocles' play, that being is Oedipus.

By this point the Corinthian who provides the definition for the name, the identity for which Oedipus has been searching, has, as we have noted, begun to assume a fatherly tone toward Oedipus: "My son, I was your savior at that time" (1030). Appropriately so, for he is in the process of fathering Oedipus' sense of his identity. Paradoxically, of course, he is also, albeit unwittingly, about to become Oedipus' destroyer. Yet this in itself should be no surprise. The notion that the definer is also the destroyer is commonplace in both Greek and Latin literature. In Statius' *Thebaid* (8.91–93), for example, the prophet Amphiaraus describes the god of death as both the great *finitor rerum*, "limiter, definer of things," and the great *sator*, "creator."[40]

In this connection it is worth noting another passage from Plato's *Cratylus* (428D) in which Socrates makes the following remark to Cratylus, after the latter has suggested, on the basis of Socrates' etymologizing skill, that he is inspired and able to give oracles (*chresmôi-dein*): "Even I myself have been overawed by my wisdom for a long time now—and I am distrustful of it. It seems proper to me, then, to take another look at what I am saying. For being the victim of self-deception is the roughest lot of all. In such circumstances the person who is going to deceive us is never even a tiny distance away, but always with us. How can this not be formidable (*deinon*)?"

We can be carried away, Socrates warns, by our apparent etymologizing skill, which enables us to make language mean anything we want it to mean. So Socrates, after having a wonderful and witty etymological romp, stops to question and reexamine. But Oedipus does not. He accepts the Corinthian's etymological explanation of his name as "swollen foot" without a quibble, even though it is by no means the only available "etymology" of his name. In fact, he reacts with anger directed against the mother and father who subjected him to the cruelty of exposure—and, perhaps, the ironic indignity of the name (1037–38):

> *Oedipus*: By the gods!
>   By mother? father? Speak!
> *Corinthian*: I don't know (*oid'*). He who (*ho dous*) gave you to me
>   will.

The first part of the messenger's reply is consistent with his claims so far and with the wordplay: "I don't know." He knows only the "where," not the "who," in Oedipus' identity. The second part is more than just inconsistent; it is a bombshell: "He who gave you to me will" (1038). But it does, curiously, echo the *OIDa POU* sound-plays from the beginning of the Corinthian's first entrance: *ouk OID' ho DOUS*.

Why does the Corinthian abruptly change his story? He no longer is the man who *found* the child; he is the man who was *given* the child. His child-finding, like his news, comes at second hand. Oedipus, for once, spots the inconsistency (1039–40):

> *Oedipus*: You got me from someone, you didn't find me?
> *Corinthian*: No, a nomad shepherd gave you to me.

But Oedipus does not pursue the issue. He is keener to track down the supposed other person than to find out why the Corinthian misled him before.

The Corinthian's admission that he did not find the child weakens, but does not delete the memory of, his claim to have been the child's immediate savior. It is a tactical, rhetorical withdrawal which may be prompted by his heightened awareness of Oedipus' fear that he is ignobly born. Oedipus is unlikely to reward an informant who finds him as a monarch's son and leaves him the child of an unknown individual, possibly a commoner. By changing his role from discoverer of the foundling to its receiver, the Corinthian reopens the inquiry his previous claim, "I found," cut off. He also readmits a chance of the foundling's nobility, and thus of Oedipus' thanks, by connecting the donor with royalty. The problem is, of course, the lowly identity of the supposed donor, as we will see. And Oedipus now wants to know the identity of this donor (1041–42):

> *Oedipus*: Who? Could you describe who this man was?
> *Corinthian*: He'd a post with Laios (*LaiOUDÊPOUtis*). Yes, that
>   was his name (*ônomazeto*).

Again, the Corinthian is evasive. This is not, of course, the first time we have seen him respond so indirectly. We have only to recall his answer to Jocasta's question: "Who do you come from?" Here, however, he is yet more clearly playing a strategic verbal game. The verb *ônomazeto* suggests he is identifying the person who gave him the child. But he does nothing of the sort. In this line containing a verb of naming, the only name mentioned is that of Laios. Yet the verb of naming, *ônomazeto*, has already been used twice in this scene with the sense of a name that assigns identity.

The identity the Corinthian is insinuating is that of Laios, not that of the donor. He is perhaps even including a hint of Oedipus' own name. Just as ODYSseus plays on the similarity of his name to *OUTIS*, "Noman," the Corinthian seems here to be playing on *laiOUDÊPOUtis* and OIDIPOUs, syllabically including Oedipus' name between LAIOS and Noman.[41] The best I could come up with was "He'd a post with Laios," which carries a slight echo of the name, Oedipus, but which does not contain the critical ligature of Oedipus' name and Laios'.

The Corinthian gives Oedipus the fatal chance to link himself with Theban royalty instead of nameless peasantry. Again we may compare Euripides' *Ion*, where Ion worries about how he will be treated in Athens as the son of an alien father and and unknown mother (593–94): "I'll have this terrible curse (*oneidos*), I'll be weak, and I'll be called . . . the child of nobodies (*oudenôn*)."

We have already seen that the Corinthian is a master of verbal skills, recalling "these violent puns," as Knox describes them, with which he made his entrance, puns "suggesting a fantastic conjugation of the verb 'to know where' formed from the name of the hero who, as Teiresias told him, does not know where he is,"[42] The echo of the syllable *POU* at the end of each of his first three lines emphasizes an alternative etymologizing play on Oedipus' name. And how fascinating it is that the *Corinthian* should be the one to produce it; for he will convince Oedipus not only of his name's swollen-foot etymology but of *where* he was born. The nameless man who enters not knowing where Oedipus is ends up persuading Oedipus that he *knows where* Oedipus was born.

It is not only Oedipus, then, who can play the interpreter of riddling language and scramble our perceptions. In this scene Oedipus has met his verbal match in the Corinthian, as the Sphinx met hers in Oedipus. Oedipus destroys the Sphinx by solving the riddle of the feet, even though he does not know the riddle of his own identity. The Corinthian "solves" another riddle of feet while guarding the secret of his own name. He can even match Oedipus' skill in anagrams. For it is worth noting that the Corinthian claims he found the swollen-footed child on KITHAIRON (1206)—an exact anagram in the fifth-century alphabet for the land Oedipus thought he was from: KORINTHIA (794).[43]

The Corinthian's vagueness about the name of the man who he says gave him the foundling child is odd, since he later testifies that he and this other anonymous individual spent six months a year for three years running their herds together on Mount Cithaeron (1133–39). It is not as if they had chanced on one another once and briefly. No less odd is Oedipus' own lack of curiosity about the donor's name. He lets the Corinthian's vague "someone or other from the house of Laios" suffice as a response. Perhaps the explanation lies in the fact that Oedipus considers, and the Corinthian realizes that he considers, this donor to be a "nobody." The name of Laios, an important and fearful name for Oedipus, will more obviously rivet his attention.

Two conflicting fears must now wage war in Oedipus: his fear of being lowly born, of being *Outis,* a "Nobody," himself and his fear of patricide and incest. Ironically, the former fear leads him inexorably to the conclusion that he has fulfilled the latter. Further, this tyrant who fears being lowly born lets his birth and his identity be determined and defined by two nameless herdsmen and an anonymous drunk.

Oedipus fixes on Laios' clearly stated name, not on the murky donor (1043–53):

    Oedipus: You mean, then, the late tyrant of this land?
Corinthian: Yes. He was a shepherd for this man.
    Oedipus: And is he still alive? Could I see him?
Corinthian: You local residents would know that best.
    Oedipus: Does anyone of you bystanders know
           the shepherd he refers to? Have you seen
           him in the countryside or in the town?
           Give me a clue. It's time this came to light.
     Chorus: I think he is no other than the one
           you sent for from the country recently.
           Jocasta here could tell you that quite well.

The anonymous donor was allegedly a shepherd in Laios' employ; but the Corinthian cannot say whether he is still alive. The locals, he claims, might be better able to answer (1046). So Oedipus throws the issue about the unnamed employee of Laios raised by the nameless Corinthian to the collective anonymity of the chorus. The chorus identifies the donor as the man Oedipus has recently sent for: a man who was allegedly the sole survivor of a murderous attack upon Laios, Oedipus' predecessor as ruler of Thebes. This man had, as we have seen, made a public statement that Laios was killed by a band of robbers (*lêistai*)—a statement that must be false if Oedipus really is Laios' killer.

In sum: the Corinthian is the only "messenger" in Greek tragedy who does not have a messenger speech. He is most likely an old man who has chanced upon the news of Polybus' death, but really knows little or nothing about the circumstances or causes of his death, and has come to Thebes in the hopes of being rewarded for bringing the good news that Oedipus will probably be invited to come back to rule his homeland. He is an opportunist determined to make what he can of the rumors and gossip he has heard. When he discovers that Oedipus is not interested in returning, he seeks to manipulate him into going back by finding out what he is afraid of and reversing the magnetic poles of his fears, and by insinuating himself into a paternal role with the anxious tyrant. The consequences of his rhetorical shrewdness will be disastrous for Oedipus and ultimately for his own hopes of reward. The play, unfortunately, gives us no verbal clue as to what his reaction is when Oedipus concludes, largely on the basis of the Corinthian's testimony, that he is Laios' son and his mother's husband. For the actor playing the part of the Corinthian has to get off stage in time to return as Creon.

Jocasta's Final Words to Oedipus

Only Jocasta, the chorus states, would know if the donor and the witness are the same man. So Oedipus turns to her and asks whether the person alluded to by the Corinthian and chorus is the man recently summoned as the alleged witness to Laios' death (1054–5):

> Good wife, you know the man we wanted here
> a while ago: is this the man he means?

Jocasta responds (1055):

> What matters who he meant? Don't dwell on it.
> Forget his words. Don't brood on them. They're lies.

We have at least two ways of interpreting Jocasta's reactions. We may assume, as critics usually do, that Jocasta is herself not telling the truth when she describes the Corinthian's words as lies. If so, we are supposing she realizes that Oedipus must be her child, the one she gave up to death so many years ago. Yet surely we must consider another possibility. Jocasta has, after all, watched and heard Oedipus' fears surfacing and being dealt with by the Corinthian throughout this scene. It is not impossible that she really suspects the Corinthian is, as she says, lying. For we have ourselves seen reasons to suspect he is. Jocasta's sense of confusion and urgency, we may argue, is based on her realization that unless Oedipus grasps that the Corinthian is lying, he will soon conclude that he is her child. Jocasta knows her late husband, Laios, gave a child to be exposed on the mountainside, and Oedipus is well on the way to concluding that he is that child. In the interests of his and her personal safety—not to mention the interests of the truth—she must induce him to stop his pursuit of an inquiry that is bound to yield a dangerously incorrect answer.

If, of course, the circumstances and gist of Jocasta's later remarks are correctly reported from offstage at 1245–50, we must favor the traditional interpretation. We will examine that report in Chapter 8. At present we must conclude that Jocasta, even though she accuses the messenger of lying, as he may well be, is a victim of her own fears of oracles and prophecies, fears leading her to conclude that her own oracle has been fulfilled.

Jocasta's pleas irritate Oedipus, who insists he will pursue his investigation (1058–63):

Oedipus: How could I *not* root out such clues as these?
so I can find my origins and roots?

Jocasta: Dear gods! I beg, if you value your life,
then stop this search. It is enough. I'm ill.

Oedipus: Cheer up! you're still noble even if
I'm proved a slave, my grandmother a slave.

Jocasta's cry that she is ill about the matter (*nosousa*) may be taken as further indication that she now suspects Oedipus is her son and is sickened by the knowledge. But it could also indicate that she is sickened at what she suspects will happen when Oedipus pursues the matter further.

Oedipus, however, understands Jocasta's words in yet another way: he thinks she is worried because he is a supposititious child—that she is married to a commoner. Hence his petulant reaction (1062–63). In response, Jocasta assumes a rather more imperious manner. And Oedipus reacts sharply and decisively, thus alienating the only remaining major character he has not yet alienated, thereby completing his isolation (1064–68):

Jocasta: Obey me, I entreat you, don't do this!

Oedipus: I couldn't obey you, leave this unresolved.

Jocasta: I'm thinking straight; I urge the best for you.

Oedipus: Your best advice has lately been a pain.

Jocasta: Accursed man! May you never learn who you are!

Oedipus is confronted, as he was once before, with a choice between believing either the word of someone he knows and presumably loves or that of someone who, as he himself says, is "(a) nothing to me." He heeded the drunk at the banquet, not Polybus and Merope. Now he heeds the Corinthian rather than Jocasta. As a result, their conversation takes a nasty turn, leaving the director or actor to decide whether Jocasta is sympathetically praying that Oedipus may never conclude, or learn, that he is her son or herself turning on him in anger and despair.

The dialogue continues (1069–75):

Oedipus: Someone go, bring the shepherd here to me.
　　　　　Leave her to revel in her wealthy roots.
Jocasta: Poor wretch! I can say only this to you.
　　　　　And I shall never speak another word.
Chorus: Oedipus, why has your wife rushed out
　　　　　so wild with grief? I fear disaster may
　　　　　burst forth from her unwillingness to speak.

It is not the Corinthian, but the chorus, that reacts to this quarrel between Jocasta and Oedipus. The mischief is afoot and taking its course without his further intervention.

Oedipus does not acknowledge the possibility that he may actually be Jocasta's son. His chief concern seems to be that he may prove of ignoble (rather than ignominious) birth (1076–85):

> Let it burst where it must burst. But I
> shall be prepared to look upon the seed
> from which I grew, however small it is.
> Perhaps she's thinking big, as women do,
> and is ashamed about my humble roots.
> Well, I declare myself the child of Luck.
> I'll not be left without a heritage.
> She is my real mother and gifts me well.
> The months, my brothers, have divided me,
> made me now great, now small. So I was born:
> I could never grow into something else
> and not search out the secret of my roots.

Agesilaus and Oedipus

Anxieties about legitimacy and lowly birth were hardly trivial matters in fifth- and fourth-century Greece. In Athens, a law of Pericles in 451–50 B.C. made a bastard, a *nothos*, of everyone not born of two Athenian parents, as Aristotle (*Constitution of Athens* 26.4) and Plutarch (*Pericles* 37.2) point out.[44] And the issue of illegitimacy becomes a major theme in Greek tragedies (*Oedipus, Hippolytus, Ion*) right after Pericles' death, and the granting of citizenship to Pericles' own illegitimate son in the early years of the Peloponnesian War.

It is in Sparta, rather than in Athens, however, that we find the closest historical parallel to the situation in *Oedipus*. After the end of the Peloponnesian War, around thirty years after *Oedipus* was produced, there was a struggle for power in Sparta following the death of King Agis (400–398 B.C.). One faction in Sparta wanted to appoint Leotychidas king, another the lame but popular Agesilaus. To complicate matters, a seer (*chrêsmologos*) who, Plutarch says (*Agesilaus* 3.4–5), was well provided with ancient prohecies, proclaimed the following oracle (*chrêsmon*) when the matter came to trial (*en têi dikêi*):

> Consider, Sparta, though you are greatly proud. Take care that there may not sprout from you, sound of foot (*artipodos*) as you are, a monarchy that is lame. For then diseases (*nousoi*) unexpected will take hold of you and a rolling wave of war that destroys men.

The oracle is repeated in much the same form in Plutarch's *Lysander* 22.11.[45]

Things looked bad for Agesilaus until Lysander found an alternative interpretation to the obvious one. The oracle was not disbarring from kingship someone who had a lame foot (*proptaisas tis ton poda*) but someone who was not a legitimate descendant of the ruling house of the Heracleidae (Plutarch, *Agesilaus* 3.5). "This is how and this is why," Plutarch continues, "Agesilaus became king." And one of his first acts was to expel his rival Leotychidas on the grounds that he was illegitimate. Mythic kings in ancient Greece weren't the only ones haunted by problems with feet and royal lineage.

7. THE WITNESS ARRIVES

When the chorus identifies Laios' herdsman-slave (who, the Corinthian claims, gave him the infant Oedipus to expose) with the houseboy summoned as the supposed survivor of the massacre of Laios and his company at the crossroads, the fabric of credibility is stretched thin even by the standards of comic recognition in Plautus or Shakespeare. Yet in *Oedipus* the potentially comic motif of foundling recognition serves rather to heighten the sense of tragic horror. The world of drama, tragedy or comedy, generally requires some tangible tokens of proof that the adult really is the long-lost child, as in Euripides' *Ion* when Creusa declares to the skeptical Ion that she is his mother (1397–1436). Oedipus, in contrast to Ion, is completely convinced by what he is told by an anonymous stranger.

Oedipus, accepting that he is a foundling, assures the chorus that Jocasta is ashamed of his ignoble birth (*dysgeneian* [1079]) and awaits the arrival of the shepherd, once Laios' slave, who supposedly handed him as an infant to the Corinthian instead of leaving him to die in the wilds of Cithaeron. Since this individual has, if the chorus is right, also been summoned in another capacity—as alleged witness to the killing of Laios—the probability looms large in our minds (and probably in Jocasta's) that the slave's answers will convince Oedipus he is the killer of Laios and the child Laios exposed.

Such thoughts presumably do not occur to the Corinthian, unless we suppose that he is deliberately luring Oedipus to disaster. There is nothing to suggest that this man knows as much as he claims to know, and thus no reason to suppose he is withholding crucial information. No one has mentioned in his presence Oedipus' fear that he may have killed Laios or Teiresias' charge that Oedipus is an incestuous parricide and a curse on the city of Thebes. If the Corinthian has a discernible vested interest, it is in manipulating Oedipus back to Corinth, not in ensuring Oedipus' destruction—which will deprive him of any possible reward.

If either Oedipus or the chorus now suspects that Oedipus will be convinced he is Laios' son and killer, their thoughts find not even covert expression. The chorus, in its brief ode preceding the arrival of the herdsman *cum* houseboy, takes a different and positive view of the impending revelations about Oedipus' parentage: "tomorrow, if I am a prophet (*mantis*)," they declare, "I shall sing a choral hymn honoring Cithaeron as nurse and mother to Oedipus," and as having done "a good service (*êra*) for our tyrants (*tyrannois*)" (1086–1109). Oedipus will be revealed their *patriôtan,* their fellow countryman (1091), the child of some mountain nymph and, say, Apollo or Pan.

Dawe describes their attitude as one of "baseless optimism" and their opening words as "designed as a frontal assault on our natural incredulity."' We might even suspect irony, given the damnation of tyranny and arrogance in the previous choral ode. The chorus has already abandoned its earlier, more sympathetic, attitude toward Oedipus in favor of a carefully phrased hostility toward tyranny. At the same time, the chorus knows something about the awaited visitor, telling Oedipus, when the man arrives, that he was "trusted as a herdsman (*pistos nomeus*) of Laios" (1118). The chorus may well recognize that the creation of Oedipus' new identity rests with this slave who is empowered by the common agreement of Oedipus and the people of Thebes to create a myth that they have committed themselves in advance to accept as correct. The slave can convert, as the chorus seems to recognize, Oedipus' feared low-birth into origins divine, as mythmakers so often do. Since the slave lives on Cithaeron, he will perhaps be able to do "good service for our tyrants" on Cithaeron's behalf. Thus the ode sung by the chorus indicates to Oedipus its willingness to participate in the creation of the new myth.

The Shepherd and the Witness

Jocasta gave us and Oedipus the only information so far about the identity and status of this alleged witness, saying he was an *oikeus tis,* "a household slave" (756), who became a shepherd in the remote areas only after seeing Oedipus "in power and Laios dead" (758–64). The chorus, however, identifies him on line 1118 as Laios' man, "trusted as a herdsman" (*nomeus*). If Jocasta was telling the truth to Oedipus earlier in the play, we are faced with some strange dispositions among the royal servants: a shepherd is brought in from the hills to become a household slave until Laios' death, then sent out again to become a shepherd once more.

Jocasta's identification of the witness as a household slave arises during her exchanges with Oedipus about Laios' death (750–54):

> *Oedipus*: Was he lightly escorted, or had he
>   many retainers, as a ruler would?
> *Jocasta*: Five was the total (*xympantes*). Of these one was just
>   a herald. Laios rode the only coach.
> *Oedipus*: Now it's coming clear. But who on earth,
>   dear wife, told you what you are telling me?
> *Jocasta*: A houseboy (*oikeus*), the sole surviver who came back.

Although Oedipus recalls killing *all* (*xympantas*) the people who accompanied the old man he encountered at the crossroads (813), he ignores the fundamental conflict between his memory and Jocasta's account of Laios' traveling party. If the survivor, on further interrogation, does not maintain his story that the assailants were many rather than one, Oedipus is prepared to accept that he himself is Laios' killer. Oedipus overlooks, or disregards, a most vital issue: whether the man who claims to be the sole survivor was ever at the scene of the killing, much less whether his report of it was true.

Since Jocasta has described the survivor as a household slave, Oedipus reasonably assumes he might be in the palace, as we have seen (757): "Does he happen to be inside right now?" Jocasta answers (758–62):

> No. The moment he came back from there
> and saw you holding power and Laios dead,
> he grasped my hand, begged me to send him to
> the countryside to look after the flocks
> so he might be well out of sight of this

> city. So I sent him. A worthy man,
> although a slave, and he deserved to get
> this act of kindness—and much more than this.

We have already discussed the contradictory nature of Jocasta's report and will recall Dawe's observations that "there are no other places where temporal relativity receives such arbitrary treatment" and that the passage is an "offence against dramatic likelihood."[2] What made this slave so special to Jocasta? Oedipus does not ask—though her statement seems to invite such a question. But we should. A man who runs away in fear while his ruler is being murdered seems hardly to merit the epithet "worthy" from the ruler's widow, much less the clear suggestion that he deserved rewards even greater than those he received—unless Jocasta wanted Laios dead, which is by no means out of the question, mythically.

The explanation usually assumed is that Jocasta is grateful to him because, in the more remote past, he exposed her child on the mountainside. But this explanation presupposes that Jocasta wanted her child killed, and that she concurred with Laios' decision to have the child killed. Lines 717–19 show that she considers Laios primarily responsible for the child's exposure:

> The child did not survive
> birth even by three days. For Laios pinned
> his feet, cast, but with others' (*allôn*) hands, the child
> away upon a trackless mountain-peak.

Jocasta does not give much detail. In fact, she seems to be withholding information. She first makes, then modifies, a statement that Laios personally bound and exposed the child: he used the hands of other people people to cast the child away. Jocasta, while attributing responsibility to Laios, concedes with the plural, *allôn,* "others'," that the actual exposure of the child was done by more than one other person, rather than by Laios himself. The detail may seem a trivial quibble over grammatical number; but much of the play focuses insistently on distinctions between singularity and plurality. It is precisely such a discrepancy between the alleged witness's account of what happened when Laios was killed and his own recollection of killing an old man and his entourage that makes Oedipus want to question the witness further (842–46).

Is, then, Jocasta's gratitude to the slave justified by his services at the time of her child's exposure? Did she instruct him to expose the infant, or to find it another home? If the latter, we must assume she is lying to Oedipus when she assures him that the infant did not survive birth by more than three days. Assuming, then, that she told Oedipus the truth, whose were the other hands that helped him? They may have been her own. When the slave arrives, he admits under pressure that someone gave him Laios' child to expose (1171–74):

> *Slave*: The child was called his. But your wife inside
> the house could best say whether this was so.
> *Oedipus*: She gives you the child?
> *Slave*:   That's so, my lord.
> *Oedipus*: With what in mind?
> *Slave*:   That I dispose of it.

Jocasta herself, at lines 717–19, is reluctant to admit to Oedipus that the vague "others' hands" that exposed the child were her own and those of her houseboy, just as she is reluctant to lift the initial blame for the action, if not the final details, from Laios' shoulders. There is, perhaps, a touch of bitterness against Laios in her words, as well as a desire to suppress Oedipus' knowledge of her guilt, in her statement about the child's exposure. Her bitterness leaves open the possibility that she might not have been overly upset when Laios died. Indeed, no one seems to have been much concerned about his death—until the plague. The inquiry about Laios' death was at best perfunctory. So perhaps Laios appeared to Jocasta as a somewhat unpleasant character. The mythic Laios, homosexual rapist of Pelops' son Chrysippus, is not one of the more sympathetic characters in Theban tradition. In some versions he is actually the *cause* of Thebes' troubles, not the victim whose death must be avenged.

Jocasta's gratitude was owed to the slave, then, because he helped her in an hour of crisis. Yet if that witness to Laios' death and the agent of the infant's exposure are one and the same, we face a dilemma. For he clearly left Jocasta the impression that the child was dead—an impression which, as we will see shortly, may not be correct. Unless Oedipus suffers from a weak memory or killed someone other than Laios, that same man lied about how Laios was killed. Even if we believe that Oedipus killed Laios, and that, his own memory to the contrary, there really was a witness who first ran away in fear (as Creon says in line 118) and then lied about the number of

Laios' killers, should we not also suspect that this witness will lie again if called on to testify again in frightening circumstances?

As we await the slave's entrance, we—and Oedipus—should be teeming with questions about him. Did he really witness Laios' death? Did he save his life by running away in fear? Will he stand by the story he told before, that Laios was killed by many robbers, not by a solitary traveler? If he changes his story, will Oedipus believe the new version unquestioningly? How could he be the same person who, as a shepherd, gave the infant Oedipus to the Corinthian? And how would the chorus know he was? Was the exposure of Jocasta's child such a public matter? Besides, do not Jocasta's own, earlier statements indicate that the alleged witness was a *household servant,* not a shepherd, until after Laios' death, when he was transferred, at his own urgent request, to distant pasturelands? Hence, presumably, Oedipus' expectation that the man would still be living in the palace.

At this point we expect the problem of the alleged witness to be resolved. But, as we will see, it never is. Before he arrives, Jocasta, who alone could tell us for certain whether the child exposed was really Laios', and whether the witness and the shepherd slave are really one and the same, rushes offstage never to return. Further, Oedipus, who alone could discover whether or not this man saw him at the crossroads, never asks him the crucial questions about Laios' death. Thus Oedipus, even though he cross-questions the alleged witness in detail and under torture, fails not only to ask about the number of killers but to mention a word about Laios' murder.

Laios' Man

As the chorus finishes its ode, Oedipus watches the old slave brought in. We should note immediately that Oedipus does not recognize a face he had seen once in a violent encounter at a crossroads, but reacts to him as to someone he has never seen before and does not suspect he might have seen before. Oedipus guesses who he is by his age (relative to that of the Corinthian) and by a process of elimination: he recognizes those who are accompanying the slave as his own retainers. But instead of keeping these thoughts to himself and testing the Corinthian to see if *he* can identify the slave, he speaks aloud and asks the *chorus* if this is the person they are looking for (1110–18):

Oedipus: (*Speaking to the chorus leader*)
    If I must judge, old sir, I think I see
    the shepherd we've been looking for of late,
    though I have not encountered him before.
    He's well on in years—same age and same
    appearance as the man next to me here (*tôide tandri*).
    Besides, I know the stewards bringing him:
    they're mine. You'd be more qualified than I to say.
    You have seen this shepherd previously.
Chorus: I know him, be assured: Laios' man,
    as trusted a herdsman as he had.

The chorus, we observe, identifies the newcomer as Laios' shepherd rather than as the man who claims to have witnessed Laios' death. This identification benefits not only Oedipus but also the Corinthian, who is standing with him on stage.

Oedipus now turns to the Corinthian, as if the questioning process had not already begun (1119–20):

Oedipus: I ask you first, Corinthian friend: Is this
    the man you mean?
Corinthian: The one you're looking at.

Even if there were two or more possible people to whom Oedipus might be referring, the Corinthian's response has him safely covered.

Oedipus now turns to question the slave, and with his first words raises our expectations—and possibly the slave's—that questioning may focus on the murder of Laios (1121–23):

Oedipus: Old man! Come! Speak and look me in the eye!
    I have some questions. Laios: Were you once his?
Slave: Yes. His slave. Reared in his house, not bought.

The reply is direct and to the point. It is thus unusual in this play, since it provides the questioner with more, clear information than he asks for. The speaker seems proud of his service to the deceased tyrant. The interrogation continues (1124–27):

Oedipus: Employed at what job? What was your living?
 Slave: Flocks. I ran them for most of my life.
Oedipus: And in what regions most particularly?
 Slave: Cithaeron and all the land around.

Again, the responses are terse and to the point. But his composure ruffles when Oedipus asks his next questions (1128–31):

Oedipus: You know the features (*OIstha têiDe POU*), then, of this
 man here (*ton andra tonde*)?
 Slave: When he did what? And which man do you mean?
Oedipus: The man beside me. Ever met him before?
 Slave: Can't say I have, straight off from memory.

Let us look at line 1128 in a more traditionally literal form alongside the wordplay in the Greek: "This man before you, do you know anywhere round here (*OIstha têiDe POU*) you might have seen him previously?" (1128). We should note not only the Oedipal echo in *OIstha têiDe POU* but the ambiguity of *ton andra tonde*, "this man here," recalling the double entendre with the same demonstrative when Oedipus first met the Corinthian. Again we have the confusion of self and other. The Corinthian is talking of himself when he says *toude tandros*, "this man standing here," in 1018. But as in 1118, the phrase can be used as it is by Oedipus in reference to the Corinthian, to indicate someone next to the speaker.

Critics often suppose the herdsman hesitates because he recognizes, but does not wish to admit he knows, the Corinthian. Yet an audience seeing the play for the first time has every reason to suppose Oedipus is referring to himself: "Have you ever seen me before?" After all, the slave has been summoned as the alleged witness to Laios' death. And Oedipus is starting the questioning in a most direct way. The slave himself must certainly be making such an assumption, since he has probably learned or guessed that he will be interrogated about Laios' death. Further, Oedipus has led off the interrogation with a mention of Laios. Perhaps the critical question is now imminent: "Did you witness Laios' death?" The Oedipal echo in Oedipus' words would reinforce that suspicion.

It is with the expression "When he did what?" that the herdsman becomes cautious. The last time he saw Oedipus was, presumably, around the time of Laios' death. He therefore has good reason to be nervous about where the questioning may lead. If he was present when Laios was killed, as people in Thebes seem to think, and as he apparently claimed, he either saw a gang of robbers killing Laios or lied about what happened. If he lied about what happened, he may have been disguising with his lie the fact that Oedipus killed Laios. Since he fled to Cithaeron to avoid this confrontation in the past, much as Creon says he had fled the skirmish in which Laios died, he would obviously rather avoid facing Oedipus now. In the nick of time, he grasps that Oedipus' "this man here" may be referring to the Corinthian, who is also on stage, or even to some member of the chorus. So he adds: "And which man do you mean?"

The slave sees—and the audience realizes—that Oedipus means the Corinthian, not himself. No, says the slave, I do not remember this man. But when the slave thought Oedipus was asking about himself, his response was not "No!" but "when he did what?" If Oedipus continued: "killing an old man at the crossroads," how differently the play would evolve! It is now the Corinthian's turn to interpose (1132–40):

> I'm not surprised, master (*despot'*). He obviously
> does not recall; I'll jog his memory.
> For I know that he knows how it was once
> on Cithaeron. He went with two herds. I,
> with one, was close to this man for three whole
> six-month seasons from the spring until
> Arcturus rises in the fall. I drove
> my flocks home for shelter in wintertime.
> He drove his off to Laios' cattle-pens.
> Do I speak fact, or do I not speak fact?

The slave answers (1141): "You speak the truth, though this was long ago."

The Corinthian's choice of *despotês*, "master," to address Oedipus here is, I think, significant. It is normally used to express the relationship of master to slave—as in line 945, when Jocasta tells a slave to fetch the master, Oedipus, outside. The word *despotês* does not properly describe the Corinthian's own relationship to Oedipus; the Corinthian seems to be a free man albeit a *thêtês*, a poor "hired hand."[3] But it does describe Oedipus' relationship to the newly arrived slave. There is an important difference in status between the two men. A slave would be at an enormous disadvantage in a public dispute with a free man. And the Corinthian has so phrased his final question that the servant cannot deny what the Corinthian says without calling him a liar.

No slave would lightly call a free man a liar during the investigation of a crime or other legal matter. In the event that there arose a difference of opinion between a slave and a free man in ancient Athens during such an investigation, the law provided that the slave be interrogated under torture. In fact, the testimony of a slave was legal evidence *only if* it was extracted under torture. Even then, the report could be taken only "from the torturers and not from the slaves in person."[4] The Greek orators, in fact, distinguish between *basanoi* (testimony extracted from tortured slaves) and *martyriai* (testimony of free witnesses): "There was a commonplace to the effect that evidence given by a slave under torture was more reliable than evidence given by a free man," as Harrison says in his study of Athenian Law.[5] We should, however, add that Harrison goes on to point out that this does not mean that such evidence was actually true.

Still, some of the details are quite chilling: "If a man extracted by torture from his own slave information incriminating a third party, such information could not be used, unless of course the slave was offered to and accepted by the opponent for torture."[6] Even the contested claim that someone was a slave offered an Athenian the chance to demand (but not necessarily get) the right to torture him or her. In Lysias 4 we hear of the refusal by a prosecutor to allow torture of a woman whom the defendant claimed was his slave.

The slave, in short, is not going to quarrel with the Corinthian unless he is prepared to be tortured. And if what Creon and Jocasta report about the character of Laios' slave is correct, he will do what he can to avoid rather than confront pain.

Let us assume, for the moment, that what the Corinthian says about the flocks running together on Cithaeron is correct. The slave has, of course, already conceded—in the Corinthian's hearing—that he ran flocks on Cithaeron most of his life. What the Corinthian adds are details about how many flocks they ran and at what period of the year they ran them. What he doesn't say is *when* this period of three years occurred. Thus the precision of the Corinthian's chronology is illusory.

The ease with which Laios' slave concedes the truth of what the Corinthian says shows, first and foremost, that he is not trying to avoid dealing with him. He could, had he feared the Corinthian in any way, simply have persisted in denying that he knew him. His complete openness may reflect his relief on not being asked the really awkward question about what happened at the crossroads. The Corinthian has now established a very crucial bridgehead: he knows *from what he has heard on stage* that the slave ran flocks on Cithaeron. He has got the slave to admit that they ran their flocks together there over a three-year period. The use of specific numbers—one flock, two flocks, three years for six-month periods—heightens the sense of accuracy in what he says. But other matters of detail that we might expect to arise do not: How long ago did all this happen? At what time of the year was the child exposed? Why does the Corinthian fail to recall the slave's name or appear so cautious in picking him out from a group?

Once the Corinthian has secured the slave's agreement that everything he has said is true, he completes his work with fiendish speed (1142–44):

> *Corinthian*: All right. You know the child you gave me then
> to bring up personally, as my own?
> *Slave*: What's this? Why are you telling this story?

The slave cannot now remain calm, especially if Jocasta gave him her child to expose. Confused, he demands to know why he's being questioned on such a subject, but gets no answer—only the declaration that Oedipus is that child (1145–51):

> *Corinthian*: This man, fool, was that child when he was young.
> *Slave*: Go to hell! Why don't you just shut up!
> *Oedipus*: Oh, don't you tongue-lash him, old man. Your words
> deserve a lashing more than his words do.
> *Slave*: Noblest of masters, what am I doing wrong?
> *Oedipus*: Not discussing the child of whom he tells.
> *Slave*: He talks, knows nothing. He's up to something else.

The servant's concluding phrase, which I have translated quite literally as "he's up to something else (*all' allôs ponei*)," is usually taken to mean "he's wasting his time," as if *allôs*, "otherwise," was the equivalent of *matên*, "in vain," which it is not.

If the recently arrived herdsman is indeed the slave responsible for exposing the child of Laios and Jocasta, he knows perfectly well what will be the consequences of conceding the Corinthian's identification of this foundling with Oedipus. Oedipus will be established as an incestuous husband, the child of his own wife. For good reason, the slave fears for his own life if he confirms that identification. He is trapped and flails about himself verbally, thereby provoking Oedipus' anger: the slave is clearly stalling. Now interrogation under torture becomes an imminent threat. The slave's protest that the Corinthian knows nothing but is up to something has been rhetorically undermined in advance by his previous agreement that what the Corinthian said about their grazing flocks together was true. In much the same way Oedipus' acceptance of Teiresias as a truthful man makes it harder for him to compete with Teiresias in a dispute over truth, as we have seen.

But is the slave really so far from the truth in his final remark? Has the Corinthian not shown us already how far he can make a little vague information go?

The Threat of Torture

Oedipus reenters the dialogue with a threat of torture which almost immediately becomes the inception of torture (1152–55):

> *Oedipus*: Speak out of kindness or you'll speak from pain.
> *Slave*: Don't, by the gods, don't torture an old man!
> *Oedipus*: One of you, twist his arms behind him now!
> *Slave*: Why should I suffer? What do you need to know?

The servant is baffled at Oedipus' insistence on extracting information that will ruin the tyrant himself and the royal house. Indeed, the last line cited above can be played in two very different ways. The slave is either verbally shrugging his shoulders and deciding that he will say whatever Oedipus wants him to say or continuing to protest the injustice of his personal suffering. The following interchanges favor the former interpretation (1156–59):

> *Oedipus*: Did you give him the child of whom he tells?
>
> *Slave*: I gave it. Oh, I wish I'd died today (*têid' hêmerâi*).
>
> *Oedipus*: You'll have your wish unless you speak the truth.
>
> *Slave*: More likely I'm dead *if* I tell the truth.

It is strange that almost all editors take the expression *têid' hêmerâi* as "that day" (i.e., the day on which I handed over the infant) rather than "this day" (i.e., today), even though throughout the play, and generally in Greek, the demonstrative *hode* tends to mean "this one here."[7] The slave imagines himself to be in a hopeless situation. The truth or falsehood of what he says will not affect his fate. Either Oedipus will not believe what he says is true and therefore kill him, or he will kill him in anger and horror at the "truth" that is revealed.

Oedipus concludes again, and I think rightly, that the slave is stalling. But note that, as he has the man tortured, the possibility lurks in Oedipus' mind, even at this late stage, that the reluctant victim might be his father (1160–62):

> *Oedipus*: This man, it seems, is trying to stall for time.
>
> *Slave*: I'm not. I just now said I gave it him.
>
> *Oedipus*: Where did you get it? Was it another's—yours?

Again we see a glimpse of an ugly side of Oedipus in his search for who his parents were. He rejoiced at the death of Polybus, whom he thought was his father; he wished that his mother Merope was dead; he was uneasy with the semi-paternal attitude of the Corinthian. We now see him torturing and threatening to kill a man who, he thinks, just might be his father. What, we wonder, might Oedipus do if the slave claimed that he was in fact Oedipus' father?

The slave responds (1163): "Mine it was not. I got it from someone." The slave, like the Corinthian, balks at claiming to be Oedipus' father. Again, the foundling is said to have been passed on from someone else's hands (1164–68):

> *Oedipus*: From what citizen and from what house?
>
> *Slave*: For god's sake, take the tale no further, lord.

Oedipus: You're dead if I've to ask this one more time.
 Slave: Then it was some child born in Laios' house.
Oedipus: A slave or born of Laios' own blood?

The vagueness of the answer rekindles Oedipus' fear of being ignobly born, outbalancing his fear that Laios might have been his father (1169–72):

> *Slave*: I'm on the formidable brink of speech (*deinôi legein*).
> *Oedipus*: And I of hearing. But I must hear it.
> *Slave*: The child was called his. But your wife inside
>   the house could best say whether this was so.

The slave has a point. Jocasta, if she was the child's mother, might be able to confirm whether Laios was in fact its father. And, of course, if Oedipus redirected his questioning to Jocasta, the slave would gain at least a respite. But Oedipus, as usual, rejects the possibility of serious discussion with the person most likely to know the answer to his question. Jocasta could best answer who Laios' child was; the slave, who allegedly witnessed the killing of Laios, could best inform Oedipus about Laios' death. But Oedipus continues undisturbed (1173–74):

> *Oedipus*: She gives you the child?
> *Slave*:   That's so, my lord.
> *Oedipus*: With what in mind?
> *Slave*:   That I dispose of it.

Again we have a curious conflict of testimony. At 717–19 Jocasta implies that Laios, not Jocasta, was the person who arranged for the disposal of the infant—unless, of course, the hands of the vaguely plural "others" are really her own:

> The child did not survive
> birth even by three days. For Laios pinned

> his feet, cast, but, with others' hands, the child
> away upon a trackless mountain-peak.

Oedipus pays no particular attention to the conflict in details. Indeed, he seems shocked not so much by the thought that Jocasta might be his mother as by the thought that she would have dared to expose her child (1175–85):

> Oedipus: His mother dared . . . ?
>   *Slave*:   No, shrank from prophecies.
> Oedipus: Which said?
>   *Servant*:   Word was he'd kill his own parents.
> Oedipus: Why then did you give him to this old man?
>   *Servant*: I pitied him, my lord. I thought the man
>   would take him to his home. But he saved him
>   for monstrous horrors. If you're who he says
>   you are, then you were born to a grim fate.
> Oedipus: Oh, oh, how it all could come so clear!
>   O sunlight, never may I see you again!
>   It now has come to light whose son I am.
>   Forbidden birth, forbidden marriage and
>   killings I should not have carried out!

Let us accept, for the moment, that whatever else may be true or false in what the Corinthian and slave say, a transaction took place between them on Cithaeron at some unspecified time in the past: a child passed from the slave to the Corinthian. The unresolved question remains: whether that child was Oedipus. This issue is one that even the slave himself, under torture, can recognize: "If you're who he says you are, then you were born to a grim fate" (1180–81). But there is no evidence that Oedipus *is* that child. We have only the anonymous Corinthian's word for it, and we have seen enough inconsistency and vagueness in his testimony to doubt its total truth. He himself admitted a selfish motive for his journey to Thebes. But the Corinthian is silent now. He has done what few messengers in Greek tragedy ever do: he has caused something to happen rather than simply reported a happening.

The slave is of course wrong when he says says that Oedipus' fate is hard if he is the person the Corinthian claims he is. Whether Oedipus really is or is not that person is irrelevant to his fate. His fate is hard because he *believes* he is that person. Indeed, by the end of this scene he is convinced not only that he is the child of Jocasta and Laios, but that he is Laios' killer. The testimony that convinces Oedipus of all these things comes from a slave whom he never questions about the death of Laios, and who must have been lying when he told Jocasta, Creon, and the people of Thebes that a gang of robbers killed Laios— provided, that is, that Oedipus really killed Laios.

Blind Belief

Here, I suggest, is the essence of Oedipus' tragedy. He will not believe Polybus and Merope when they name him as their child, but he will believe an anonymous drunk at a party, an anonymous Corinthian who is seeking to line his own pockets. He will even believe, on secondhand testimony, that he has killed Laios, despite the fact that his own memory of a similar killing differs in several important details. And we readers draw the same conclusions on the same flimsy grounds. Sophocles' great achievement here is to make us do what Oedipus does: to disregard or rationalize away everything that might demonstrate the hero's innocence.

The anonymous drunk was the beginning of Oedipus' destructive inquiry; the slave-herdsman-witness and the Corinthian are, of course, the end. But, between, there are three no less influential forces of rather greater nobility working on him: the oracle of Apollo at Delphi, Creon, and Teiresias. And they can be paired with their three anonymous counterparts: the drunk causes Oedipus to go to the oracle; Creon, like the Corinthian, arrives with news from abroad and may hope to gain personal profit from the situation. Teiresias, like the supposed witness, claims to have knowledge of something that is believed to be causing the plague that blights Thebes, and he may have some old hostility toward Oedipus. The motives of the drunk and of the oracle lie beyond critical reach. But those of Creon and Teiresias do not. Oedipus rules a realm that could be, and by the end of the play is, Creon's. Like the Corinthian, Creon may well have a motive of personal gain. Teiresias is a professional seer, surpassed in mantic skills only once, in the riddle of the Sphinx, by Oedipus.

In this play he may well take his revenge.

8. THE PALACE MESSENGER AND THE COUP D'ETAT

Jocasta leaves the stage at line 1072, well aware that if Oedipus pursues his investigations further he will conclude he is her son. Most critics would add that Jocasta now believes Oedipus is her child, although she herself does not say so. What sets that opinion firmly in our minds is the arrival of a messenger from inside the palace to announce her death, a messenger who clearly wishes to suggest that Jocasta thought herself Oedipus' mother. This palace messenger, more than any other character in the play, "fixes" our perceptions of Oedipus and prepares us for the transition to Creon's monarchy. Unlike his Corinthian predecessor, this messenger presents not just enigmatic hints about what may have happened but detailed descriptions of movements and motivations. By this point, however, we ought to be suspicious of "messengers" and their reports, and examine any messenger's words carefully before accepting them as true.

Oblique Oration

Reported messages in *Oedipus* are, compared with those in Sophocles' other plays, unusually vague and oblique. The messenger announcing Oedipus' death in *Oedipus at Colonus,* for example, maintains an illusion of vividness and immediacy by citing Oedipus' last words "exactly" (1610–19, 1631–45, 1640–44). Similarly, the messenger reporting Haemon's death in *Antigone* quotes Creon word for word (1211–18, 1228–30). In *Electra* 289–98, Electra cites Clytemnestra's abuse in direct speech, suggesting it is emblazoned on her mind. When she conjures up in words for her sister the imagined glory she will earn for avenging Agamemnon's death, she sets the anticipated praise of their compatriots in direct speech (*Electra* 977–80). Indeed, her verbatim quotation of a speech not yet composed is a measure of her total absorption in fantasy.

Indirect speech, on the other hand, particularly when reported in the optative, the Greek verbal mood used for potential action, wishes, and conditions that are remote or contrary, decreases our sense of the immediacy of what is reported. The optative in Sophoclean indirect speech warns us that the speaker is distancing himself or herself from the report, disguising feelings, or otherwise dissimulating, even lying.[1] In *Trachiniae,* for example, when Heracles' friend Lichas describes to Deianeira, Heracles' wife, why her husband attacked Eurytus' city, he says he was provoked by Eurytus' mockery of Heracles' skill as an archer and his own forced servile obedience to a lesser man, Eurystheus. Our suspicions are aroused because Lichas cites Eurytus' supposed taunts in indirect statement (*Trachiniae* 265–68). He is later obliged to admit he was not telling the truth (*Trachiniae* 472–89). The real reason for Heracles' actions was his passion for Iole, which Lichas prefers, for obvious reasons, not to mention to Heracles' wife.

Characters in Greek tragedy do not always tell the truth, and ancient writers do not always explain overtly to us, as modern writers tend to, who is and who isn't being truthful on each given occasion. But they do provide clues. Some passages from Sophocles' *Philoctetes* may help us discern some of those clues.

Obliquity in *Philoctetes*

In *Philoctetes,* Odysseus attempts to get Philoctetes, who has inherited the bow of Heracles, to come to Troy with the Greek army. Without the hero and his bow, Troy cannot be taken. It will be hard for Odysseus to win Philoctetes' help. As Aristotle points out, if you are to convince someone to do something, you must be able to present your argument in terms appealing to the person you wish to persuade: "Something is persuasive because it persuades the particular person" (*to pithanon tini pithanon* [*Rhetoric* 1.7. [1365B]). The speaker of persuasive words must also be credible to the person to be persuaded. Philoctetes has been abandoned by the Greeks, with the special connivance of Odysseus, on a deserted island because of an evil-smelling wound he has. Philoctetes therefore hates Odysseus, and Odysseus thus has no rhetorical credibility with the person he must persuade.

Odysseus enlists the help of a persuader with perfect credentials for the task: Achilles' son Neoptolemus, who has good reasons of his own to resent Odysseus. For Odysseus had persuaded the Greeks to give him, not Neoptolemus, Achilles' famous armor after Achilles' death. Fundamental to Odysseus' strategy is his knowledge that Neoptolemus' alienation from him is counterpoised by the young man's military ambition and by his wish to express his quite genuine resentment of Odysseus. The dangers in the strategy are that Neoptolemus will be impeded by his sense of military honor and by personal pain at helping Odysseus defraud yet another person of his inheritance of weapons.

Odysseus is well aware, then, that conventional persuasion or violence will be useless (*Philoctetes* 100–107). He must, with Neoptolemus' help, *trick* Philoctetes into coming with them. He therefore uses the energy of Neoptolemus' hatred for him as the means of moving Philoctetes to Troy. He specifically permits Neoptolemus to abuse him as much as he wishes in the matter of Achilles' arms if that will help win the day.

Neoptolemus is persuaded and cooperates. At Odysseus' prompting, he insinuates himself into Philoctetes' good graces. As he wins Philoctetes' confidence, he recalls for the latter's benefit what was said when the Greeks awarded his father's arms not to himself but to Odysseus (364–66). He also cites *verbatim* both his own tearful reaction to (369–70) and Odysseus' justification of that award, including Odysseus' rejection of Neoptolemus' own claims (372–73 and 379–81). He thus establishes a most solid and credible basis for persuading Philoctetes that he too hates Odysseus, and for good reason.

But when Neoptolemus goes on to mention a fiery and abusive retort he made to Odysseus in the dispute over his father's arms (374–76), he does so in *indirect* speech replete with optatives. The optatives in this reported speech betray the extraneous element in Neoptolemus' account. He does not report his searing reply to Odysseus in direct speech, I would suggest, either because he never actually made it or because he worries that Odysseus may be eavesdropping. Perhaps both considerations affect his choice. Neoptolemus extends a known truth into a plausible falsehood, a strategy set forth by Odysseus himself, who told Neoptolemus in instructions set in indirect speech, though without optatives, what lies to feed Philoctetes (57–64).

Odysseus is offstage during these exchanges. Yet, not much later, a man saying he is a merchant presents himself to Neoptolemus and Philoctetes, announcing that Odysseus and Diomedes are coming to get Philoctetes (*Philoctetes* 591–621). The statement is only partially true, since Odysseus' partner in deception on this occasion is not the usual Diomedes but Neoptolemus, the very man now winning Philoctetes' trust. The report is an elaborately orchestrated lie, known (at least partially) to Neoptolemus, but unknown to Philoctetes.[2] The merchant (who could well be Odysseus himself diguised) reports that a captured Trojan, the prophet Helenus, said Philoctetes must be *persuaded* to come to Troy if the city is to be captured (608–13). Attributions of such statements to divine sources often carry special conviction to the targets of persuasion. But Odysseus told Neoptolemus that neither persuasion nor violence would lure Philoctetes to Troy. The strategy must be deceit. And the merchant's appearance is part of that strategy. The presumably invented words attributed to Helenus are presented in indirect speech with optatives.

Toioutos and *Tosoutos*

Perhaps his awareness of the false element in his narrative prompts Neoptolemus to sum up the dispute over the arms of Achilles with the expression *toiaut' akousas* ("having heard things of that sort" [*Philoctetes* 382]). Sophocles often has a speaker use forms of the adjective *toioutos* ("of such a kind" or "to this effect") to comment on an interchange the speaker believes dubious or dangerous. In contrast, when a speaker sums up his report with *tosoutos* ("such was the extent" of what was said), we can usually suppose he or she thinks the report true.

In *Trachiniae*, when Hyllus recalls his father Heracles' dying words, he captures their vividness in direct speech and summarizes them with *tosoutos*: "such was the extent of his instructions" (797–802, 803). Similarly the nurse, when she announces Deianeira's death, uses direct speech and summarizes with the neuter plural of *tosoutos, tosauta* (920–23). Yet the same nurse's report of Hyllus' reaction to the loss of both parents is in indirect discourse. It is not clear whether the nurse is reporting the actual words spoken or just explaining Hyllus' motivation. This time she summarizes with *toiauta*, "of such a kind" (940–43):

> Chest next to chest he lay, groaning a lot
> because he'd stupidly and wrongly struck
> at her with blame, weeping because his life
> would now be orphaned of both his father
> and her. Such (*toiauta*) is the state of things inside...

The use of indirect speech allows the nurse to incorporate covert criticism of Hyllus' folly into her report and to suggest, at the same time, her own affection for Deianeira. We cannot be sure that Hyllus actually said: "How wrongfully I've blamed you..."

Deianeira's recollection of the centaur Nessus' dying words offers an interesting variant on the pattern. Her use of direct quotation introduced by *tosouton* shows that she believes Nessus' words and that they are vividly present in her mind (*Trachiniae* 569–77). Yet the centaur was not telling the truth except in the most Delphic way: if Heracles puts on, as Nessus suggests, the cloak dipped in the centaur's blood, he will never love another woman again—not because of a novel fidelity to his wife but because he will die in agony. We might argue that, in strict logic, the report of a lie should also be in indirect speech. But if Sophocles had chosen such an approach, he would have lost the all-important sense that Deianeira accepted Nessus' words as truthful and well intentioned.[3]

We find self-protective use of indirect statement in *Ajax* too. The messenger who announces the arrival of Teucer, Ajax's half-brother, to Ajax's sailors understandably wants to dissociate himself from the insulting remarks other Greeks have made about Ajax and Teucer (*Ajax* 724–28). Indirect speech protects him from any suggestion that he shares the negative views he reports; at the same time, it allows him the freedom to report those views. When the same messenger, however, reports Calchas' advice, which he obviously considers crucial if Ajax's life is to be saved, he uses *direct* speech and closes his summary with *tosauta* (*Ajax* 756–80).

Let us return now to the messenger from the palace in the *Oedipus* with special concern for the distinctions between direct and indirect speech.

What the Palace Messenger Saw

Sophocles cuts his second "messenger" in *Oedipus* from more traditional theatrical cloth than the first. The palace messenger makes a speech. He has numerous and lurid details for us, in contrast to the Corinthian's sparse and ambiguous one-line mention of Polybus' death. He indulges in a tragic messenger's characteristic love of hyperbole. Although he is, like the Corinthian, anonymous, he knows whom he is addressing, whereas the Corinthian does not. Further, the chorus seems either to know him or to be *unconcerned* that it does not. The palace messenger's uncertain identity is less of a problem than the Corinthian's, since his words do not have such an obvious impact on the play's characters as do the Corinthian's. Yet his words seriously affect how the chorus and we, the audience, interpret what happened.

The palace messenger reports, among other thing things, that Oedipus has put his eyes out. Since Oedipus enters, blinded, immediately after the messenger finishes his speech, his truthfulness seems beyond dispute on this score. But we must be careful. The truth of one statement is no guarantee that everything else said is true. As we have already noticed in *Oedipus,* there is no better mask for rhetorical deception than to couch an untruth in a generally "truthful" setting.

Some interesting inconsistencies in the palace messenger's report invite closer inspection. Sophocles, as usual, offers the necessary clues about what to look for. The messenger begins with a melodramatic warning about what we will hear about and see (1223–25):

> You, always men most honored in this land,
> what actions you will hear about and see!
> and what great sorrow you will have to bear!

Yet it is precisely in the distinction between what the messenger seems to have heard and seen with his own eyes and what he reports as apparent fact that the critical chasm opens.

Jocasta's Lament

The chorus, noting that events so far are quite horrible enough, asks what else has happened and receives a very terse reply from the messenger (1234–35):

> Stated succinctly, it's succinctly grasped:
> Jocasta, our divine head, is now dead.

When asked how the death actually occurred, the palace messenger, like the Corinthian, becomes a little confused. He wants to appear informed but does not quite go so far as to pretend he has seen what he has not seen (1237–40):

> She killed herself. The worst of what occurred
> is distanced. There were no eyewitnesses.
> But you will learn as much as I recall
> about what that poor woman suffered then . . .

The palace messenger is *not* saying that he himself saw Jocasta take her life, as some translators imply. David Grene, for instance, renders the same lines as follows:

> By her own hand. The worst of what was done
> you cannot know. You did not see the sight.
> Yet in so far as I remember it
> you'll hear the end of our unlucky queen.[4]

Grene assumes, as others have done, that the messenger is drawing a distinction between the pain he himself has experienced, having seen Jocasta's death, and the (lesser) pain of the chorus, who did not see her die. But it is clear from the text a few lines later, even in Grene's translation, that the messenger did not see Jocasta killing herself (1251): "How after that she died I do not know." This statement contradicts what the messenger has just said. Why does he claim not to know how Jocasta died after opening with a dramatic announcement of her suicide? He is either coy or cautious.

We must look more closely at his account (1239–54):

Palace Messenger:
> But you will learn as much as I recall
> about what that poor woman suffered then:
> how, angry and distraught she passed into
> the hall and went straight to her bridal bed,

ripping her hair with fingers of both hands;
and how she closed the doors and went inside,
calling on the late Laios (*Laion palai*), long since dead,
remembering the late man's (*palaion*) sowing, long
   ago,
of seed that *he would die* by, *leaving* her
to bring to birth cursed children by that seed.
She bemoaned the nuptials where she, accursed,
bore double offspring, husband from husband,
child from child.
           How, after this, she perished
I still don't know. For Oedipus burst in,
shouting, making it impossible
for us to watch her troubles to the end (*ektheasasthai*),
for we were watching him as he strode in.

Jocasta, then, went into the bed-chamber and out of the messenger's sight. From this point, he is *not* reporting what he saw. Nor is he reporting what he heard uttered behind closed doors, but rather what he imagines, or wishes to imply, were Jocasta's thoughts. And those thoughts are reported in the optative mood, so often used, as we have seen, when a speaker in Sophocles is not being wholly truthful or is, like the nurse in the *Trachiniae* as she reports Hyllus' last words, attributing motives for actions rather than reporting exactly what was said. To help the reader in translation, I have italicized the English verbs that render Greek optatives.

The messenger gives the chorus a vivid, but not necessarily correct, series of suggestions about what Jocasta might have been remembering and groaning about. At the same time he leaves traces that show he did not really see and hear what he tells us. He probably would not be unhappy if we took his account as definitive, as if it really were an account of someone whose eyes and ears were at the chamber's keyhole. But we should not be tricked by him, as some translators have been.

E. F. Watling, for example, renders lines 1237–50 as follows:

> Her own hand did it. You that have not seen,
> And shall not see, this worst, shall suffer the less.
> *But I that saw*, will remember, and will tell what I
>   remember

Of her last agony.
You saw her cross the threshold
In desperate passion. Straight to her bridal-bed
She hurried, fastening her fingers in her hair.
There in her chamber, the doors flung sharply to,
She cried aloud to Laios long since dead,
Remembering the son she bore long since, the son
By whom the sire was slain, the son to whom
The mother bore yet other children, fruit of
Luckless misbegetting. There she bewailed
The twice confounded issue of her wifehood—
husband begotten of husband, child of child.
So much we heard.[5]

This passage includes several serious misrepresentations, which I have italicized. Not only does Watling have the messenger claim he saw Jocasta's death (which the messenger specifically denies, even in Watling's own translation: "Her death was hidden from us"), but he introduces a gratuitous "You saw" when describing Jocasta's entry into her chamber. He also adds a decisive, final sentence not in the Greek text: "So much we heard." There is no warrant for the assumption underlying Watling's interpolation, namely that the messenger is reporting words actually spoken by Jocasta. He most emphatically is not. Watling is re-creating his original on the assumption that what the messenger says about Jocasta is, essentially, accurate. So his concern about whether Jocasta spoke the words or not is diminished.

Watling may also have been drawn off track by the curious confusion in the messenger's account. Let us look again at the concluding lines of the passage cited (1251–54):

How after this, she perished
I still don't know. For Oedipus burst in,
shouting, making it impossible
for us to watch her troubles to the end (*ektheasasthai*),
for we were watching *him* as he strode in.

The messenger's use of *ektheasasthai*, "to watch through to the end," perhaps, lured Watling into supposing that the messenger had actually followed Jocasta into her chamber and seen her die. But it quickly becomes evident that he did not. The most we can reasonably infer is that if Oedipus had not arrived, the messenger would have followed

Jocasta inside and watched. He makes himself part of an inner group of spectators who, like the outer audience he addresses, can watch, can even be addressed by the protagonists, but who cannot intervene. There is no hint that he or anyone else might try to *prevent* the queen from killing herself, as, if only for an instant, the chorus of Euripides' *Hippolytus* contemplates doing (*Hippolytus* 782–83).

Thus the palace messenger in a way represents the dramatist's sardonic comment at his audience's expense, perhaps anticipating that we, like the chorus, will lose interest in Jocasta's fate as Oedipus moves into narrative view. It is part of the play's constantly narrowing focus, as everything, from the plague devastating Thebes to the fate of Jocasta, is subsumed in the intense concentration not only of Oedipus on himself but of us on Oedipus. We are lured into overlooking the same sort of detail that Oedipus overlooks until, at the end, we share his conviction of guilt and thus, I would suggest, his blindness.

We do not "see" Jocasta through the palace messenger's narrative eyes until Oedipus arrives outside her chamber (1255–66):

> He comes round, begs us for a sword and asks
> where he *might find* that wife who was no wife,
> that maternal field yielding double
> harvest of himself and his children.
> As he raves on, some god points him the way—
> no man of us did who were standing near.
> Roaring horribly as if some force
> were leading him, he hurled himself against
> the double entrance, bent and burst the hollow
> doors and plunged into the room.
> >   And there
> > we saw his wife hanging entangled in
> > woven cords that raised her, swung her round.

As Oedipus burst through the locked doors that separate him—and the messenger—from Jocasta's room, he brings Jocasta back into the messenger's view. The messenger obviously intends us to conclude that Jocasta hanged herself, that she committed suicide, as, in fact, he stated at the outset. And this intent adds to the problem raised by his comment just seconds earlier (1251): "How after that she died I still don't know." More on this shortly. There are other issues we must tackle first.

I have italicized in my translation the ambiguous optative *kichoi,*

"might find." Is this the messenger's comment about Oedipus, Oedipus' comment about himself, or both? It would be more in keeping
with Sophocles' practice elsewhere for the optative to indicate something other than a genuine quotation of one speaker by another. I
suspect that the messenger is, once again, adding his own creative
touch. Our resistance to his rhetorical inference is low since we know
Oedipus now believes he is Jocasta's son. Yet if we take the words
to be Oedipus', we attribute to him a very harsh comment about
Jocasta, which leads to what I think are mistaken conclusions about
his request for a sword.

What does Oedipus want the sword for? The answer is made trick-
ier because because he never gets the requested weapon—though we
occasionally find it in modern translations.[6] That is why he must *untie*
the noose around Jocasta's neck, not cut it. Dawe comments (on 1255):
"In this rapid recital we have not time to ask ourselves what Oedipus
intended to do with the sword. If we do ask ourselves, we cannot
avoid the answer that he intended to kill his wife/mother."[7] How
often one hears this argument: that one does not have time in tragedy
to ask those questions that the commentator would rather not deal
with. But at least Dawe acknowledges that such questions arise and
attempts to answer them, as in this case. If he is right, Jocasta's
presumably self-inflicted death occurs just in time to prevent her dying
at Oedipus' hands. Such an Oedipus would indeed make the kind of
comments that appear in the messenger's ambiguously optatival
statement.

But the issue is not as clear as Dawe makes it seem. In Euripides'
Hippolytus, which shares so many motifs with this play, a handmaid
cries out for a sword to cut the rope with which Phaedra hangs herself
(*Hippolytus* 780–81):

> Oh won't you hurry? Won't anyone bring us
> a two-edged sword to free her neck?

The chorus' response is a fearsome and grimly humorous reminder
of its reluctance to "get involved" (782–85):

> *Half-chorus*: Friends, what shall we do? Enter the house,
>   you think, to free our queen from strangling ropes?

Half-chorus: Why? Doesn't she have young maids there with her?
    Getting involved is no safe way of life.

Oedipus' request for a sword is as unsuccessful as is the maid's in
Hippolytus. Indeed, his request might suggest he suspects Jocasta has
tried to hang herself. Oedipus' anger, we should note, even as narrated
by the messenger, is directed against *himself*, not against Jocasta. He
releases her from the rope. He shows no rage at her in either word
or action, in the messenger's report or subsequently when he reenters,
despite the messenger's foreboding tone (1266–67):

> But when she lay upon the ground, poor thing,
> what happened next was hideous to see.

Instead of turning on Jocasta with verbal or physical violence, Oedipus removes the pins from her robe to destroy his eyesight (1268–
70):

> He tore away from her and from her clothes
> gold-pinned brooches that kept her dress draped.
> lifted them up and struck the moving orbs
> of his own eyes . . .

We might better argue that Oedipus was hunting all along for some
instrument with which to attack himself, not Jocasta. Sophocles' heroes are remarkably prone to self-destruction.[8] He even provides us
with the only protagonist in surviving ancient tragedy who commits
suicide on stage: Ajax.

It would be surprising to find the Oedipus of this play ready to
kill, with his own hand and deliberately, the woman he believes to
be his mother. We should not draw false conclusions by comparing
his reaction to the death of Polybus. He is happy that Polybus died
because he will not therefore be his father's killer. Finding Jocasta
hanging, and denied a sword either to cut her down or kill himself,
he uses her brooches to strike out his eyes.

Brooches are the instruments of blinding in the only other scene
in Greek tragedy where a man is blinded offstage: Euripides' *Hecuba*—
a play that dates to within a few years of Sophocles' *Oedipus*, around
425 B.C. The attack on Polymestor is an act of revenge for his treach-

erous killing of Polydorus, Hecuba's last surviving son, and is carried out by Trojan women who have swords (*phasgana*) available and use them to kill Polymestor's children. But Polymestor's eyes they destroy with their *porpai,* the clasps of their dresses (1169–71).

Oedipus' use of dress-clasps for this act of female vengeance is grimly appropriate. For he is, in a sense, undressing her. The pins that hold the dress in place and keep the breasts from view are removed so that they can deny him sight forever: "gold-pinned brooches" (*chrysêlatous peronas* [*Oedipus* 1268–69]). In Euripides' *Phoenician Women* (written after 410 B.C.), we might add, Oedipus is described by Jocasta herself as using precisely such clasps, "gold-pinned clasps" (*chrysêlatois . . . porpaisi*), to blind himself (62).

In the poetic diction of tragedy, the language of death and the language of blindness are very close. To live is "to see the light." To be alive but sightless is thus a kind of living death. Oedipus, deprived of the means of killing himself, deprives himself of the light in the other, more terrifying way recognized by Greek thought.

Jocasta and Eurydice

We may gain a further perspective on this puzzling scene from *Oedipus* if we compare the far less dramatically important suicide of Eurydice in Sophocles' *Antigone*—a play in which three of the characters kill themselves. Eurydice vanishes from the stage at *Antigone* 1243, to the chorus' puzzlement, after she has learned of her son Haemon's suicide. A messenger from the palace soon enters and announces that she has killed herself, after denouncing and cursing Creon as her own destroyer and destroyer of her son. But the messenger in *Antigone* also produces Eurydice's body (1293): "See for yourself. She is not hidden now." Eurydice kills herself with a sword, just as her son Haemon did (*Antigone* 1236). So there is a curious appropriateness about the way the messenger puns on *paisasa* ("striking") and *pais* ("child") which are, respectively, the first words of *Antigone* 1311 and 1312, when he reports to Creon:

> She heard sharp moans of grief for her own son (*paidos*)
> and struck (*paisas'*) with her own hand (*autocheir*) beneath her heart.

I have also singled out the word *autocheir,* "by her own hand," because this report of Eurydice's death is echoed in Oedipus' account of his own self-blinding in *Oedipus* 1331. The expressions are virtually identical:

> Yet no-one struck (*epaise*) me with his hands (*autocheir*) but I, my miserable self.

Comparison between *Oedipus* and *Antigone* on this issue shows how subtly Sophocles deploys the suggestive range of language and invites further questions about Jocasta's death. In *Antigone* there is no reasonable doubt that Eurydice is dead. The audience, not just Creon, is invited to view the corpse, as is usually the case in Greek tragedy.[9] But in *Oedipus* the palace messenger invites the chorus to view not Jocasta's corpse but Oedipus blinded (1294–96):

> The gates are now being unbarred, and you
> will soon see such a spectacle as even
> one who hates (*stygount'*) him *could feel pity*
> *for* (*epoiktisai*).

How curious that his last verb is an optative, and that the last thought he has for Oedipus is that he might seem pitiable even to someone who hated him.

Critics have been uneasy with these lines. Jebb, commenting on 1296, takes the unstated (in Greek) object of "loathes" to be "it," that is, the spectacle, rather than Oedipus himself. So he translates: "for lo, the bars of the gates are withdrawn, and soon then shalt thou behold a sight which even he who abhors it must pity."[10] Dawe, in a note on the same line, seems to accept that "Oedipus" is the object, since he adduces the parallel of the suicidal Ajax (*Ajax* 924) who is described as "worthy a farewell lament even among his foes."[11] But Ajax really is lamented as a hero by his greatest foe, Odysseus, in that play. In *Oedipus,* beneath the superficial courtesy that cloaks the initial encounters among the characters, there is a strong sense of dislike and hatred, which emerges most clearly when Oedipus finally accedes to Jocasta and the chorus in their request that Creon not be killed or banished. Pity and hatred are blended here as they are at the end of the palace messenger's speech and nowhere else in this play or in Sophocles' other surviving works (669–75):

Oedipus: Then let him go, even if I must die
or be thrown out by violence from this land.
I'm moved to pity (*epoikteirô*) by your words, not his.
He will be hated (*stygêsetai*) wherever he may be.
Creon: You're full of hate (*or*: hateful—*stygnos*) when clement,
oppressive
when enraged. But then, natures like yours
are hardest on themselves. And rightly so.

The palace messenger's final words, then, echo the earlier parting of
Creon and Oedipus and presage the new encounter of these two men
as roles and positions are reversed. For nowhere else in the play do
we find the verb *stygeô,* "hate," or words based on it, except here.
How curious that this palace messenger, who so recalls the language
of Creon, does not go on to mention that Creon has become tyrant
now that Oedipus seems unfit to rule.

In the midst of all this, Jocasta's apparent death is forgotten. Indeed,
no one after the palace messenger mentions her at all except Oedipus.
In lines 1446–48, Oedipus, who in his last instants of vision found
Jocasta hanging and naturally assumed she was dead, asks Creon to
permit her burial—a precaution not necessarily superfluous, given
Creon's notoriety in myth, and in Sophocles' own earlier *Antigone,*
for refusing burial to relatives. Oddly enough, Creon totally ignores
the request, and Oedipus does not pursue the matter. The queen's
apparent death is taken very casually.

I say "apparent" for two reasons. First, as we noted earlier, the
palace messenger contradicts himself. One moment he says Jocasta
committed suicide, the next he denies knowing how she died. The
second reason is that poets do not always set Jocasta's death at this
particular point in the tale of Thebes. Elsewhere she dies much later,
after the duel between Eteocles and Polyneices, her sons by Oedipus.
Questions may well cross our minds as to how and why Jocasta died,
even about *whether* Jocasta really did die. A messenger who brings
such a confused report deserves at least a little suspicion.

Oedipus' Self-Blinding

In contrast with the Corinthian, who can stretch the little knowledge
he has only to a few lines, the palace messenger is quite ready to
divagate into detail, even though he trips from time to time. It is as

if he knows more than he is saying and is intent on misleading both chorus and audience. We have already seen that the report of Jocasta's self-condemnation is his imaginary reconstruction of her thoughts, couched in the careful distance of indirect statement. Nonetheless, he has fixed it in readers' minds for many years that Jocasta killed herself through guilt about marriage with her son; and that Oedipus would himself have killed Jocasta if a sword had been available, and if she had not anticipated such an attack by her own suicide. In short, the palace messenger reaffirms Oedipus' image as parent-killer. And he seems to be doing so deliberately.

The messenger now perfects his rhetorical illusion by a disarming final ploy which we must examine. As he goes on to present Oedipus' words as the latter blinds himself, the messenger opens and closes with *toiauta*, "to this effect," and uses the future optatives of indirect speech which usually indicate, as we have seen, that the speaker is in some way distancing himself from his report. He makes no pretence of citing Oedipus exactly (1271–76):

> He spoke to this effect:
> that they'd never more see any evil
> that he was doing or experiencing;
> that from then on they'd see in darkness those
> they had no right to see and they would fail
> to recognize people they should have known.
> To this effect he made his ritual
> lament and kept raising his hands to strike
> his lidded eyes again.

Is indirect speech used here simply because Sophocles does not want to "upstage" Oedipus himself, who is about to enter in one of the most shattering scenes in Greek tragedy?[12] If so, this passage differs from other similar passages in Sophocles where indirect speech with optatives *distances* narrator from narrative. Such reporting occurs, we have seen, when the speaker consciously engages in rhetorical dissimulation: protecting himself or herself from hostile response, as with the messenger in the *Ajax*; offering covert criticism, as with the nurse in the *Trachiniae*; actually lying, as with the merchant and Neoptolemus in the *Philoctetes*, and Lichas in the *Trachiniae*. The present passage from *Oedipus* contains *three* future optatives, forms rare enough that they attract attention.

There is no reason to suppose the palace messenger is mistaken in his summary of Oedipus' reasons for blinding himself. Oedipus' comments onstage in the following scene show that the report is essentially correct. The optatives, on this occasion, suggest not that the messenger is reporting things unsaid as if they were said, as he does in Jocasta's case. Rather, they reveal his own doubts about the validity of Oedipus' reasons for the attack upon his sight. In short, the obliqueness of this passage is the reverse of Deianeira's use of direct speech to report Nessus' dying words. Her direct quotation with *tosouton* shows, as we have seen, that she believes Nessus' words, even though the centaur was lying (*Trachiniae* 569–77). The messenger's indirect speech, in contrast, suggests that he disbelieves or doubts what he is reporting.

The palace messenger knows more than he admits—and not just about the reasons for Oedipus' self-blinding. After all, his descriptions of the brutal savagery in the palace mask a major political change: the man who would not be king has taken control of Thebes. And everyone, from displaced monarch to scholarly critic, takes Creon's access to power in stride. We do not even worry that the palace messenger fails to mention that Creon has assumed the crown, even though his strange observations about pity and hatred, so resonant of the earlier argument between Oedipus and Creon, seem to suggest that Creon's words are on his mind. Nor do we worry that the chorus knows all about the succession without leaving the stage and without having been told (1416–18).

9. CREON KREON

The chorus, which remains onstage during the changes and interchanges described by the palace messenger, suggests that Creon became guardian of the state by default (1416–18):

> The man you ask for to fulfill your need,
> the action and the planning, has arrived:
> Creon. Only he is left as guardian
> for the country now instead of you.

The Oedipus tradition, as we have noted, is by no means unanimous about when Creon assumed power. He is more usually shown as ruling *after* Laios' death and *before* Oedipus' succession to the throne and, again, after the deaths of Oedipus' sons Eteocles and Polyneices.[1] Sophocles was certainly not obliged to make Creon ruler *now*. In other versions, such as Statius' in the *Thebaid* or Euripides' in the *Phoenician Women,* Oedipus sons take over, not Creon—as they do in Sophocles' own earlier *Antigone* and later *Oedipus at Colonus.* Tradition defers Creon's principal period of monarchy until after the civil war between Eteocles and his brother, Polyneices. But here, as we will see, Oedipus assumes when he reemerges that Eteocles and Polyneices will not rule in his place. In sum, the *only* version of the Oedipus myth in which Creon becomes ruler of Thebes immediately after Oedipus' self-blinding is that of Sophocles' *Oedipus.* The innovation is less noticeable to us than it would have been to his contemporaries because Sophocles' *Oedipus* is now *the* canonical definition of the Oedipus myth.

Sophocles' Oedipus, far from protesting Creon's assumption of power, not only takes it for granted but is embarrassed about his earlier rough treatment of his brother-in-law (1419–21):

> Ah! But what then shall I say to him?
> What just reason will he have to trust
> in me? In all my past dealings with him
> it's evident that I have been wicked.

No sooner is the admission made than Creon speaks, echoing some of Oedipus' words (1422–23):

> It's not to laugh at you that I have come,
> Oedipus, nor to abuse you at all
> for past, wicked dealings.

Creon is clearer about what he does *not* intend to do than about what he intends. Instead of elaborating plans for Oedipus, he takes the chorus to task for allowing Oedipus to remain outside (1424–31);

> But if you men
> have not yet learned respect (*aideisth'*) for things that die
> and come to birth, at least protect the fire
> of the lord Sun, which nurses everything,
> from sights that shame the eye. So don't display
> all unconcealed before him such a thing (*agos*)
> accursed, which earth and holy rain and light
> will not tolerate. Get it inside
> the house. Only those kin by birth may see
> and hear the disgrace borne by their kinfolk
> and still be acting reverently and well.

Here is a forceful reminder not just of the inversion of power but of something we noticed about Creon when he first came on stage in this play: he asked whether Oedipus wanted to hear the oracle's response indoors or outdoors. We may also recall that the chorus had ordered Jocasta to take Oedipus inside the house when he was wildly, and without evidence, accusing Creon earlier in the play.

The shift from Creon's sympathetic tone to impersonal coldness is abrupt and stark. Oedipus suddenly becomes something subhuman: an object, a thing. The transition is marked by the punning use of the neuter *agos* ("thing accursed"), accented on the first syllable, instead of the masculine *agos* ("king" or "leader"), accented on the last syllable. The notion that Oedipus ought not to be seen by the sun is reinforced by the wordplay on *aidôs* ("shame") and the root *aid-* ("unseen"). Sophocles is extending the earlier play Oedipus himself makes (perhaps with unconscious irony on Oedipus' part, if not on Sophocles') between "seeing" (*proseidon*) and "Hades" (*Haidou*) in 1372–73. In these lines Oedipus explains to the chorus why it is better that he has blinded rather than hanged himself:

> Could I see with my eyes, I don't know how
> I'd face (*proseidon*) my father in faceless Hades (*Haidou*).

Plays on Hades as "the unseen" or "unseeing" are common in Greek literature and most overtly made by Sophocles himself in *Ajax* 608: *aidêlon Aidan,* "Hades that makes unseen [or: destroys]."[2]

What emerges forcefully in the present passage of the *Oedipus,* however, is the contrast between Oedipus' reluctance to see the world around him and Creon's reluctance that Oedipus be seen. Creon treats him as a monster to be kept out of the light (and sight) of the Sun. But in Greek tragedy, to look upon the Sun or to see the light are often synonymous with being alive. And curiously Apollo, the god usually identified with the Sun by Greek tragedians, is in Oedipus' opinion the author of his misfortunes.[3] Before proceeding with our treatments of Oedipus and Creon, we must explore some further verbal resonances in the matter of Oedipus' blindness.

Oedipus and Odysseus

When the blinded Oedipus reenters and is asked by the chorus which god brought his misfortunes upon him, he responds (1329–31):

> This was Apollo, Apollo, friends (*philoi*),
> who achieved all these evil, evil
> sufferings of mine. But no one (*Outis*) struck
> me with his hands but I my miserable self.

There is a strange Homeric echo here. Oedipus' response to the chorus' question recalls the Cyclopes' reaction to the cries of the blinded

Polyphemus in *Odyssey* 9.403–12: "Is not someone (*mê tis*), we thought, killing you by treachery or violence?" (406). Polyphemus replies (408): "Friends (*philoi*), No one (*Outis*) is killing me by treachery or violence." Oedipus, then, seems to be verbally playing Polyphemus to the chorus' "other Cyclopes."

Polyphemus, of course, has been duped by the wordplaying Odysseus into believing that Odysseus' name is Outis, "No one." So Polyphemus' answer leaves his fellow Cyclopes baffled (9.410–12): "If then no one (*mê tis*) does you violence when you are alone, there is no way that you can escape the sickness that comes from Great Zeus. So pray to your father, Lord Poseidon." As W. B. Stanford pointed out long ago, there is a further wordplay lurking in this scene from the *Odyssey* between *mê tis*, "no one," and *mêtis*, "thought."[4] What the Cyclopes mean is that Polyphemus is going mad: "If then your thought (*mêtis*) and no person (*mê tis*) does you violence when you are alone, there is no way that you can escape the sickness that comes from Great Zeus." Odysseus himself takes double delight in that "my name (*onoma*) and my cunning thought (*mêtis*) deceived him" (*Odyssey* 9.416). Indeed, Homer gives him the epithet Poly*mêtis* ("Man of Much Cunning Thought") so often that it is almost his second name.[5] Thus his triumph over Poly*phêmus*, "Man of much speech," has a special appropriateness.

We find a similar Homeric parallel in Euripides. In a bizarre exchange between the chorus and the blinded Polyphemus in *Cyclops* (672–75), the Cyclops cries out:

Polyphemus: No one (*Outis*) ruined me.
 Chorus: Nobody's wronged you?
Polyphemus: No one (*Outis*) blinded my eye.
 Chorus: Then you're not blind.
Polyphemus: You . . .
 Chorus: How could no one make you blind?
Polyphemus: You're mocking. Where is No one (*Outis pou'stin*)?
 Chorus: Nowhere (*oudamou*).

Euripides' puns on *Outis* recall the cascade of puns in the opening comments of Sophocles' Corinthian messenger who wants to know where Oedipus is.

Sophocles' Oedipus, on the other hand, whose words echo those of the deluded Polyphemus, really does blind himself. It is he himself and his own thoughts, more than the actions of others, that bring him suffering, as Teiresias observed earlier: "Creon is not your problem. You are your own." But surely lurking behind Oedipus' confident "No one" are real people whose words have tricked him as certainly as Odysseus tricked Polyphemus. The difference is that Polyphemus thinks "No one" is a person's name, whereas Oedipus concludes, on the basis of statements by "Nobodies," that no one but himself is the cause of his blinding. He does not recall that it was the blind Teiresias who first suggested that he might put out his own eyes. Again we see his confusion of self and "other."

The verbal parallel between Homer's Odysseus and Sophocles' Oedipus should not surprise us. When talking of stories involving the killing of kinsmen, Aristotle in *Poetics* 1453B.33 mentions not only Oedipus but Alcmaeon in Astydamas' *Alcmaeon* and Telegonus in *The Wounded Odysseus,* quite possibly the lost tragedy *Odysseus Akanthoplex,* by Sophocles. The tradition that Odysseus was killed in error by Telegonus, his son by Circe, dates back at least to the epic *Telegonia* (around the middle of the sixth century B.C.), of which we have only fragments.[6]

The *Telegonia* developed a theme from *Odyssey* 11.126–37, in which it is forecast that Odysseus' death will come to him from the sea—a prophecy given him in Homer by the ghost of Teiresias. Sophocles' *Odysseus Akanthoplex* seems to have told that while Odysseus was on his journey to make ritual appeasement to Poseidon in accordance with Teiresias' prophecy (fragment 453), he learned from the oracle of Zeus at Dodona that he would die at the hands of his son. He worried, according to Dictys of Crete (6.15), that Telemachus might be his assailant. So he was grateful, when mortally wounded by a young man who attacked him in Ithaca, that Telemachus, who fought at his side, was not blood-guilty. But on asking his killer's identity, he discovered him to be Telegonus, his own son by Circe. Telegonus, accompanied by Penelope and Telemachus, took Odysseus' body to Circe's island. There Telemachus married Circe, his father's former mistress, and Telegonus married Penelope, his father's widow.

The story of Odysseus and Telegonus is an interesting variant of the Oedipal tale of killing one's father and marrying one's mother. Or vice versa. Dana Sutton observes that "the resemblance of this play to the *Oedipus Tyrannus* must have been remarkably close."[7] But, to reverse Sutton's observation, we should note that Sophocles seems equally keen on having us think of Odysseus as we hear his *Oedipus.*

The Final Encounter between
Oedipus and Creon

It was Creon who first established the link between the death of Laios
and the plague upon Thebes (now long forgotten in the play) when
he offered an interpretation of his own report of the Delphic oracle's
response (102–7):

> *Oedipus*: What man does he declare (*mênyei*) has earned this fate?
>   *Creon*: We had a ruler once called Laios
>   before you set our city on its course.
> *Oedipus*: I've heard the name, but never seen the face.
>   *Creon*: He's dead. God clearly now instructs a hand
>   to act as agent of revenge upon
>   those who killed him, whoever killed him.

Creon, we suggested, was playing oracle to Oedipus during their
first encounter in the play. He does much the same at the beginning
of their final encounter. But by this later point Oedipus is not cher-
ishing the suspicions, which, we learn, he had entertained about
Creon's loyalty. Oedipus has now concluded that he himself is vile
and that Creon is noble (1432–43):

> *Oedipus*: By the gods, since you have torn me from
>   my expectations just by coming here,
>   in your excellence to all my wickedness,
>   Do what I say! For your sake, not for mine!
>   *Creon*: What is your prayer that needs response (*chreia*) from
>   me?
> *Oedipus*: Hurl me from this land quick as you can,
>   to where no man will see or speak to me.
>   *Creon*: Be sure that I'd have done so, if I'd not
>   needed (*echrêizon*) first of all to learn clearly
>   from the god what really must be done.
> *Oedipus*: But surely now: his prophecy was made
>   entirely plain—appalling death (*apollynai*) for me,
>   the impious man, the father-killing man.
>   *Creon*: Thus these things were said. But still, given
>   our need of answers (*chreias*), it is better now
>   to learn quite clearly what must be performed.

Many aspects of this interchange need comment. But let us begin
with what is probably the most easily overlooked.

Creon and *Chreiai*

The word *chreia,* which Creon uses of Oedipus' request, means not only "need" but also a "devastating response" to a challenging interlocutor. A *chreia* is a pithy retort, repartee, aptly attributed to and characteristic of a particular person, as Aphthonius, a rhetorician of the late fourth century A.D., points out; it is also, Aphthonius contends, useful (*chreiodês*) in guiding the conduct of life.[8] Hence the Roman rhetorician Priscian translates *chreia* as *usus.*[9] We might also contend that a *chreia* has something in common with an oracle, a *chrêsmos,* a divine response. Hence, perhaps, Jocasta's comment to Oedipus at lines 724–25:

> The things that god
> has need (*chreia*) to answer and track down, he will
> quite easily reveal all by himself.[10]

Chreiai are attributed most commonly to philosophers, especially to the Cynic Diogenes. But characters in the tragedies of Sophocles and Euripides make sententious statements that find their way into the collections of *chreiai.* Two lines from Sophocles' *Ajax* that have an obviously proverbial force—"affection (*charis*) is always parent to affection" (522) and "those who are sound of mind hold the power everywhere" (1252)—are cited by ancient rhetoricians as examples of *chreiai.*[11] Indeed, Sophocles himself coined some *chreiai* in his everyday life. Perhaps the most famous is cited in Plato, *Republic* 1.329B–C: Sophocles' supposed witty response to an interlocutor who asked him about his sex life in old age: Could he still have sex with a woman? the question arises. "How nice to have escaped such a fierce master," the reply comes.[12]

One *chreia* with a particular bearing on the Oedipus myth is attributed by Diogenes Laertius (6.40) to the Cynic Diogenes. Diogenes ridiculed Plato's definition of man as a living creature with two feet and no wings (*zôon dipoun apteron*) by plucking a cockerel and presenting it at the school with the comment: "This is Plato's man." This *chreia* evokes not only the Oedipus myth but also Aristophanes' various rooster jests about Socratic learning in the *Clouds.* The Aristophanic Socrates, as we have seen, fails to detect the intrusive rooster among Strepsiades' quadrupreds, and his warring arguments appear on stage as fighting cocks.

In most *chreiai*, the victorious speaker is the one who delivers the final crushing retort which an adversary cannot counter, the one who has the last word. This is quite appropriate. Nicolaus of Myra, a grammarian of the early fifth century A.D., observes of the *chreia* that "it should be placed after the narrative (*diêgêma*), for this would be the best position."[13] And Creon certainly has the last word in the exchanges with Oedipus in Sophocles' tragedy.

Oedipus' First Request

Creon's use of *chreia* should be on our minds when he declares that he needs to consult Delphi before deciding what should be done about Oedipus. Let us look again at these interchanges which contain the substance of Oedipus' first request from Creon:

Oedipus: Hurl me from this land quick as you can,
    to where no man will see or speak to me.
  Creon: Be sure that I'd have done so, if I'd not
    needed (*echrêizon*) first of all to learn clearly
    from the god what really must be done.
Oedipus: But surely now: his prophecy was made
    entirely plain—appalling death (*apollynai*) for me,
    the impious man, the father-killing man.
  Creon: Thus these things were said. But still, given
    our need of answers (*chreias*), it is better now
    to learn quite clearly what must be performed.

Oedipus seems surer than Creon about what the god commands, even though Creon, not Oedipus, made the most recent and critical consultation of Apollo. Creon's report said nothing about finding a father-killer and was vague about the kind of punishment to be inflicted on the polluter of the land: death or banishment. The "plainness" that Oedipus finds comes from his conflation of the oracle with Creon's interpretation of it and with his own, earlier consultation of Delphi. Even on that earlier occasion, the god was far from explicit. In response to Oedipus' question "Who are my parents?" the oracle had responded: "You will kill your father and marry your mother."

Creon, of course, knows better than we or Oedipus what was said when he consulted Delphi, since we depend entirely on his report. Why, then, does he cast such a shadow of ambiguity over the situation, if not to draw Oedipus' (and our) attention to the fact that matters are not as clear-cut as Oedipus imagines? Creon's "thus these things were said" is imprecise. Said by whom? By the oracle, or by Oedipus, Creon, and others?

Oedipus *takes it for granted that Creon's words imply the latter's intention to consult the oracle again*. What surprises him is Creon's concern for precision in the case of so contemptible a wretch as himself (1444): "You will inquire about a wretch like me?" Scholars take for granted, as Oedipus does, that Creon is piously motivated and "playing it safe" by deciding to consult Delphi. But then, oddly enough, many scholars feel that Creon finally grants Oedipus' first request of banishment on Cithaeron and does *not*, after all, consult Delphi before releasing him. Neither of these two mutually contradictory assumptions is beyond question. By sending Oedipus into the house, even temporarily, Creon subjects himself to Oedipus' curse on anyone who harbors Laios' killer—unless, of course, Oedipus is not that killer.

Let us begin, however, by presuming that both assumptions are right. What changes Creon's mind? Perhaps he is probing the extent of Oedipus' conviction of his own sinfulness, just as he earlier attempted to penetrate and undermine Oedipus' conviction that he, Creon, was plotting a coup d'etat. Does Oedipus doubt his guilt—as he earlier doubted his innocence? After hearing his reply in line 1444, Creon apparently concludes he does not. With Oedipus' self-abasing response, Creon feels secure from further changes of mind. Hence his reply in line 1445 would be both a summation and a taunt: "Well, even you would now trust in god's word." He can drop all suggestion of consulting Delphi again and let Oedipus go. He is empowered to act on his own: Oedipus will not challenge him on the issue of prophecy again. Dawe calls Creon's remark here "unsympathetic."[4] So be it. But Oedipus' own earlier treatment of Creon was hardly such as to earn the latter's sympathy and goodwill.

It may be, however, that Creon's proposal to consult the oracle is more than just a rhetorical ploy to test the depths of Oedipus' self-conviction. Perhaps we, like Oedipus, are missing the point about Creon's doubts. Creon reveals few details about his recent consultation of the oracle and about what happened at Thebes when Laios died, and Creon earlier characterized Teiresias' charges against Oedipus as lies. He is not necessarily as convinced as Oedipus that the oracle has been fulfilled and makes no direct allusion to *any* of the counts upon which Oedipus finds himself guilty. Creon may suspect—or know—that Oedipus' self-condemnation is based on a mistaken judgment, and that consultation of the oracle would be a wise precaution. He will not mock Oedipus, as Odysseus mocks the Cyclops—and in this we see what is both his cool self-interest and an apparent act of charity to his humbled and hated rival. When Homer's Odysseus casts aside his anonymity and tells the Cyclops that his name is Odysseus, not Nobody, he brings himself within range of Polyphemus' curses and the wrath of Polyphemus' father, Poseidon. A curse on "Nobody" achieves nothing. But the curse on Odysseus finds its mark. Similarly, if Creon were to break cover now, he would become the target of Odysseus' curses and would lose favor with the people. His newfound tyranny would be short-lived. On the other hand, Creon's ambiguity spares Oedipus the horror of realizing that he has been deluded, that he has deluded himself—if we grant that Oedipus, like Othello, has been lured by his own folly and others' jealousy and self-interest into drawing a dubious, perhaps terribly wrong conclusion.

Creon's sharp tone and hesitancy in granting his request for exile do not pass unnoticed by Oedipus, who seems caught between two reactions, as his words in 1446 show: "Well, now I charge you formally (*episkeptô*) I beg upon my knees (*prostrephomai*) . . . " Oedipus' first verb, *episkeptô,* means not only "make a forceful request" but also "strike with lightning," "curse with dying breath," and "lodge a charge of perjury against." His expression is powerful and ironic. He is laying a strong obligation on Creon to do his bidding, in his new guise as the man taking leave of the world of cities and men: it is his will and testament, designed to include the kind of provisions a dying man would make for his family. But for a fleeting moment there is also the undertone (perhaps unconscious on Oedipus' part but hardly on Sophocles') of an accusation of perjury against Creon. Given the popular association of thunderbolts with the punishment of perjury, as in Aristophanes' *Clouds* 394–403, the additional meaning of "strike with lightning" reinforces the connection between the legal and religious shades of meaning in the word.

Oedipus' second verb here, *prostrephomai,* is used not just of a suppliant but of someone begging mercy from an *enemy*. It acknowledges hostility as well as inferiority in power. Oedipus *knows* he is not addressing a friend. Compare, for example, the tone Alcestis uses when making her dying requests of Admetus in *Alcestis* 280–325. She asks her husband to *remember* (*apomnêsai*) what he owes her (299) and says she will ask him to pay back (*aitêsomai*) his due to her (300). Alcestis bases her expressed hope for the petition's fulfillment on Admetus' obligations to her. Her words reflect the curious nature of her relationship with Admetus, the man for whom she is dying, and who will shortly break most of the vows he makes to her in response to her request. Oedipus' words show a more overt awareness of his heritage of hostility toward Creon. He realizes he needs heavier verbal force to get Creon to do his bidding. The battle for control is not yet over. It has just changed in nature.

Oedipus' Second, Third, and Fourth Requests

Oedipus' second request is that Jocasta be buried, a request charged with irony for anyone who remembers Sophocles' earlier *Antigone* in which Creon denies burial to the body of Polyneices. Oedipus broaches the matter in this way (1447–48):

> Bury as you will
> her who is in the house. It's only right
> you set your own kin properly to rest.

Creon never responds verbally. And a gesture would be lost on the now blind Oedipus. Perhaps he feels an answer is not needed; perhaps burial would be premature. Oedipus, however, does not pursue the issue.

Oedipus' third request is an amplified reiteration of his first: a plea that he be allowed to live and die in Cithaeron, away from Thebes (1449–58):

> Let this, my father-city, never think
> it right that I should dwell here while alive.
> Permit me to live in the mountains where
> Cithaeron is now called mine, and which
> my mother and my father, when they lived,
> chose as the grave to master me. Then I
> may die at the hands of those who tried
> so hard to kill me. Yet I know this much:
> that it won't be disease or any such
> doom that will destroy me. I would never
> have been saved when on the point of death,
> unless for some formidable (*deinon*) evil.
>
> My lot, then—let it go where it will go.

Oedipus sees his life, then, in terms of a larger, *formidable*, importance. He defines for himself, and accepts, a role as a Sphinxlike creature, marked supernaturally for a special, if dire, destiny. Whether destiny (or Creon) sees him this way is another matter. Oedipus has, curiously, no requests to make on his sons' behalf (1459–61):

> And don't worry yourself about my sons,
> Creon. They're male and will not lack a stake
> in life wherever they may be.

Oedipus' casual reference to his sons' ability to manage by themselves is charged with mythic irony. Eteocles and Polyneices bring the plague of civil war upon the city in every other version of the Theban myth. Since they would, presumably, have been his heirs to the tyranny at Thebes, he is virtually disinheriting them by making no requests on their behalf. His reticence on this point effectively concedes rulership of Thebes to Creon and would probably have surprised his audience, since almost every other version of the Theban myth has Eteocles gaining power after Oedipus' loss of power.

Oedipus' attention, affection, and fourth request are reserved entirely for his daughters whom he refers to insistently in the Greek dual person. Nowhere else in Greek literature do so many dual forms occur in such close proximity, and the effect simply cannot be adequately reproduced in translation (1462–70):

> But these,
> my two poor, pitiful virgin daughters—
> my table was never set with food
> without the two of them, without me.
> They always shared, these two, whatever I
> touched. Look after them for me. Let them,
> please, touch me now with both their hands,
> and weep for our misfortune. Come, my lord!
> Come, noble in your birth! If I could feel
> them with my hands, I'd think I had them as
> when I could see.

The reason for the insistent duals, I suspect, lies in what is not said rather than in what is actually expressed. So let us first look at a similar dramatic situation where the imagery is blatant, rather than underlying.

When Euripides, in his *Hecuba*, describes Polymestor's blinding by the Trojan Women, he uses the common Greek wordplay on *korê*, "daughter," and *korê*, "pupil of the eye." The herald Talthybius calls the women Trojan *korai* (485), and the chorus, playing on the two senses of the word, talks of Helen as the "Spartan *korê* much wept for in her home" (651). As Hecuba lures Polymestor into her trap, she claims she cannot, as a woman, look him "straight in the eye," *orthais korais* (972). And when Polymestor is blinded, Hecuba boasts that he will never more put bright sight in his pupils (*korais*) or look again upon his children living (1045). The litany continues throughout the central section of the play. Polymestor curses the Phrygian *korai* who have blinded him (1064) and describes how the same *korai* (1152) destroyed his eyesight, *koras* (1170).

Even more to the present point, when Euripides' Jocasta in *Phoenician Women* 55–62 describes her family, she says she bore two daughters, *dissas koras* (57), and that Oedipus bloodied his eyes, *koras,* with brooches (62).

Sophocles *never* makes this wordplay explicitly in the surviving tragedies. But the idea is present implicitly in this passage as it is later in *Oedipus at Colonus,* when Creon, having abducted Oedipus' daughter Ismene, drags his other daughter, Antigone, away from Oedipus too. Oedipus cries out that Creon has torn away his *psilon omma,* the one poor eye left to him now that his own eyes are lost (*Oedipus at Colonus* 866–67). Thus he complains about Creon: "You go off, taking my *koras* with you" (1009).

In Sophocles' *Oedipus,* then, when Creon brings Oedipus' two daughters, their eyes streaming with tears, to comfort Oedipus, he is giving him, in a sense, his two eyes back. And Oedipus' gratitude is great (1471–83):

> What am I saying? Gods!
> Do I not hear my two darlings somewhere,
> both teeming with tears? You pitied me,
> Creon, sent me my two dearest offspring?
> Am I right?
>
> Creon: You're right. I am the one who brought them here,
> knowing the joy they are and were to you.
>
> Oedipus: May you be blessed, and on your journey may
> god's luck guard you better than it did me!
> My children, where are you? Come, come here
> into these arms of mine, these brother's arms
> which now must substitute for sight
> in place of your father's once active eyes
> so I can see you.

Creon does not produce Oedipus' sons, only his daughters. And, as they come into his arms, which now substitute for his lost sight, he speaks like a man declaring his last wishes from the deathbed. Or perhaps a woman. For we have already noted a resemblance between Oedipus' requests to Creon and those made by Alcestis to Admetus in Euripides' *Alcestis*. The comparison may be extended. If Jocasta and the chorus had not implored Oedipus to change his mind about killing Creon, Creon, not Oedipus himself, would have been treated as the murderer of Laios. Similarly, if Admetus had been willing to die, Alcestis would not be dying in his place. As Alcestis is more concerned about what will happen to her daughter than her son once her protective care is removed (*Alcestis* 311–19), so too is Oedipus. He continues now to address his daughters in terms recalling almost exactly those Alcestis uses (1484–1502):

> This man who begat
> you, children: he—I—am proved to have
> fathered you within the very womb
> in which my seed was sown, although I did
> not see, did not perceive, that this was so.
> I greet you both with tears. Though I lack power
> to see you, my mind grasps what still remains:
> the bitterness of life which you must both
> endure from fellow humans throughout life.
> What social contact will you come to have
> with those in town, and what festivities
> will you attend—from which you'll not return
> home, and in tears, instead of staying out
> to watch the spectacles? Then, when you come
> of age to get married, who will there be?
> Who will shrug off, children, all the abuse
> he'll take because of my role in your birth,
> the ruin it will bring? What element
> of evil is missing? "Your father killed
> his father, then he sowed his seed where he
> himself was sown, and so begat you where
> he too was once conceived." These are the slurs
> you'll have to bear. Then who will marry you?
> No one at all, children. Oh no, you must
> wither and rot, unmarried and barren.

Oedipus now reiterates his fourth request to Creon, that he look after the two girls (1503–10):

> Menoeceus' son, since you alone are left
> as father to these two—for we, the two
> of us who brought them into life, are gone,
> don't look away as they, your relatives,
> these two, wander as beggars, husbandless.
> Do not reduce them to my evil plight,
> but pity them, seeing how young they are,
> bereft of everything except for what
> you have to give. Agree, O noble sir,
> give me your hand on it.

The question, of course, arises as to what the status would be for children born of an incestuous marriage. The matter has been hotly and inconclusively debated by scholars.[15] But certainly Oedipus himself seems to fear that they may be disenfranchised in some way in the aftermath of his self-condemnation and self-punishment, and clearly expresses the hope that the girls will *not* be condemned to the life of wandering he desires for himself. We are not yet in the world of *Oedipus at Colonus* where Antigone and Ismene accompany him into exile. However, there is no more verbal indication of Creon's assent to this request than of his assent to Jocasta's burial.

    Oedipus continues (1511–14):

> My two children, could you yet understand,
> I'd tell you much. But now, pray this for me:
> that I may live where each instant allows,
> that you may win a better life than this,
> the one your father, who begat you, leads.

Oedipus implies that the girls are as yet very young—too young to grasp what is happening around them.

    At this point he either ends his monologue or, more likely, is interrupted by Creon. I suspect interruption because, among other things, the meter of the Greek suddenly changes from iambic trimeter to trochaic tetrameter, from a three-foot to a four-foot line, and with reversed rhythm.[16] Creon sets a new mood and a new tempo (1515–16):

> *Creon*: Now you have wept enough. Now go inside the house!
> *Oedipus*: There's no joy in your words, but I'll obey.
> *Creon*: All things have their instant (*kairos*) of beauty.

Creon's thin mask of sympathy is dropped, especially in his sarcastic parody of Oedipus' "living for the instant." There is still no indication that any of Oedipus' requests will be granted. In fact, the command that he enter the house reaffirms Creon's intention to hold Oedipus until the oracle has been consulted again (1517–19):

> *Oedipus*: You know my terms for going?
> *Creon*:   You'll tell. I'll hear, then know.
> *Oedipus*: Send me from here in exile.
> *Creon*:   That's god's gift not mine.
> *Oedipus*: Gods? they loathe me so.
> *Creon*:   Then you'll soon have your wish.

Dawe, who considers lines 1515–23 to be written by someone other than Sophocles, finds the logic of line 519 "altogether baffling." He thinks Oedipus means: "I am hateful to all gods, of whom Apollo is one, and in that case they, and he, are sure to favour my expulsion."[17] On the contrary, Oedipus' logic runs as follows: exile is a blessing, therefore the gods will deny him this blessing because they hate him. Most people, however, regard exile as a *punishment,* not a reward, something they would not wish the gods to give them. This thinking is the basis of *Creon*'s logic: since Oedipus wants something usually considered bad, the gods will readily grant it if they hate him as much as he thinks they do. Oedipus thus misconstrues Creon's response as consent to his exile (1520): "Your answer's yes?" But Creon only replies (1520): "I don't waste time saying what I don't mean." There is nothing in Creon's response to justify the common assumption that he has changed his mind on the matter of Oedipus' exile. Indeed, he would prove to have been "saying what he did not mean" if he were not to continue insisting that he consult the god first. And, let us recall, Creon has avoided any explicit accession to Oedipus' requests during this scene.

We should not suppose Oedipus is reassured by Creon's noncommittal response when he continues (1521): "Lead me from here right now." Oedipus' "lead me from here" can more easily mean "into the house"—where Creon ordered him to go at 1515—than "lead me off to Cithaeron." Oedipus is, rather, angrily conceding defeat. Oliver Taplin, citing Colin Macleod, observes that "the tragedy does *not* end with the final departure. . . . The point is that Oedipus, formerly the king, now cannot even control his own destiny: he has to be in Creon's hands."[18]

He is about to be humbled again (1521–23):

> Creon: Go now. But leave the girls.
> Oedipus: No, don't take them from me!
> Creon: Don't yearn for command all the time!
>   What you commanded did not follow you through life.

It is unlikely Oedipus has now also changed his own mind and wants to take Antigone and Ismene to Cithaeron with him, especially after just imploring Creon to look after them and not leave them wandering as beggars. Rather, he hopes for their company as he goes into the palace to wait until the oracle decides his fate. If Creon restored Oedipus' sight by giving him his daughters, he now robs him of the same loving and friendly eyes without ever pledging to look after them as his own children, as Oedipus had asked.

This last moment of humiliation and pathos is crowned by Creon's concluding words, about which Dawe comments: "On the face of them . . . they seem brusque . . . a needlessly sharp rebuff to a man who has just made a mild and pathetic request."[19] He is being less than fair to Creon. Oedipus has spared little thought throughout the play to the consequences upon others of his own obsessive search and self-punishment. He has rejoiced in Polybus' death, accused Teiresias and Creon of conspiracy, condemned (then pardoned) Creon without evidence or trial, and abused Jocasta as a snob when she tried to deflect him from his self-destructive course. Above all, he has forgotten about the plague on Thebes. It is only for his daughters that he has expressed, belatedly, any affection. He is indeed still trying to control the conditions and terms of his own and others' existence. Dawe, who considers the whole trochaic passage from 1515 onward spurious, and thus feels free to condemn its structure and style, comments that Creon's last line "looks to be little better than a jibe, and a clumsily phrased jibe at that."[20] I would suggest, rather, that it is a statement of Creon's exasperation and of his sense of irony. Oedipus' power was his mastery over words. But however well it served him in solving the riddle of the Sphinx, it has abandoned him now in the three-footed dialectic of the play, and even in these final four-footed measures which serve to move Oedipus back into symbolic infancy, not onward into three-footed old age.

The Final Chorus

Some scholars doubt that lines 1524–30 are the original ending of *Oedipus,* since they so resemble Euripides' *Phoenician Women* 1758–63.[21] But William Calder III, and now Brian Arkins, D. A. Hester, and S. Douglas Olson have made a strong case for the authenticity of at least the first two of these lines.[22] Those rejecting their authenticity usually maintain that they replace an original ending, rather than constitute an extension of the play beyond its "original" conclusion. The effect of the final chorus as we have it is, nonetheless, powerful, though I set off in brackets everything after line 1525, since many scholars reject the passage:

> Look, inhabitants of our ancestral Thebes:
> This is Oedipus who knew the famous riddles
> and was a very powerful man. [Who, surely no one,
> of our citizens saw his luck without envy?
> Look how he has met a wave of formidable
> catastrophe. And so, since you are mortal, watch
> for the final day, and, looking carefully,
> count no one blessed before he has crossed over
> life's finishing line without enduring pain.]

The chorus of Theban citizens steps out of character to address an Athenian audience with a reworking of the advice given to Croesus of Lydia by Solon, the Athenian wise man, in Herodotus' *Histories* 1.32.7–8: "Count no one blessed until he is dead, just lucky." Part of the problem, of course, is that the chorus is passing final judgment on Oedipus prematurely. He is not yet dead, even though he no longer sees the light. And every version of the Theban myth, including Sophocles' own *Antigone,* warns us of much direr days ahead for the house of Oedipus, for Creon, and for Thebes. Here, of course, is the heart of the matter.

The chorus, like Oedipus, has focused its attention on Oedipus instead of Thebes. The vast sufferings of a plague-ridden city outlined by the priest at the beginning of the play have been subsumed into an obsession with one man and the question of his origins. And to the various illnesses, of plague and tyranny, will be added that of civil war.

The Herodotean echo has a peculiar appropriateness to Sophocles' play and its immediate times. Herodotus himself seems to have died, possibly of the plague, shortly before *Oedipus* was produced—and in Thurii in Italy rather than in Athens because he was denied Athenian citizenship under the law of 451 which revoked the generous terms for enfranchisement granted to foreigners since the days of Solon. The closer the composition of these final lines in the text of Oedipus is set to the time of Herodotus' death, then, the greater their potential poignancy for an Athenian audience. Indeed, the story of Solon and Croesus is a somber warning to Athens, itself engaged, as Herodotus and Sophocles wrote, in imperialistic designs with uncertain outcome. The anxieties about tyranny that appear in Sophocles' *Oedipus* recall Solon's anxieties about tyranny as he was laying the groundwork for a more democratic Athenian state with equable laws and denouncing the folly of those who championed Peisistratus in his coups.[23]

Sophocles' Oedipus, like Herodotus' Croesus, meets disaster through oracular ambiguity, by interpreting too literally the Delphic responses given him. The playwright's reworking of the Oedipus myth involves a profound sense of the Solonian adage " 'nothing in excess' or 'know yourself' " (*mêden agân ê gnôthi sauton*), mentioned by the Suda (under "Solon") as Solon's particular apothegm. In fact, this double maxim is described by Pausanias as the collective wisdom sung (*aidomena*) by the Seven Sages and dedicated by them to Apollo at Delphi (10.24.1). Sophocles' Oedipus is keenly aware of his own offenses against that proverbial wisdom. In his dialogue with Jocasta at 767–68, as we saw in Chapter 5, he says he has done "much in excess" (*poll' . . . agân*). He is no less aware that others too have violated that wisdom: he accuses Teiresias at 439 of having done "everything in excess" (*pant'agân*). In Oedipus' case, no one would dispute his excess. The dispute centers, rather, on the question: excess in what?

10. ORACULAR WORDPLAY

In all arts no less than in magic," W. R. Halliday observed, "there is a tendency particularly strong where tradition demands conformity to a specific form, for the art to assume a paramount importance, for the artificer to succeed to the artist, for the priest to oust the prophet, for formalism to supersede *mana*. It is this understanding which accounts for the fact that magic arts came into being, and magical words or actions tend to acquire a power *per se* independent of the personality which sets them in motion."[1] He adds later: "Every word spoken is potentially a word of power and is liable to produce an effect."[2]

Few Greek poets were more aware of the power of words than Sophocles. As A. A. Long notes in the introduction to his study of Sophoclean language: "Sophocles is a supreme artist of language. This is a judgment which few if any would dispute. On it I base the assumption that he writes in a manner which is highly appropriate; that he chooses his vocabulary and manner of expression for reasons which are eminently worth investigating."[3] Similarly, Long writes in his conclusion: "If we fail to understand the subtle ways in which he expresses his thought, we may find him dispassionate, or even complacent. But if this is our verdict, we shall have mistaken control for insensitivity. . . . Read critically he is among the most disturbing writers. Imperceptibly we are involved in the lives of his characters. Sophocles evokes this response by his delicate use of language."[4]

"Delicate use of language" might reasonably be expected to include etymologizing wordplay. Indeed, Long adds: "Sophocles clearly likes to exploit the etymological connexions between words" and "Sophocles . . . is exploiting the etymological connexion between abstract nouns and other words."[5] But he stays clear of the elaborate wordplay Knox detects, well aware, no doubt, that most classicists—unlike most ancients—take etymologizing play to be coarse, heavy-handed, and unscholarly. Although Long makes occasional reference to wordplay, he does not take the subject too far beyond what G. M. Kirkwood calls "words or phrases that strikingly recall significant previous occurrences of the word or word group."[6] "Such play on words," Long adds, "is a favourite Sophoclean device for stressing a specific theme."[7]

It is surely more than just a literary device as far as the ancients themselves were concerned. In Plato's *Cratylus* 428C, Cratylus calls Socrates' etymologizing *chrêsmôidein* ("giving oracles"), just as Hermogenes, Socrates' interlocutor in the first part of that dialogue, calls Cratylus' own etymologizing interpretations of language *manteia* ("prophecy") at 384B.[8] Connections are established in the listener's mind among similar-sounding words. If two words sound alike, there must be, many ancients thought, some relationship in meaning between them.[9] Thus we find Hades (*Haides*) described as *aidêlos* ("making unseen, unseen, hidden") in Sophocles' *Ajax* 608, recalling the etymology suggested for it in Plato's *Cratylus* 403E–404B.[10] The priest in *Oedipus* 29–30 makes a further Cratylan play when he observes that Hades *ploutizetai* ("grows plutocrat"), thus echoing Hades' other name, Ploutôn, which derives, according to *Cratylus* 403A, from *ploutos* ("wealth"). In a more extended soundplay on *aidôs* ("shame, modesty") and the idea of concealment in the *aid-* element, Creon in *Oedipus* 1426–27 asks people to respect (*aideisth'*) the fire of the Sun by not displaying Oedipus uncovered (*akalypton*).

Oedipus is himself highly sensitive to such verbal play, as we might expect, since he solved the riddle of the Sphinx. Unfortunately, his Cratylan faith in the true nature of names and the meaning of words and his self-preoccupation make it easier for others to define him than for him to define them, as we will see as we examine some of the wordplay on oracular subjects. He becomes an extreme instance of

Protagorean man to whom reality is what it appears to him to be (*Cratylus* 386C), and who becomes convinced of that reality by what Cratylus regarded as the connection by nature's "fathering" (*physei*) between the thing named and the etymological explanation of the name.

Chrêsmoi

It is not only the obvious matter of the connection between Oedipus' name, etymologized by the Corinthian as "swollen foot," that must concern us. For there is some crucial etymologizing on the root *chrê* itself which appeared to yield a link between a *chrêsmos* ("oracle") and the verb *chrê* ("it is necessary"). What is prophesied *must* be. That is why, when Oedipus talks to the Corinthian about the oracle Apollo had given him years ago about marrying his mother, he states it in the following terms (994–96):

> Loxias once said that I must (*chrênai*) have sexual
> intercourse with my mother and take my father's
> blood with my own hands.

Chrê(nai) ("must") is important because some of its forms echo the verb *chraomai* ("use"), the verb *chrêizô* ("need, desire"), and the verb *chraô* ("give oracles"). And Jebb recognizes such wordplay in *Oedipus* 878–79.[11]

We have seen something of the force of these blurred semantic boundaries in Chapter 9, in our discussion of *chreia*. But we should now move further. *Chreos,* for instance, may mean "debt" or "something necessary and desired" (*Oedipus* 157). *Chreos* is also used of prophecy—and Teiresias' prophecy at that, in Homer's *Odyssey* (11.479). Similarly, the scholiast on *Antigone* 887 glosses *chrê* ("need") in the expression *chrê thanein* ("need to die") with "if she needs (*chrêizei*) and wishes (*thelei*)." Some editors in fact prefer to read *chrêi* ("desires"). Indeed, the scholiast on *Oedipus at Colonus* 1426 incorrectly explains *chrêizei* ("wishes") as *chrêsmôidei* ("gives oracles"), so widespread is the confusion.

What is surely most telling in *Oedipus,* however, is the insistence with which both Oedipus and Jocasta refer to oracular utterances (*chrêsmoi*) with the verb *chrênai*. Lines 994–96, cited above, are not the first time Oedipus has formulated the oracle this way. Consider line 791, when Oedipus tells Jocasta what the oracle announced to him: "Saying that I must (*chrêie*) have intercourse with my mother..." That, in fact, was why he left home, he says, so that "I might never see the scourge of these oracles (*chrêsmoi*) fulfilled" (796–97). Jocasta also reports her own terrible oracle in much the same way (711): "There came once an oracle (*chrêsmos*) to Laios..." She later continues (853–54): "[Laios] whom Loxias said must (*chrênai*) die by my child." Fulfillment is syllabically built into the oracular utterance as it is described in Greek. But so too is the *desire* to fulfill the oracle. Jocasta presumably recognizes the proximity of Oedipus' fears to his desires when she tells him not to fear (*mê phobou*) marriage with his mother, since "many a mortal before you has slept with mother in dream fantasies" (980–81). Freud, it would appear, was not so far off the mark:

> There is an unmistakable indication in the text of Sophocles' tragedy itself that the legend of Oedipus sprang from some primaeval dream-material which had as its content the distressing disturbance of a child's relation to his parents owing to the first stirrings of sexuality... And just as these dreams, when dreamt by adults, are accompanied by feelings of repulsion, so too the legend must include horror and self-punishment. Its further modification originates once again in a misconceived secondary revision of the material, which has sought to exploit it for theological purposes.[12]

It is not, however, only modern interpreters who exploit such desires and fears in a theological way. Sophocles' Teiresias does so in his refutation of Oedipus. And, above all, Oedipus himself theologizes his desires and fears, as we will see shortly.

Among the most striking plays on the base *chrê* in *Oedipus* are surely those produced by *Creon* at the beginning of the play's final episode, some aspects of which we discussed earlier. Creon asks the blinded Oedipus what need, *chreia,* Oedipus has of him (1435). When Oedipus asks that he be banished, Creon responds (1438–39):

> Be sure that I'd have done so, if I'd not
> needed (*echrêizon*) first of all to learn clearly
> from the god what really must be done.

A passage from Dio Chrysostom (*Discourse* 10.2) offers a further dimension on these words. The Cynic Diogenes is talking with a traveler who was distracted from his journey to Delphi "to make use of," "consult" (*chrêsomenos*) the oracle of Apollo because his slave ran away. The traveler had therefore headed off toward Corinth looking for the boy. Diogenes retorts that the man was an idiot, attempting to *chrêsthai*, "use" (i.e., "consult"), the god when he does not know how to *chrêsasthai*, "use" (i.e., "employ"), a slave. Diogenes goes on to point out that people must understand whatever it is they are trying to use—be it animal, man, or god—before they can really "use" (*chrêsthai*) it.

The problem of how to use oracles is particularly complex, since they are notoriously ambiguous (*Discourse* 10.17–31). The meaning must be sought out; it is not self-evident. Yet Oedipus assumes that the meaning of his oracle is perfectly clear. That is why Creon's reply to his request for banishment takes Oedipus by surprise and prompts Oedipus' response and Creon's next, chilling, retort (1440–43):

> Oedipus: But surely now: his prophecy was made
>   entirely plain—appalling death (*apollynai*) for me,
>   the impious man, the father-killing man.
>
> Creon: Thus these things were said. But still, given
>   our need of answers (*chreias*), it is better now
>   to learn quite clearly what must be performed.

We should be less surprised. We know Creon's interpretation of the oracle, not the oracle itself, linked the plague to the murder of Laios. Creon himself thus became the oracular force of necessity that drove Oedipus on, the substitute voice of necessity whose words Oedipus obeyed.

Oedipus' confidence that Apollo wishes to destroy him emerges in his wordplay on the god's name and the verb meaning "destroy": *apollynai* (1441). For it is Apollo whom Oedipus blames for his suffering when he comes back on stage, having blinded himself (*Oedipus* 1229–30). Apollo's name is commonly explained in these terms by Greek writers. Aeschylus and Euripides both etymologize the destruction, *apol-*, in "Apollo." Aeschylus has *Apollôn . . . apôlesas,* "Apollo, you have destroyed (*apôlesas*)", in *Agamemnon* 1081–82, and Euripides does the same in *Phaethon* 224–25.[13] We may also note the play on *polis* ("city") and *ollymi* ("destroy") in *Antigone* 673: *hautê (sc.*

anarchia) poleis ollysin ("it [i.e., anarchy] destroys many cities"). The identical wordplay is in *Oedipus* 179: *hôn polis anarithmos ollytai* ("the city is destroyed, numberless in its dead"), where there is also, I suspect, a play on the base *pol* ("many") in the juxtaposition of *polis* to *anarithmos* ("numberless").

Phoebus and Phobias

Socrates comments in *Cratylus* 404C that many people (*polloi*) fear (*phobountai*) Apollo because of the apparent connection of his name with destruction. That is why, Socrates continues in 405E, the second *la(m)bda* was inserted into "Apollo" because otherwise it looked too much like "a harsh name," too much like such forms as *apôlesa* ("destroyed"). Socrates continues: "And so, even now some people suspect that there is (an underlying element of destruction in Apollo's name) because they do not consider the force of the name (*onoma*) correctly (*orthôs*), and they fear (*phobountai*) it as signifying some kind of catastrophe." Apollo, then, is feared because of his name. And Oedipus, when his own terrible fears seem realized, naturally associates their fulfillment with the god who symbolizes his fears. We recall Jocasta's complaint in 914–17 that Oedipus is vulnerable to a speaker who plays on his fears. Among the most obviously formidable voices for Oedipus is, as we have seen, the oracle of Apollo. The close relationship in *Oedipus* between fear and the god is perhaps best illustrated by a comparison of two statements by Oedipus. First (296):

> A man who took no fright (*tarbos*) at doing
> the deed will not fear (*phobei*) the spoken word.

Second (1011):

> Phoebus (*Phoibos*) frightens (*tarbôn*) me—he may turn out
> to have been obviously right.

Phoebus, the oracular god's name, occurs twenty-two times in the extant plays of Sophocles, and more than half of the occurrences are in *Oedipus*. As we have seen in Chapter 6 *phobos*, "fear," and words from the base *phob* occur more frequently in *Oedipus* than in any other

Sophoclean play: seventeen of the fifty-three instances. *Phoibos,* like *phobos,* suggests fear to Oedipus, as their common association with *tarbos* ("fright") shows in lines 296 and 1011.[14] The chorus also uses wordplay to establish the connection between Apollo and the two words it employs to describe fear (153–55):

> I am stretched on the rack, trembling (*pallôn*)
> with terror in my fearful (*phoberan*) mind,
> O Paean of Delos [i.e., Apollo], in awe before you.

Phoebus is the divine symbol of Oedipus' fears not only because of a connection in soundplay between *Phoibos* and *phobos,* but because an explicit etymologizing relationship is established by both Oedipus and Creon between the Pythian oracle of the god and the search for knowledge itself. Oedipus announces (70–72):

> I've sent Menoeceus' son, my brother-in-law
> Creon, off to Phoebus' Delphic (*Pythika*) shrine,
> to delve into the question (*pythoith'*) as to what
> I might do or say to guard this town.

Creon challenges (603–4):

> As proof of this, go to the Pythian (*Pythôd'*) seer:
> you'll find (*peuthou*) if I reported her response,
> its pith and substance.

Since, however, the Pythian Apollo (and those who report his words) speak fears (*phobous*) to Oedipus, Oedipus does not feel the need to go and ask again. He belongs to those who "speak fears."[15]

Destructive Ambiguity

Like Oedipus, scholars often treat Greek *chrêsmoi* ("oracles") as if they had an absolute, "fixed" meaning for the listener to interpret either correctly or incorrectly. Ancient writers, in contrast, generally suggest that oracles formulate rather than resolve the questioner's dilemma and so formulate it that the questioner must make his or her own choice and decision. Most famous oracles found in Greek and Roman literary texts are ambiguous and designed to appear "right" regardless of the choice or decision made by the questioner. Thus it is not the oracle itself that defines, but the oracle's interpreter who, like a scholar, decides *which* of the possible meanings must apply and rejects the others. The interpreter's choice, his decision, destroys the oracle's ambiguity and makes the utterance mean what he wants it to mean until such time as events prove him right—or, more usually, wrong.[16]

Herodotus' Croesus, for example, wants to march against the Persians and asks the oracles of Apollo and Amphiaraus if he should do so (1.53–54). When told by both that if he marches against the Persians he will destroy a great empire, he interprets the ambiguity in accordance with his own expansionist ambitions. He is, after all, the first person to whom Herodotus applies the term *tyrannos* (*Histories* 1.7.4). The boundary between Croesus' Lydian empire and that of the Persian Cyrus is the river Halys (*Histories* 1.72). The name of the river itself suggests a nice wordplay on *katALYSein* ("destroy"), rather like Chaucer's prophetic wordplay that Calkas "knewe by calkulynge" that "Troie sholde destroied be" (*Troilus and Criseyde* 71, 68). We know, with historical hindsight, that the empire Croesus destroys will be his own. But the oracle's integrity, of course, is safeguarded by its ambiguity regardless of the outcome of Croesus' invasion.

As we saw in Lysander's explanation of the oracle warning Sparta to beware of the "Lame Rule," the most literal interpretation of an oracle is not necessarily the one favored by those called upon to evaluate it even in a historical setting. Lysander persuades the Spartans to select Agesilaus, who is lame, over Leotychidas, who is only metaphorically "lame," in the sense that he is illegitimate. What makes Lysander's triumphant interpretation so appealing to the mythicizing historian is that his successful interpretation proves both his own undoing and Sparta's. The scheming Lysander rapidly falls from Agesilaus' favor, and Agesilaus is himself the last king of Sparta's "great days," who dies when eighty years old as a mercenary in Egypt. Plutarch underscores the irony by pairing Agesilaus in his parallel *Lives* with Pompey, the general and politician symbolic of the Roman Republic in its final days, who also dies pathetically in Egypt.

Corinthian Lameness

The myth of Oedipus calls to mind, as J.-P. Vernant shows, another passage in Herodotus: *Histories* 5.92, where a Corinthian, Sosicles, tells of a fellow-Corinthian, Amphion, a nobleman from the ruling

Bacchiad family who had "a lame daughter whose name was Labda."[17] Let us pursue this parallel a little further. Although the Bacchiads normally married within their own clan, Labda's lameness discouraged suitors—except for an undistinguished man, Eetion, from the *dêmos* (i.e., people) of Petra ("rock") and a descendant of the Lapith Caeneus. Being childless, Eetion consulted the Delphic oracle and was told that Labda would produce a child who would be an *oloitrochos*, "a [destructive] boulder," that would fall upon the rulers of Corinth and bring justice. (Homer in *Iliad* 13.137 shows the "parental" relationship between *petra* and *oloitrochos* in a simile comparing Hector to "a boulder from a rock"—*olooitrochos hôs apo petrês*.) When the other members of the Bacchiad clan heard about this oracle, they were not pleased, since it gave a plausible explanation to a hitherto inexplicable oracle of their own that an "eagle (*aietos*) among the rocks (*petrêisi*)" would bring forth a lion destructive to Corinth. The proximity of *aietos*, "eagle," to Aetion, the Doric dialect form of Eetion's name, and the fact that Eetion was born in Petra, convinced the Bacchiads they should do away with the child of Eetion and Labda, whose name was Cypselus.

These "rock" motifs also occur in the Theban legend of Laios. According to Apollodorus, the Theban Amphion, with his twin brother Zethus, expelled the Cadmean Laios, son of Labdacus, from Thebes (3.44.7 [3.55–66]): "They built walls around the city since, when Amphion played the lyre, he was followed by the stones (*lithôn*). Laios they threw out." Apollodorus seems to be making an etymological jest when he juxtaposes Laios' name with *lithôn*, as if Laios meant "Rocky." Apollodorus was himself familiar with the well-known Greek etymology associating *laas* ("stone") with *laos* ("people"), which he uses (*Library* 1.48.10 [1.7.2]) when he, like Pindar in *Olympian* 9.42–6, describes Deucalion and Pyrrha's regeneration of the human race from stones: "Hence *laoi* (peoples) were named, metaphorically, from *laas*, that is *lithos* (stone)."

Labda and the Labdacids

The similarities between Herodotus' tale of Labda and her son Cypselus and Sophocles' *Oedipus* are striking, not least because the Cypselus tradition incorporates many *Theban* elements just as the Oedipus tradition has many Corinthian elements. We notice, for instance, that Sosicles' *Corinthian* Amphion has a name most obviously evocative of the *Theban* minstrel Amphion, Cadmus' rival as "founder of

Thebes" and husband of the ill-fated Niobe. Niobe, the *Theban* Amphion's wife, was daughter of *Corinthian* Tantalus (Apollodorus 3.5.5–6). Theban Amphion exiled Laios, who went to Corinth, where he was hospitably received, Apollodorus adds, by Pelops, son of Tantalus—Niobe's brother. Laios stayed in Corinth until Amphion's death. And his return to Thebes was marred by his crime of abducting Chrysippus, Corinthian Pelops' son (Athenaeus, *Deipnosophists* 13.602). In short, Laios has a secondary mythic connection with Corinth as Oedipus does with Thebes.

Sophocles' Oedipus, of course, chooses between a Corinthian and a Theban identity: son of Polybus or son of Laios. According to Herodotus (*Histories* 5.67) and the scholiast on Pindar's *Nemean 9*, Polybus, king of Corinth and its territories, including Sicyon, was the grandfather of Adrastus, king of Argos—the leader of the Seven against Thebes and father-in-law of Oedipus' son Polyneices.[18] Laios was son of Labdacus, son of Polydorus, son of Cadmus, son of Agenor from Phoenicia, according not only to Herodotus (5.59) but to Oedipus in *Oedipus* 267–68. Cadmus, of course, was the mythical introducer of alphabetic writing to Greece. He was also non-Hellenic.[19]

Labdacus, Laios' father, also has a name with special force, derived, some think, from the Greek letter Lambda, or, more correctly, Labda. The *Etymologicum Magnum,* under *blaisos,* says that Labda is the name given those who are lame because their feet (*podas*) are turned outward like the "feet" of the letter lambda.[20] Labdacus' name parallels that of the lame Labda in Corinthian tradition. The child born to Labda will be destructive to the people of Corinth; the child born to Labdacus' son, Laios, will, the oracle forecasts, kill his father.

In both myths the dangerous child is saved from attempts to destroy him at birth and bears a name whose traditional "etymology" is a reminder of his childhood brush with death. Laios' child is exposed but, in some versions, rescued by a herdsman. The soldiers sent to kill Labda's baby could not at first bring themselves to do the murder. So Labda hid the child away in a *kypselê,* a "chest," and thus saved his life. The chest, in fact, gave the infant his name: Cypselus, in honor of the *kypselê,* in which his mother concealed him—and which he subsequently dedicated in the temple of Hera in Olympia. Pausanias describes it in great detail (5.17.5–19.10). Cypselus grew up to be the founder of a dynasty of particularly cruel Corinthian tyrants which ruled the city from approximately 655 to 581 B.C.

Perhaps the most curious similarity between Herodotus' narrative of Cypselus and Sophocles' *Oedipus* is their mutual preoccupation with tyranny. Sosicles tells the story of Labda, Eetion, and Cypselus in a successful speech advising the Spartans and their allies about the evils of tyranny; for the Spartans were planning to keep Athens in order by reimposing the tyrant Hippias, descendant of Peisistratus (tyrant of Athens 560–27 B.C.) The Athenians had expelled Hippias in 510 B.C. Yet, ironically, the man who reorganized and democratized Athens after the expulsion of Hippias was Cleisthenes, the grandson and namesake of the tyrant of Sicyon, a city once ruled by Polybus of Corinth (Herodotus 5.66–69). Cleisthenes of Athens owed his name and tyrannical heritage to the fact that his father, Megacles, was the preferred suitor for the daughter of Cleisthenes of Sicyon; Megacles' chief rival, related to the house of Cypselus, had disgraced himself. The same marriage also produced the Athenian Cleisthenes' brother, Hippocrates, the grandfather of Pericles (Herodotus 6.123–31).

There is, then, in Herodotus a direct connection between Corinthian tradition and the threat of a restored tyranny in late sixth-century Athens. This theme of tyrannical power and its use and abuse are, as we have seen, omnipresent in Sophocles' *Oedipus*. The play was probably produced around the same time as Herodotus' *Histories*—which was available for Aristophanic parody when the *Acharnians* was produced in 425 B.C. and was fresh on Athenian minds.

We have seen how Sophocles interweaves the themes of disease and tyranny, as Plato does, and seems to share Plato's view that tyranny arises from the abuse of power by a champion, a *prostatês*, of the people. We have also suggested that there may be an allusion to the Athenian demagogue and *prostatês* Cleon in Teiresias' comment that he does not need Creon as his *prostatês*, since the speech impediment known as Labdacism converts Creon to Cleon (see Chapter 3). Labdacid wordplay, then, focuses all the myths and legends of Theban and Corinthian tyranny on Sophocles' contemporary Athens.

Laios

Labdacus' name suggests a curious, multiple deformity: "Labdacism" both physical and verbal. His son Laios' name has its own kind of polyphony. J.-P. Vernant observed that "Laios" suggests the king's "left-handedness" and alludes to his sexual deviancy, since *laios* means "left."[21] True, the cause of the curse upon Laios' house is said by some ancient writers to have been his abduction, while exiled from Thebes, of Pelops' son, Chrysippus (Athenaeus, *Deipnosophists*

13.602). Plato mentions Laios' act of homosexual rape as something of a turning point in Greek sexual mores, since before that time pederasty was considered not in accord with *physis,* natural "fathering" (*Laws* 8.836C). But Sophocles himself never uses *laios* as "left," and the only possible hint of wordplay on Laios' unnaturalness is the ironic (and presumably unintentional) jest in Oedipus' question to Jocasta (740–41): "Laios' nature (*physin*) tell me what was he like?"[22] There is, however, very clearly much wordplay in Sophocles between Laios and *laos,* "people," and between Laios and the adjective *palaios,* "ancient," and its adverb *palai.*

The cause of the plague at Thebes, according to Creon, the oracle's interpreter in *Oedipus,* was not Laios himself but the *killing* of Laios many years ago (*palai*) by plural bandits (*lêistai*), as he and others insist, or by a singular bandit (*lêistês*), as Oedipus maintains. When Oedipus summons the ordinary people to hear what steps he has taken to find the killer of Laios, whose presence is causing death and disease among them, he refers to them as the *laos* of Thebes. This is one of only two instances of the form *laos,* "people," in Sophocles. Elsewhere he uses the Attic form *leôs.*[23] The other instance is *Philoctetes* 1241–43, where Odysseus threatens Neoptolemus, who intends to give Philoctetes back his bow:

> *Odysseus*: There is, there's someone who'll stop you from this.
> *Neoptolemos*: What's this? Who will there be who will stop me?
> *Odysseus*: The whole Achaean host (*laos*)—among them, me.

Odysseus prudently (and humorously) avoids challenging Neoptolemos directly. Hence he produces not a specific individual but the *laos,* in its Iliadic sense of the army, the "host of the Achaeans," as in *Iliad* 7.434, rather than the tamer Athenian *leôs,* usually meaning "people." He hides himself inside its protective, armed plurality.[24]

The use of *laos* rather than *leôs* in *Oedipus* has different resonances. Oedipus requests that the *laos* of Cadmus be summoned (144) to aid his quest for the man who murdered *Laios* (cf. 223–24) and who is, appropriately enough, a *lêistês.* We find here one of the most important series of wordplays in Sophocles' *Oedipus*: Laios is murdered by a *lêistês,* "bandit, taker of booty (*leia*)" (124), or by *lêistai,* "bandits" (122). *Leia* literally means "the people's plunder," and its relationship to *laos* is comparable to that of the Latin *populus* ("people") and *populari* ("plunder"). The point is important since Laios' killer has allegedly brought a blight upon the *Kadmou laon,* "the people (laity) of Cadmus" (144). Oedipus is reputedly son of Laios, grandfather of Laodamas, "tamer of people," and, in Sophocles' version, reared by Merope, whose name means "articulate human" and is used adjectivally by Aeschylus to qualify *laos* ("people"): *meropessi laois* (*Suppliants* 90). Little wonder Oedipus is so interested in words; great wonder that he does not believe himself the child of articulate speech.

The issue, then, of singular versus plural which so preoccupies Oedipus in the play may just as well be applied to the killed as to the killer: is the plague to be ended by discovering who killed the singular king, Laios, or what is destroying the plural people, the *laos*? It is not just a matter of whether the murderer was an individual *lêistês* or multiple *lêistai*. Since *laos* is more usually rendered as *leôs* in Attic Greek, there is a connection between *leôs* ("people") and *lêistês* ("killer of people") through *leia* ("plunder [of the people]"), just as there is in Latin between *populus* ("people") and *populari* ("to plunder"): to take from the people what is rightly theirs. Significantly, Oedipus accuses Creon of being a "*lêistês* of my power as tyrant (*tyrannidos*)" (*Oedipus* 535). Surely, then, Oedipus too must be a *lêistês* in that he, as tyrant, has taken from the *laos*, the people, what is properly theirs regardless of whether he killed the ancient Laios. And tyranny is itself, as Plato suggests, a disease, a *nosos*, upon the city.

Laios' name suggests not only "people" and "plunder," but "antiquity" and "the ancient," *palai(os)*. When Oedipus asks the name of the man who allegedly gave him as an infant to the Corinthian he receives the following reply and reacts accordingly (1042–43):

Corinthian: He'd a post with Laios. Yes, that was his name.
Oedipus: You mean, then, the late (*palai*) tyrant of this land

The palace messenger juxtaposes Laios and *palai* and fills out the effect with *palaios* (1245–46):

calling on the late Laios (*Laion palai*), long since dead,
remembering the late man's (*palaion*) sowing, long ago,

Since there is antiquity in Laios' very name, Creon can rely on it when he answers, most vaguely, a specific question from Oedipus (558–61):

Oedipus: How much time (*chronon*), then, now since Laios . . .
Creon: Did what? I do not understand your point.
Oedipus: Was mortally wounded by hand unknown?

Creon: Years (*chronoi*) deeply layered (*palaioi*) could be measured
　　　back.

Palai(os), "ancient," is often juxtaposed by Sophocles with words
indicating things new or recent, as in the opening line of *Oedipus:*
"Children of Cadmus the ancient (*palai*), new (*nea*) offspring..."
Jocasta, similarly, maintains that Oedipus (915–16):

> turns not where
> the rational man turns, to evaluate
> the new (*ta kaina*) against his past (*tois palai*)
> experience.

Perhaps, then, Jocasta is not completely accurate in her diagnosis of
Oedipus' condition, if we bear in mind the wordplay between Laios
and *palaios*. For Oedipus becomes quite obsessed with Laios and ancient prophecies. In *Oedipus* 906–7, for example, we find reference,
depending on whether we follow the manuscripts or Hermann's
emendation, either to the "ancient oracles of Laios" (*Laiou palaia
thesphat'*) or to "the anciently told oracles of Laios" (*Laiou palaiphata
thesphat'*). Similarly, the quest for Laios' killer is a search for "the
traces of an old (*palaias*) crime" (108).

Sophocles' characters extend the soundplays beyond Laios and *pa-
lai(os)* to embrace *palin* ("again"), *polis* ("city"), and *polys, polloi*
("much, many") not only in *Oedipus* but in other plays too. In *Antigone* 162–67, for instance, Creon makes his entrance with the following words:

> Men: the gods have set affairs of state (*poleôs*),
> after much (*pollôi*) turmoil, back in line again (*palin*).
> I sent for you for two main reasons. First,
> I knew you honored Laios' (*Laiou*) power throughout
> his reign, and that again, when Oedipus
> restored the city (*polin*)...

A little later Creon complains that he has "long ago noticed men of
the city (*palai poleôs andres*) bridling at his rule" (*Antigone* 289–90).
The latent notion of "many" (*polloi*) in the one "city" (*polis*) can also
be released by juxtaposition, as when Antigone cries out: "O city, o
men of the city who possess much" (*o polis, o poleôs polyktêmonês*
[*Antigone* 841]).

Similarly in *Oedipus,* Jocasta plays on *palin* and the implicit plurality of *polis* to show that the "witness" to Laios' death cannot retract his testimony again (*palin*): "the city (*polis*) heard it. It was not just me" (849–50). It may well be a sense of the traditional competitiveness that arises from the plurality of the *polis* which prompts the chorus in *Oedipus* 880 to pray that "the god will never destroy the [ancient tradition of] competition (*palaisma*) in the state (*polei*)."

Ultimately Oedipus defines himself in terms of antiquity and in terms of "ancient Laios" as "the child of Laios," *pais Laiou*, even if he does not learn from things past, *ta palai*. In *Oedipus at Colonus* 553 and 1507 Sophocles' Theseus refers to Oedipus as "child of Laios," *pai Laiou*, and juxtaposes the phrase first to *tanyn*, "recently" (553), then to *neorton*, "new" (1507), as if intending, paradoxically, to suggest Oedipus' age by the implicit play between *pai Laiou* and *palaiou* ("ancient"): "I recognized you, child of Laios, recently (*pai Laiou, tanyn*) . . . "; "What is now, child of Laios, new (*pai Laiou, neorton*) . . . ."

Sophocles' use of *palaios* not only when Oedipus or others seek to connect Oedipus with Laios and the past but also in juxtaposition with *palin* ("again") suggests his reiteration or repetition of the past and may make us think of Philoctetes' complaint about the recurrence of his "old pain again and again": *palin palin palaion algêma* (*Philoctetes* 1169–70).

But *palin* has associations beyond those with *palai(os)*, as we have already seen. We may recall *Oedipus* 100–101, where Creon announces the gist of the oracle's response:

> By banishing or paying out again (*palin*)
> killing for killing. Death's a hemorrhage
> whose rage makes wintry days for the city (*polin*).

We have discussed in Chapter 1 the "oracular" tone of these lines and their similarity to Plato's *Republic* 3.399E–401A, where Socrates also talks of removing pollution, of "thoroughly cleansing again (*palin*) the city (*polin*)." And among the reforms envisaged are, as we have seen, the banning of complex, riddling music and diction: in effect, the banning of the Sphinx, the banning of mythic poetry, and the suppression of the irrational, tyrannical soul.

But there was no easy escape in antiquity from the plural, vatic, nature of language itself—least of all in Plato himself, who was, like his Christian counterpart, St. Augustine, never averse to using the rhetorical pluralism he criticized in others. Those who believed in oracles appear to have had a special interest in such disputes over individual letters. And solving such verbal enigmas is, as Teiresias sarcastically points out, Oedipus' specialty, as it is Cratylus' in Plato's dialogue of that name. Oedipus, in fact, is named by the Corinthian who uses a Cratylan etymology: "swollen foot." He is similarly presented with a potential set of Cratylan etymologies to help him solve the riddle: the LAos of Thebes is destroyed because a LÊISTÊS has killed LAIOS. Here is where Thucydides' idea of people adapting their interpretation of an oracle to suit their own experiences may be usefully adduced. Even before Teiresias makes his entrance into the play, Oedipus, anxious to stop the destruction of the Theban LAos, has accepted that the only thing that remains between him and guilt in the murder of LAIOs is a question of whether LAios was killed by a singular LÊISTÊS or plural LÊISTAI. Since he knows he killed a man on the highway, and is thus a LÊISTÊS, he might well be prone to accept that the man he killed was LAIOS.

The world of Oedipus is a Cratylan world where one is constantly subverted by language—where not only a person's name but every word used might somehow be considered to have a vatic quality. It is a world of spells and of bewitchment, to which the incautious inquirer might readily fall prey. And that, in a sense, is the dilemma of Oedipus, who, however much he seeks to escape the irrational, vatic subcurrents of language, is nonetheless their slave. In seeking out meaning, in assuming that words examined in isolation from fact will solve rather than generate riddles, he falls prey to those who exploit, often cynically, the multivalence of language for their own personal benefit: a respected, professional seer, offended by Oedipus' amateur and single success, a demagogue whose power lies in dissimulation and double-talk, a shepherd who sees a chance to live his remaining years in comfort, and a cowardly slave who will say what he has to say to preserve his life.

CONCLUSION

The tragic irony in *Oedipus,* Pietro Pucci comments, "emerges ... most often in the form of an ambiguity when the expression ... allows the audience to detect a different meaning from that which is intended by a character."[1] The difficulty is that it is not always clear what meaning a given character intends to convey to another character within the play itself. Sadly, the rhetorical force of Sophocles' *Oedipus* has been considerably lessened for modern readers by the assumption that the intentions, that is to say motives, of characters within the tragedy are fairly simple and explicit. Sophocles, like the great writers of Roman epic, practices not only dramatic irony but its reverse: where characters know things that we do not know and never learn.

Sophocles does not permit quick and easy resolutions of the dilemmas he poses in *Oedipus* or other plays. He is himself a practitioner of what Demetrius (*On Style* 279) called *deinotês,* the art of being *deinos* ("formidable") in speech, "asking questions of one's listeners without revealing one's own position on the issue, driving them to perplexity by what amounts to cross-examination." As the Sphinx's poetic riddle and the no less complex-riddle-singing oracle at Delphi are problems for Oedipus to solve, so Sophocles' plays are for us. This is perhaps why Sophocles refers to the Sphinx in poetic terms as the *sklêras aoidou,* "unyielding singer of poetry" (36), *rhapsôidos kyôn,* "the rhapsode dog" (391), *poikilôidos Sphinx,* "the complex-riddle-singing Sphinx" (130).

Nonetheless, a curious linguistic and thematic scenario emerges in Sophocles' *Oedipus.* Corinthian and Theban identities blend, lines between generations and, above all, between the individual and the general are crossed and blurred. Was Laios killed by one or many assailants, and what, if any, connection is there between Laios' death long ago (*palai*) and the present suffering of the Theban laity? In the complex, riddling language of Sophocles' play, Laios is presented by Creon and other Thebans not as the criminal *cause* of a blight upon Thebes, of the Sphinx's presence and depredations, as he is in other traditions. Rather, he is a *victim,* whose murder pollutes the land, whose death brings suffering upon the *laos,* the "people." Oedipus is transformed in the words of Creon, Teiresias, and the Corinthian, and by his own thoughts from savior of the land and solver of the Sphinx's riddle of the feet to the man whose swollen feet make him symbolic of the plague. He becomes Sphinxlike, even, perhaps, a Sphinx himself.

As tyrant of Thebes, of course, Oedipus could be considered, in Platonic terms, the disease that lies heavy on the city regardless of whether he really killed his father and married his mother. The tyrannic soul, as Plato shows it, is capable of transgressing all boundaries, of committing acts not only of parricide and incest, but of cannibalism. The incestuous dreams of the tyrant Hippias and of Caesar, soon to be "perpetual dictator" of Rome, are taken by the dreamers themselves to be good omens, symbolizing their own close intimacy and control of their motherland and the displacement of ancestral traditions. But they have a less than pleasant political import for the state, since the tyrant's position is wrested or plundered from the people by men who have, in a figurative, Platonic sense, killed their fathers and married their mothers.

Oedipus attacks his symbolic "father" in other ways too. Most obviously, he rejects his legitimacy and accepts bastardy when he gives more weight to the assertions of an anonymous drunk than to the denials of Polybus and Merope, who claimed to be his real parents. For a fleeting moment he senses that he could have caused Polybus' death by staying away from Corinth: the old man might have died of grief. Most often, however, he does not seem conscious of his parricidal and incestuous reactions to Polybus and Merope: his ghoulish delight in Polybus' death, his fear that if he stays in Corinth he will have a sexual relationship with Merope. When Oedipus finally draws the dubious or false conclusion that Laios and Jocasta were his parents, and that he *has*, therefore, killed his father and married his mother, he has allowed himself to think he has consummated the acts he most fears and thus, in some ways, most desires.

It is, then, possible that Sophocles' Oedipus was never wholeheartedly trying to establish his innocence at all, but that he felt compelled to make the prophecy that he would kill his father and marry his mother come true, to find what had to be (*chrê*) in the oracle (*chrêsmos*). To see oneself marked even as a thing accursed by the gods or by luck is to take a very high view of one's own importance. Oedipus comes to see himself as singled out to be a kind of scapegoat, a *pharmakos,* to Apollo, such as those offered by Athens at Apollo's festival of the Thargelia. A *pharmakos,* however, though the chosen scapegoat for the ills of the community, is not necessarily the *real* cause of the community's sufferings or guilt even if he or she is the atonement for them.[2] And we should not for a moment forget that Greek mythic tradition is unanimous on the issue that Thebes' troubles became even worse after Oedipus' removal from power. The *nosos*—the plague and the city's various other ills—continued without abatement. One could contend that had Oedipus stayed in power, the disastrous wars between his sons and the subsequent crimes of Creon would never have occurred at all. Indeed, Oedipus makes no greater and more callous mistake than assuming that his sons can look after themselves. Rather than removing the blight from the city, his self-punishment intensifies it.

In his quest to escape the fulfillment of his fears, Oedipus leaves Thebes, as Jocasta points out, a ship without a helmsman. He abandons his sons as recklessly as he had abandoned Polybus and Merope at Corinth, and cruelly rejects Jocasta, who tries to protect him from the damaging force of his own anxieties. He threatens to torture an old slave to death if that slave will not give him the answers he wants. And whether he killed Laios at a crossroads or not, he killed an old man and other members of his company. He is egocentric and paranoid: the very embodiment of Plato's tyrannical soul in so many ways.

Yet there is another side to him too. Oedipus' sense of personal guilt allows him to take on the responsibility for the guilt of the community as a whole and thus, he hopes, to become its savior again, as he was once before in the days of the Sphinx. When someone chooses a painful and apparently humiliating path despite numerous opportunities to escape it, people strongly incline to accept that he must be either what he proclaims himself to be, as Sophocles' readers generally believe, or a madman, as Creon suggests to the chorus. And this is where there is a curiously Christlike element in the Oedipus myth. Crucial to Christ's claim to be the Messiah in the New Testament is his willingness to accept public humiliation and execution, to become a scapegoat and be a ritual offering for the community's sins. To be god, he must also be the lamb of god and fulfill even the most terrifying prophecies in conformity with messianic expectations. He must, then, make himself the slave of "the word," of destiny. That, in a sense, is his "heroic" choice of achieving divinity through suffering.

Greek and Jewish writers were not alone in understanding this "heroic choice." Roman poets did so too. They often represent historical figures yearning to be "offerings" for the community—notably Cato the Younger, who killed himself rather than compromise with Caesar. Cato's goal, like Christ's, was to make himself a sacrifice for the benefit of humanity. Lucan has him declare in *Pharsalia* 2.312–13: "May this blood of mine redeem the peoples (*hic redimat sanguis populos*). Let the slaughtering of me atone for any punishment the Roman way of life has earned." Later, he eulogizes Cato as follows (9.601–4): "Here was a real father of his country, a man by whose name you will never be ashamed to swear. If ever you stand free again with neck unchained, one day you will make this man a god (*nunc olim, factura deum es . . .*)." Lucan's perception of the divinity of his ideal man appealed to Christians too. Dante (*Convivio* 4.28) thought no mere human more worthy to symbolize god than Cato.[3]

Lucan also grasped, however, that such mythic, divine status could be achieved by men with less public-spirited motives. His Julius Caesar, when facing the possibility of death at sea, does not burst into tears and lament his impending and potentially unheroic death, as do Odysseus and Aeneas (*Odyssey* 5.299–312; *Aeneid* 1.94–101). Rather, he asks the gods (*Pharsalia* 5.668–71): "Keep my shredded body in the midst of the sea! Deprive me of pyre and cremation, so long as I am always feared, and people expect me to appear from every corner of the world." The yearning for power that extends beyond the physical boundaries of life is the yearning to escape from time, from history, into myth. Caesar is confident that he has achieved enough to be remembered and feared, provided no proof of his death remains.

Similarly, the disappearance of Christ's body from the tomb becomes, for the faithful, proof that he arose from the dead. And Sophocles will later, in *Oedipus at Colonus,* grant Oedipus a similar "disappearance" instead of death.

Unlike the gospel-writers, however, Sophocles draws attention to his hero's delusions and irrationality rather than suggests his judgment is correct. Oedipus chooses to accept that Laios and Jocasta were his parents, and that he killed Laios—even though no substantiating evidence emerges to confirm either him or us in that belief. On the contrary, there is much to suggest that he is misled by his own fears, his faulty inquiries, and the ambiguous statements and complex motives of his interlocutors. Yet he believes.

We do not in any way diminish Oedipus' heroism if we concede that this play is not about his final self-discovery but about his ultimate self-deception. He is misled by others but is, above all, self-deluded. His missing the mark, his error, *hamartia,* is tragic enough. Shakespeare's far from rational Othello is no less grand because he is deceived by the jealous Iago. True, Othello learns he has been deceived and takes his own life. Oedipus does not. He is protected from that knowledge because not even Creon overtly mocks him with it. But the unspoken consequences of the hero's downfall in either play are much the same. Othello's death deprives Cyprus of its protection against the Turks, who, as Shakespeare and his contemporaries well knew, went on to capture Cyprus in 1571. They are not "all drowned" in a storm, as even Othello supposes (*Othello* 2.1.194–95). Similarly, Oedipus' self-punishment brings about not the end of misfortune and suffering for the people of Thebes, but civil war among his heirs.

Because no one points out explicitly that Oedipus has erred, Sophocles' audiences often assume he has not. Indeed, what makes *Oedipus* perhaps the most astonishing of all Greek tragedies is its success in inducing readers to climb over all the obstacles of missing evidence, answers that do not match questions, and irrational arguments to share with Oedipus the conviction that he has proven himself to be no son of Polybus and Merope, but the parricidal and incestuous child of Laios and Jocasta. In short, we become Oedipus.

Sophocles' *Oedipus,* I submit, is a play about the genesis of a myth, not simply the dramatization of a myth. Its texture is woven from the cross-threads of so many individual lives, both lowly and mighty, by Oedipus. Oedipus is wholly self-obsessed, preoccupied with his own identity, not with the fate of Thebes, which passes from his care quite early on. Like the Sphinx, who, tradition has it, destroyed herself after Oedipus, "who knows nothing," solved her riddle, he too is a rhapsode, a weaver of song who destroys himself when he thinks his riddle is solved. As the Sphinx's riddle is one of feet, so Oedipus' riddle appears to be one of feet. And Oedipus' most immediate destroyer is, like the Sphinx's destroyer, a "know nothing" man from Corinth who "solves" the riddle of Oedipus' feet.

In another sense, of course, the metrical feet of Sophoclean tragedy pose a riddle and a challenge for us. Sophocles wrote, as did many other ancients, in a self-consciously vatic, Delphic way, presenting a complex, polyphonic song for his audiences to contemplate, analyse, and attempt to solve.[4] Like the complex-riddle-singing Sphinx, the poet sings a song that carries, in a single vocal utterance, more than one meaning, inscribed in a reverse form of musical notation which compresses concordant, even dissonant themes into one line rather than expresses them in the multiple lines of an orchestral score. Ambiguous words and characters become pivotal chords for shifting themes. That is how his art imitates the complex pluralities of life. If we follow only one part of his harmony in our insistence on unity and unison, we will transcribe no more than one line of its musical score. If we mistake that one line for "the answer" to its riddle, we follow the path of Croesus and Oedipus.

Oedipus' doom, like that of the Sphinx's generalized man, becomes the doom of all men through the poetic form of Sophocles' play as readers struggle to believe, and so often do believe, that Oedipus' guilt is proved. If every character in *Oedipus* becomes another Sphinx whose riddle Oedipus fails to solve, so too we readers may become Oedipuslike if we assume that the myth is a "given," that it is "fate," and that the hero, "the self," is the only character who has motives and ambitions. We can remain as oblivious to its pluralism as Oedipus. But we do not have to.

NOTES

Introduction

1. Peter Rudnytsky, *Freud and Oedipus* (New York, 1987), 337.
2. See Stefan Radt, *Tragicorum Graecorum Fragmenta*, vol. 4: *Sophocles* (Göttingen, 1977), 50.
3. Rudnytsky, *Freud and Oedipus*, 108–9.
4. Ibid., 97.
5. I have outlined my views on Seneca in *Seneca: Three Tragedies* (Ithaca, 1986), 9–32.
6. As, for example, in *Punica* 17.184–86 and 223–24, where Hannibal, as he is ordered by the Carthaginian senate to leave Italy and come back to Carthage after an absence of thirty-six years, wonders whether "Carthage is worth such a sacrifice" (*an tanti Carthago foret*) and "whether it would not be better if Carthage had been destroyed and Elissa's [Dido's] name forgotten" (*flagrasset subdita taedis / Carthago, et potius cecidisset nomen Elissae*). See F. Ahl, M. Davis, A. Pomeroy, "Silius Italicus," *Aufstieg und Niedergang der römischen Welt* 2.32 (1986):2492–561.
7. Sigmund Freud, *The Interpretation of Dreams*, ed. and trans. James Strachey (New York, 1955). See also Thomas Gould, *The Ancient Quarrel between Poetry and Philosophy* (Princeton, 1990), 80–86.
8. For a useful, general overview of Sophoclean scholarship, see R. G. A. Buxton, *Sophocles (Greece and Rome,* New Surveys in the Classics No. 16) (Oxford, 1984); also Valdis Leinieks, *The Plays of Sophocles* (Amsterdam, 1982) and Ruth Scodel, *Sophocles* (Boston, 1984). Some important, divergent interpretations are: Philip Vellacott's eccentric but often brilliant *Sophocles and Oedipus* (London, 1971); Karl Harshbarger, *Sophocles' Oedipus* (Washington, D.C., 1979); John Hay, *Lame Knowledge and the Homosporic Womb* (Washington, D.C., 1979); Robert Eisner, *The Road to Daulis: Psychoanalysis, Psychology, and Classical Mythology* (Syracuse, 1987), especially 1–47; René Girard, "Symetrie et dissymetrie dans le mythe d'Oedipe," *Critique* 249 (1968):99–135; Girard, "Dionysus and the Violent Generation of the Sacred," *Boundary* 2 (1977):487–505; Girard, *Violence and the Sacred*, trans. P. Gregory (Baltimore, 1977);

J.-P. Vernant, "Ambiguity and Reversal: On the Enigmatic Structure of Oedipus Rex," *New Literary History* 9 (1978):474; Charles Segal, "Tragedy and Civilization: An Interpretation of Sophocles," *Yale Classical Studies* 25(1977): 99–158; Sandor Goodhart, "*Leistas Ephaske*: Oedipus and Laius' Many Murderers," *Diacritics* 8.1 (1978): 55–71; Cynthia Chase, "Oedipal Textuality: Reading Freud's Reading of Oedipus," *Diacritics* 9.4 (1979):54–68; Pietro Pucci, "Reading the Riddles of *Oedipus Rex*," in *Language and the Tragic Hero: Essays in Greek Tragedy in Honor of Gordon M. Kirkwood*, ed. Pietro Pucci (Atlanta, 1988), 131–54; see also R. G. A. Buxton, *Persuasion in Greek Tragedy* (Cambridge, 1982).

9. Fragment 191 (Edmonds), 1–8, cited by Athenaeus in *Deipnosophists* 6.222A.

10. E. R. Dodds, "On Misunderstanding the *Oedipus Rex*," *Greece and Rome* 13 (1966):37–49.

11. M. S. Silk and J. P. Stern, *Nietzsche on Tragedy* (Cambridge, 1981), 309. For Friedrich von Schelling, see his *Samtliche Werke,* 14 vols. (Stuttgart, 1856–61), 5:693–94, and his *Werke,* ed. H. Büchner et al., 3 vols. (Stuttgart, 1976), vol. 1, part 3, 106–7. For an opposing view, see Rudnytsky, *Freud and Oedipus,* 105–10.

12. On the psychological implications of Oedipus' self-blinding, see Richard Caldwell, "The Blindness of Oedipus," *International Review of Psycho-Analysis* 1 (1974): 207–18.

13. Similarly, the Sphinx, according to Diodorus Siculus 4.64, hanged herself when Oedipus solved her riddle.

14. For a detailed account of all the variants in the Oedipus tradition, see Carl Robert, *Oedipus: Geschichte eines Poetischen Stoffs im Griechischen Altertum,* 2 vols. (Berlin, 1915).

15. There is even a variance about what sword Jocasta used to kill herself. In Euripides' *Phoenician Women* 1455 ff., she uses the sword belonging to her dead son; in Seneca's *Oedipus* and Statius' *Thebaid,* she uses the sword with which Oedipus killed Laios. See Paola Venini's note on *Thebaid* 11.6 in *P. Papini Stati Thebaidos liber undecimus* (Florence, 1970).

16. See J. C. Kamerbeek, *The Plays of Sophocles: Commentaries,* Part 3: *The Antigone* (Leiden 1978), 2, citing the scholia on Sophocles' *Antigone* 1351.

17. Aeschylus, fragment 122 in Stefan Radt, *Tragicorum Graecorum Fragmenta,* vol. 3: *Aeschylus* (Göttingen, 1985).

18. R. C. Jebb, *Sophocles: The Plays and Fragments,* Part I: *Oedipus Tyrannus* (Cambridge, 1893), 150 (on lines 1136–37) and R. D. Dawe, *Sophocles: Oedipus Rex* (Cambridge, 1982), 210–11. For more on Arcturus as the boundary between winter and summer for dating purposes, see A. W. Gomme, *A Historical Commentary on Thucydides,* vol. 3 (Oxford, 1956), 699–715, especially 707–8.

19. Patrick L. Fermor, *Roumeli: Travels in Northern Greece* (London, 1966), 36.

20. For a recent discussion, see G. O. Hutchinson, *Aeschylus: Septem contra Thebas* (Oxford, 1985), xvii–xxx.

21. There are no references to the Sphinx in Homer. M. L. West, *Hesiod, Works and Days* (Oxford, 1978), note on line 533 (which alludes to the riddle), argues that the Sphinx is not pre-Hesiodic. In Hesiod's *Theogony* 326 she is called Phix which, Plato notes in *Cratylus* 414C–D, is what the Boeotians call her (cf. M. L. West, *Hesiod, Theogony* [Oxford, 1966] on *Theogony* 326). The Sphinx, or Phix, is part of Theban geography: Sphinx Mountain—also called *Phoinikion,* "Phoenician Mountain," according to Strabo 9.2.26 and Pausanias 9.26.1–5,—went through a variety of spelling changes in various ancient and Byzantine sources before becoming Mount Phagas, as it is called today (in the Hesiodic *Shield of Heracles* 33, it is *Phikeion*). See Paul

Wallace, *Strabo's Description of Boeotia,* Bibliothek der Klassischen Altertumwissenschaften, NF, 2. Reihe, Band 65 (Heidelberg, 1979), 108–9. The Sphinx and her mountain (or rock) remained a symbol of political banditry in Hellenistic times (Athenaeus, *Deipnosophists* 6.253 E–F). See, in general, Lowell Edmunds, *The Sphinx in the Oedipus Legend,* Beiträge zur Klassischen Philologie, Heft 127 (Königstein/Ts, 1981), especially 1–29.

22. Victor Ehrenberg, *Sophocles and Pericles* (Oxford, 1954), 9.

23. See Pietro Pucci, "Euripides Heautontimoroumenos," *Transactions and Proceedings of the American Philological Association* 98 (1967):365–71.

24. See Emily McDermottt, *Euripides' "Medea": The Incarnation of Disorder* (University Park, Pa., 1989), especially 9–17.

25. Eckart Schütrumpf, "Traditional Elements in the Concept of *Hamartia,*" *Harvard Studies in Classical Philology* 92 (1989):154; cf. P. van Braam, "Aristotle's Use of *Hamartia,*" *Classical Quarterly* 6 (1912):272; O. Hey, "*Hamartia,* Zur Bedeutungsgeschichte des Wortes," *Philologus* 83 (1928):5; Martin Ostwald, "Aristotle on *Hamartia* and Sophocles' *Oedipus Tyrannos,*" in *Festschrift Ernst Kapp* (Hamburg, 1958), 104. Schütrumpf's article also contains an excellent overview of recent discussions of *hamartia* and a useful bibliography in footnote 1.

26. Cedric Whitman, *Sophocles: A Study of Heroic Humanism* (Cambridge, Mass., 1971), 123.

27. C. M. Bowra, *Sophoclean Tragedy* (Oxford, 1944), 360–62.; cf. Ehrenberg, *Sophocles and Pericles,* 24, n. 1 and 25, n. 1.

28. Schütrumpf, "Traditional Elements," 154.

29. Bernard Knox, *Oedipus at Thebes* (New Haven, 1957), 31.

30. Thomas Tyrwhitt, *De Poetica Liber* (Oxford, 1794); his comment on Aristotle's *Poetics* 1452A25 reads as follows: *Bene factum est quod ipsam tragoediam adhuc superstitem habemus, nam alioquoi ex Aristotelis verbis credere deberemus Nuntium venisse eo consilio ut Oedipum a metu circa matrem liberaret.*

31. Dawe, *Oedipus,* 190.

32. Ibid., 192 (on line 940).

33. Carlo Gallavotti, "Ma non bisogna cavillare sulle parole . . . ," *Aristotele, Dell' Arte Poetica* (Verona, 1974), 147.

34. Lane Cooper, *The Rhetoric of Aristotle* (Ithaca, 1926) (translation of *Rhetoric* 3.14 [1415A]); E. M. Cope, *The Rhetoric of Aristotle,* revised by J. E. Sandys, 3 vols. (Cambridge, 1877), 3:167–68.

35. Frederic Parsons, *The Rhetoric of Aristotle* (Oxford, 1836), 325 n.

36. Anthony Fitton-Brown, *Proceedings of the Cambridge Philological Society,* n.s. 12 (1966): 22; Dawe, *Oedipus,* 200.

37. A. A. Long, *Language and Thought in Sophocles* (London, 1968), 161. See also R. G. Lewis, "The Procedural Basis of *Oedipus Tyrannus,*" *Greek, Roman, and Byzantine Studies* 30 (1989):41–66.

38. Knox, *Oedipus at Thebes,* 78.

39. J.-P. Vernant, P. Vidal-Naquet, *Tragedy and Myth in Ancient Greece,* trans. Janet Lloyd (Brighton, 1981), 3.

40. Joseph Fontenrose, *The Delphic Oracle* (Berkeley and Los Angeles, 1978), incidentally, accepts the historicity of Chaerephon's consultation of Delphi about Socrates (245).

41. D. MacDowell, *The Law in Classical Athens* (Ithaca, 1978), 243.

42. A. R. W. Harrison, *The Law and Life of Athens,* vol. 2: *Procedure* (Oxford, 1971), 145.

43. R. J. Bonner, *Evidence in Athenian Courts* (Chicago, 1905), 20–22; Aristotle, *Rhetoric* 2.1375A24 f.; cf. MacDowell, *The Law in Classical Athens*, 243.

44. Harrison, *The Law of Athens*, 133.

45. I owe the ingenious translation "cock" and "cockette" to Professor Frederick Williams of the University of Southern Illinois.

46. For a fuller discussion, see my "Art of Safe Criticism in Greece and Rome," *American Journal of Philology* 105 (1984):174–208.

47. R. Hackforth in *Plato's Phaedo* (Cambridge, 1955), 30–31, ignores it; J. Burnet, *Plato's Phaedo* (Oxford, 1911), 10–11, disputes it.

48. Hackforth, *Plato's Phaedo*, 30–31.

49. Knox, *Oedipus at Thebes*, 120.

50. Fontenrose, *The Delphic Oracle*, 44.

51. Knox, *Oedipus at Thebes*, 121.

52. On the curative power of words, see Pedro Lain Entralgo's still classic study, *La Curación por la Palabra en la Antigüedad Clásica* (Madrid, 1958). It is available in translation as *The Therapy of the Word in Classical Antiquity*, ed. and trans. L. J. Rather and John M. Sharp (New Haven and London, 1970).

53. Jebb, *Oedipus Tyrannus*, 21.

54. Roland Barthes, *S/Z*, trans. R. Miller (London, 1975), 178.

55. Pat Easterling, "Constructing Character in Greek Tragedy," in *Characterization and Individuality in Greek Literature*, ed. C. B. R. Pelling (Oxford, 1990), 83.

56. Ibid., 84. See also Easterling's references to modern discussions of the person in footnotes 4–7 on that page, especially: B. A. O. Williams, *Problems of the Self* (Cambridge, 1973); R. Harré, *Personal Being* (Oxford, 1983); E. Goffman, *Frame Analysis* (Cambridge, Mass., 1977); J. Lacan, *The Language of the Self*, trans. A. Wilden (Baltimore, 1968).

57. Simon Goldhill, "Character and Action, Representation and Reading: Greek Tragedy and Its Critics," in *Characterization and Individuality*, 108.

58. Colin Renfrew, *Archaeology and Language: the Puzzle of Indo-European Origins* (Cambridge, 1987), 1.

59. For a discussion, see my "Homer, Vergil, and Complex Narrative Structures in Latin Epic," *Illinois Classical Studies* 14 (1989):1–31.

60. See ibid., 21–31.

Chapter 1. Oracles and Plagues

1. Joseph Fontenrose, *The Delphic Oracle* (Berkeley and Los Angeles, 1978), 363 (Response L 18 = no. 149 in H. W. Parke and D. E. W. Wormell, *The Delphic Oracle* [Oxford, 1956]), vol. 1.

2. Thucydides 2.47–51 and 3.87.

3. Victor Ehrenberg, *Sophocles and Pericles* (Oxford, 1954), 11; see also O. Longo, *Edipo e Nicia* (Padua, 1975) for more on Sophocles and contemporary events.

4. Parke and Wormell, *The Delphic Oracle* 1:189; compare G. E. R. Lloyd, *Polarity and Analogy* (Cambridge, 1966), 206–7.

5. Calamis' works, however, as Parke and Wormell point out (*The Delphic Oracle*, 190), "are all to be dated to the first part of the fifth century." Pausanias, they suggest, either is thinking of another plague or has got the sculptor wrong.

6. See John Gould, "On Making Sense of Greek Religion," in *Greek Religion and Society*, ed. P. Easterling and J. V. Muir (Cambridge, 1985), 1–33.

7. Parke and Wormell, *The Delphic Oracle* 1:90.

8. John Burnet, *Plato's Euthyphro, Apology of Socrates, and Crito,* ed. with notes by John Burnet (Oxford, 1924), 92.

9. The Greek text is in Stefan Radt, *Tragicorum Graecorum Fragmenta,* vol. 3: *Aeschylus* (Göttingen, 1985): *Incertarum Fabularum,* fragment 350.

10. In other areas of religion, aside from Delphic prophecy, the Athenian populace remained generally fearful of hostile divine intervention, as we can see from the mass reaction to the mutilation of the herms in Athens in 415 B.C. See Thucydides 6.27–29, with the comments in A. W. Gomme, A. Andrewes, and K. J. Dover, *A Historical Commentary on Thucydides* (Oxford, 1970), 4:264–90 (cf. Andocides, *On the Mysteries*). But an act of sacrilege was a different matter from the utterance of a suspect oracle. As Martin Nilsson observes of the Athenians: "Belief in the oracles . . . was weakened. The prejudices shown by the oracles, as in the case of the favor shown by the Delphic oracle for the Spartans, contributed to the disbelief" (*Greek Popular Religion* [New York, 1940], 136).

11. R. D. Dawe, *Sophocles: Oedipus Rex* (Cambridge, 1982), 111, commenting on line 181. For discussion of the plague and its nature, see A. J. Holladay and J. F. C. Poole, "Thucydides and the Plague of Athens," *Classical Quarterly* n.s. 29 (1979): 282–300 and "Thucydides and the Plague: A Further Footnote," *Classical Quarterly* n.s. 34 (1984):483–85; also J. A. H. Wylie and H. W. Stubbs, "The Plague of Athens, 430–28 B.C.: Epidemic and Epizootic," *Classical Quarterly* n.s. 33 (1983):6–11.

12. Fontenrose, *The Delphic Oracle,* 40.

13. The same story is found in Plutarch, *Pericles* 10, and is also told of the orator Demades by Athenaeus (*Deipnosophists* 3. 99D). To at least some ancient ears, eta and iota, and the diphthong omicron iota, were as indistinguishable as in modern Greek.

14. Fontenrose, *The Delphic Oracle,* 41.

15. Ibid., 43; cf. Xenophon, *Memorabilia* 1.3.1.

16. See R. C. Jebb, *Sophocles: The Plays and Fragments,* Part I: *Oedipus Tyrannus* (Cambridge, 1893), 21.

17. Compare Herodotus 1.54.3, where Croesus sends a delegation to the *Pytho* and makes a gift to the Delphians of two staters per person, having ascertained (*pythomenos*) their number.

18. Dawe, *Oedipus,* 93.

19. See my *Metaformations: Soundplay and Wordplay in Ovid and Other Classical Poets* (Ithaca, 1985), 22–63.

20. See R. G. A. Buxton, *Persuasion in Greek Tragedy: A Study of Peitho* (Cambridge, 1982), 20; Plutarch, *Lives of the Ten Orators* 833C–D. See also, in general, Pedro Lain Entralgo, *The Therapy of the Word in Classical Antiquity,* ed. and trans. L. J. Rather and John M. Sharp (New Haven, 1970).

21. The textual problem with the final choral passage in the play is discussed in Chapter 9.

22. Alcmaeon fragment 24B4 (Diehls Kranz), cited by G. E. R. Lloyd, *Polarity and Analogy* (Cambridge, 1966), 20.

23. T. B. L. Webster, *An Introduction to Sophocles,* 2d ed. (London, 1969), 45–46.

24. Plutarch, *Pericles* 7.4, 8.3, 16.1; compare Thucydides 2.63.2 and 65.8–10; and 63.2; Aristophanes' *Acharnians* 530–39; Diodorus 12.38.2–39.3; Ehrenberg, *Sophocles and Pericles,* 85, and, more generally, 75–98; Martin Ostwald, *From Popular Sovereignty to the Sovereignty of Law: Law, Society, and Politics in Fifth-Century Athens* (Berkeley and Los Angeles, 1986), 185, 201–2. For a different view of Pericles, see A. Andrewes, "The Opposition to Pericles," *Journal of Hellenic Studies* 98 (1978):1–8 which minimizes

the value of Plutarch's testimony and which Ostwald, rightly I believe, finds "too radical a solution for a real historical problem" (*Popular Sovereignty*, 185 n.). Pericles, in fact, had some troubles not only with champions of the people (*prostatai tou dêmou*) but with more conservative opponents such as Thucydides, son of Melesias (as distinct from the historian Thucydides), whom Aristotle describes as *prostatês* for the affluent (*Constitution of Athens*, 28.2).

25. Cf. my earlier treatment in *Metaformations*, especially chap. 1.

26. Robert J. White, *The Interpretation of Dreams: Oneirocritica by Artemidorus* (Park Ridge, N.J., 1975), 81; cf. Roger Pack, *Artemidori Daldiani Onirocriticon Libri V* (Leipzig, 1963), 91.

27. Ibid.

28. See ibid., and E. R. Dodds, *The Greeks and the Irrational* (Berkeley and Los Angeles, 1963), 43 and 61–62. On Freud and Artemidorus, see Cesare Musatti, *Artemidoro di Daldi: Dell' Interpretazione de' Sogni* (Milan, 1976), 7–23.

29. See Jules Brody, *"Fate" in Oedipus Tyrannus: A Textual Approach*, Arethusa Monographs 11 (Buffalo, 1985), 36–42.

30. Edward A. Lippman, *Musical Thought in Ancient Greece* (New York, 1964), 45. For a more detailed discussion of Greek polyphony, see my "Pindar and the Sphinx: Celtic Polyphony and Greek Music," in *Harmonia Mundi*, ed. Robert W. Wallace and Bonnie MacLachlan (Rome, 1991), 78–98.

31. In a curious way, even dedicatory tripods speak. Herodotus (5.59–61) says he saw writing in Cadmean letters on tripods in the temple of Apollo Ismenias in Thebes, dating to the times of Laios, Oedipus, and Laodamas (Oedipus' grandson).

Chapter 2. Ambassador Creon

1. Bernard Knox, *Oedipus at Thebes* (New Haven, 1957), 11.

2. Ibid., 29.

3. Ibid., 3, 5.

4. *The Oedipus Tyrannus of Sophocles*, ed. John Williams White (Boston, 1894), 90.

5. Knox, *Oedipus at Thebes*, 11–12.

6. White, *The Oedipus Tyrannus of Sophocles*, 90.

7. For the *Oedipodeia* epic, see *Poetarum Epicorum Graecorum Testimonia et Fragmenta, Pars 1*, ed. A. Bernabé, and with an iconographical appendix by A. R. Olmos (Leipzig, 1987), 17–20; Malcolm Davis, *The Epic Cycle* (Bristol, 1989), 19–29.

8. In Sophocles' *Antigone*, Haemon's epic sacrifice (or self-sacrifice) becomes a suicide. And the motif of the Sphinx's self-destruction by hanging herself when her riddle is solved is replaced by Antigone's hanging. Epic tradition was quite tenacious about the self-immolation of one of Creon's children. In Statius' *Thebaid*, Creon's son Menoeceus hurls himself from the walls of Thebes in ritual self-offering to sanctify the city's defenses. And his action embitters Creon, who demands that Oedipus' son Eteocles must also confront death for his homeland (*Thebaid* 10.756–82). See David Vessey, *Statius and the Thebaid* (Cambridge, 1973), 131, and F. M. Ahl, "Statius' *Thebaid*: A Reconsideration,"*Aufstieg und Niedergang der römischen Welt* 2.32 (1986): 2803–12, especially 2808.

9. For *mênyei* in the technical, legal sense of "lays information," see R. G. Lewis, "The Procedural Basis of *Oedipus Tyrannus*," *Greek, Roman, and Byzantine Studies* 30 (1989):53 and n. 4.

10. Sandor Goodhart, "Leistas Ephaske," *Diacritics* 8.1 (1978):55–71.

11. See Martin Ostwald, "The Athenian Legislation against Tyranny and Subversion," *Transactions and Proceedings of the American Philological Association* 86 (1955):103–28 and *From Popular Sovereignty to the Sovereignty of Law: Law, Society, and Politics in Fifth-Century Athens* (Berkeley and Los Angeles, 1986), 8 and 185; Michael Gagarin, "The Thesmothetai and the Earliest Athenian Tyranny Law," *Transactions and Proceedings of the American Philological Association* 111 (1981):71–77; P. J. Rhodes, *A Commentary on the Aristotelian Athenaion Politeia* (Oxford, 1981), 156. Oedipus, however, later refers to Laios as a king, *basileus*, in line 257 when invoking a curse on the supposed killer(s).

12. We may also notice that Oedipus, as he summons the ordinary people of Thebes, calls them the *laos*. This is one of only two instances of the form *laos* in Sophocles (the other is *Philoctetes* 1243). Elsewhere he uses the Attic form *leôs*. For further discussion of this matter, see Chapter 10 of the present volume.

Chapter 3. Oedipus and Teiresias

1. Oedipus also uses the verb later (in the form *ephthito*) to summarize what he has concluded from the Corinthian's ambiguous description of Polybus' death (962). Oedipus supposes Polybus must have died either through treachery or of disease and, after the messenger speaks, concludes that the cause was disease.

2. See H. W. Parke, *Festivals of the Athenians* (Ithaca, 1977), 17: "In Athens, as in Rome, when the kingship was abolished as a political institution, it was still retained for ritual functions."

3. R. G. Lewis, "The Procedural Basis of *Oedipus Tyrannus*," *Greek, Roman, and Byzantine Studies* 30 (1989):44.

4. Parke, *Festivals of the Athenians*, 110.

5. Ibid., 110–11.

6. See the notes by R. C. Jebb, *Sophocles: The Plays and Fragments*, Part I: *Oedipus Tyrannus* (Cambridge, 1893), 49, and R. D. Dawe, *Sophocles: Oedipus Rex* (Cambridge, 1982), 121–22. Dawe mentions M. Schmidt's emendation *eiasamên* as one solution to the "dilemma."

7. Dawe, *Oedipus*, 123.

8. Ibid., 124.

9. For a detailed study of the Teiresias myth in antiquity, see Luc Brisson, *Le mythe de Tirésias: Essai d'analyse structurale* (Leiden, 1976).

10. Dawe, *Oedipus*, 124.

11. Marcel Detienne discusses the connection between *LÊTHÊ* and *aLÊTHEia* in "La notion mythique d'ALÊTHEIA," *Revue des Études Grecques* 73 (1960):27–35, and "*Les maîtres de verité dans la Grèce archaique*" (Paris, 1967), 75–77. W. G. Thalmann, *Conventions of Form and Thought in Early Greek Epic Poetry* (Baltimore, 1984), 147–49, expresses the idea this way: "*Aletheia* personified is thus a mythic double of Mnemosyne, Memory, and the Muses are intimately associated with it" (147). See also my discussion in *Metaformations: Soundplay and Wordplay in Ovid and Other Classical Poets* (Ithaca, 1985), 47 and 321–22, and "*Ars est Celare Artem*: Art in Puns and Anagrams Engraved," in *On Puns: The Foundation of Letters*, ed. Jonathan Culler (Oxford, 1988), 17–43.

12. See, for example, *Electra* 637 and *Trachiniae* 209.

13. Dawe, *Oedipus*, 124.

14. Victor Ehrenberg, *The People of Aristophanes* (Oxford, 1951), 353; cf. 146 and 355–57 and his long discussion in *Sophocles and Pericles* (Oxford, 1954), 75–105. See also Gerhard Thür, "Wo wohnen die Metöken?" *Demokratie und Architektur: Der Hippodamische Stadtebau und die Entstehung der Demokratie,* ed. W. Schutter, W. Hoepner, E. L. Schwander (Munich, 1989), 117–22.

15. Jebb, *Oedipus Tyrannus,* 65.

16. Ehrenberg, *Sophocles and Pericles,* 7.

17. See P. Karavites, "Tradition, Skepticism, and Sophocles' Political Career," *Klio* 58 (1976):359–65; M. H. Jameson, "Sophocles and the Four Hundred," *Historia* 20 (1971):541–68; Martin Ostwald, *From Popular Sovereignty to the Sovereignty of Law: Law, Society, and Politics in Fifth-Century Athens* (Berkeley and Los Angeles, 1986), 340–41. For a different view, see Harry Avery, "Sophocles' Political Career," *Historia* 22 (1973):509–14.

18. F. J. Parsons, *The Rhetoric of Aristotle* (Oxford, 1836), 287–88.

19. Aristophanes, *Knights* 1–5, 137, 191–93, 256, 275–76, 296–98, 392; *Wasps* 592–93; *Acharnians* 215–17, 223–32, 289–91, 299–302; *Peace* 637, for example. Aristotle in *Constitution of Athens* 28.3 speaks of Cleon's manner and approach to politics in highly disparaging terms, and Thucydides, who had personal reasons for his hatred of Cleon, gives him perhaps the roughest treatment of all (3.36.6; 5.10.9). See W. R. Connor, *The New Politicians of Fifth-Century Athens* (Princeton, 1971), especially 132–34; also Ostwald, *Popular Sovereignty,* 201–34.

20. Major work on this wordplay has now appeared in articles by Michael Vickers (who kindly gave me the opportunity to see some of them prior to publication): "Alcibiades on Stage: *Philoctetes* and *Cyclops,*" *Historia* 36 (1987):171–97; "Lambdacism at Aristophanes *Clouds* 1381–82," *Liverpool Classical Monthly* 12 (1987):143; "Alcibiades on Stage: *Thesmophoriazusae* and *Helen,*" *Historia* 36 (1989):267–99; and "Alcibiades on Stage: Aristophanes' *Birds,*" forthcoming in *Historia*.

21. Bdelycleon pretends to be Cleon himself and sings the song about Harmodius, the tyrant-killer. "What a man!" sings Bdelycleon. "What a thief!" his father responds (1223–27). Bdelycleon warns his father to be careful what he sings about Cleon, since the latter threatens to "destroy you, wipe you out, and banish you from the land" (1228–29); Plutarch also records the story in *Alcibiades* 1.3–4.

22. One might reach this erroneous conclusion from reading A. D. MacDowell's note on *Aristophanes' Wasps* (Oxford, 1971), 133–34.

23. Joseph Fontenrose, *The Delphic Oracle* (Berkeley and Los Angeles, 1978), 159.

Chapter 4. Creon, Oedipus, and Jocasta

1. For the tritagonist, see R. C. Jebb, *Sophocles: The Plays and Fragments,* Part I: *Oedipus Tyrannus* (Cambridge, 1893), 7. The same actor would also play the Corinthian, as we will see in Chapter 5. On stage conventions in Sophocles, see David Seale, *Vision and Stagecraft in Sophocles* (Chicago, 1982), especially 12–25 and 215–60.

2. For Teiresias' lineage, see Luc Brisson, *Le mythe de Tirésias: Essai d'analyse structurale* (Leiden, 1976), 37, n. 44.

3. See also the comments of U. Albini, *Edipo,* ed. Bruno Gentili and Roberto Pretagostini (Rome, 1986), 124 and 161.

4. Cedric H. Whitman, *Sophocles: A Study of Heroic Humanism* (Cambridge, Mass., 1951), 131.

5. T. Zielinski, "Exkurse," *Philologus* 55 (1896):523 and n. 7.

6. See Whitman, *Sophocles,* 46–55 and the sources cited there.

7. For Hippolytus as an aristocrat with snobbish, gentlemanly goals in life, see A. N. Michelini, *Euripides and the Tragic Tradition* (Madison, 1987), 307–8.

8. For Creon as an *onoma epônymon,* see Max Sulzberger, "Onoma Epônymon: Les noms propres chez Homère et dans la mythologie grecque," *Revue des Études Grecques* 39 (1926):398.

9. Pietro Pucci, "Reading the Riddles of *Oedipus Rex,*" in *Language and the Tragic Hero: Essays in Honor of Gordon M. Kirkwood,* ed. Pietro Pucci (Atlanta, 1988), 149, n. 35.

10. For Oedipus as "Knowfoot" and "Swollenfoot," see ibid., 149–52, and "La vertigine dell'enigma," in *Il cavallo di Troia* 9 (1988):113–14.

11. See Thomas Gould, "The Innocence of Oedipus: The Philosophers on Oedipus the King," *Arion* 5 (1966):502–6.

12. Thucydides 1.24–55; cf. Diodorus Siculus 12.30–33.

13. The order and nature of the last two lines is disputed by editors. See R. D. Dawe, *Sophocles: Oedipus Rex* (Cambridge, 1982), 124–25.

14. Joseph Plescia, *The Oath and Perjury in Ancient Greece* (Tallahassee, 1970), 12.

15. Ibid.

Chapter 5. Jocasta

1. For the divisions, see R. C. Jebb, *Sophocles: The Plays and Fragments,* Part I: *Oedipus Tyrannus* (Cambridge, 1893), 7.

2. We will discuss the force of the term *chreia* in Chapter 9.

3. Euripides, *Phoenician Women* 21–22; Apollodorus, *Library* 3.5.7.

4. Or "big man," depending on whether we read *melas,* "dark," or *megas,* "big."

5. Plutarch, *On the E at Delphi.* The letter epsilon, used by the Greeks as the number five, was of great symbolic importance at Delphi.

6. R. D. Dawe, *Sophocles: Oedipus Rex* (Cambridge, 1982), 160.

7. Jebb, *Oedipus Tyrannus,* 104–5.

8. Dawe, *Oedipus,* 175.

9. Sandor Goodhart, "*Leistas Ephaske*: Oedipus and Laius' Many Murderers," *Diacritics* 8.1 (1978):55–71. See also Cynthia Chase, "Oedipal Textuality: Reading Freud's Reading of *Oedipus,*" *Diacritics* 9.4 (1979):54–68.

10. *Sophocles: Oedipus the King,* trans. Stephen Berg and Diskin Clay (New York, 1978), 7.

11. Apollodorus, *Library* 3.5.7, says Laios was drunk when he fathered Oedipus; in Euripides, *Phoenician Women* 21–22, Jocasta says much the same.

12. Wilhelm Dindorf, *Lexicon Sophocleum* (Leipzig, 1870).

Chapter 6. An Anonymous Namer

1. I am not persuaded by R. D. Dawe's argument in *Sophocles: Oedipus Rex* (Cambridge, 1982), 182, that we should emend the text to read *hybrin phyteuei tyrannos* ("the tyrant father's uncontrolled arrogance") since the traditional reading poses no particular problem. The argument that a *transgression* of normal rules of

political, social, and personal behavior produces disease is commonplace in Athenian literature.

2. Bernard Knox, *Oedipus at Thebes* (New Haven, 1957), 184. See also Thomas Gould, *Oedipus the King: A Translation with Commentary* (Englewood Cliffs, N.J., 1970), 63.

3. Simon Goldhill, "Exegesis: *Oedipus (R)ex,*" *Arethusa* 17 (1984):182–83.

4. Bernard Knox, *Sophocles, Oedipus the King* (New York, 1959), 62.

5. Dawe, *Oedipus,* 190.

6. *Oedipus Tyrannus,* trans. and ed. Luci Berkowitz and Theodore F. Brunner (New York, 1970), 21.

7. *Sophocles: The Three Theban Plays,* trans. Robert Fagles, with introduction and notes by Bernard Knox (New York, 1982), 212.

8. Forms of the verb *audao* generally express the idea of not necessarily well-informed talk in the *Oedipus.* In line 731, Jocasta, commenting on the report that Laios was killed at a place where three roads meet, says: "Such was the rumor (*êudato*) that has not yet stopped." Similarly, in line 527 the chorus, talking to Creon about accusations that he "set up" Teiresias to accuse Oedipus, comments: *êudato men tade, oida d'ou gnômêi tini* ("words were uttered to that effect. But I / don't know what reason they were based upon").

9. *Sophocles: Oedipus the King,* trans. Kenneth Cavander with an introduction by Tom Driver (San Francisco, 1961), 29.

10. Berkowitz and Brunner, *Oedipus Tyrannus,* 21.

11. Dawe, *Oedipus,* 192.

12. The forms of the Greek demonstrative *hode* ("this," "this person,") are marked in the translation to alert the reader to its double use: as a reference by the speaker to himself and as a reference by the speaker to someone standing beside him onstage. Sophocles exploits this ambiguity at a crucial juncture, as we will see in Chapter 7.

13. Dawe, *Oedipus,* 194.

14. Knox, *Oedipus at Thebes,* 143 and n. 15 (on p. 247) with the ancient sources cited there, notably Hippocrates, *Epidemics* 1.26: *rhopas* ("turns") for the better or the worse; Aristotle, *Problems* 1.861A uses the same expression as Sophocles' messenger in reference to the aged: *mikra . . . rhopê*; Aretaeus 3.12: "old men . . . need only a short turn (*bracheias rhopês*) for the sleep of death."

15. *Sophocles: The Oedipus Cycle,* trans. Dudley Fitts and Robert Fitzgerald (New York, 1965), 48.

16. Cavander, *Sophocles: Oedipus the King,* 30.

17. Peter L. Rudnytsky, *Freud and Oedipus* (New York, 1987), 6–14. For the text of Freud, see *The Standard Edition of the Complete Psychological Works of Sigmund Freud,* ed. and trans. James Strachey, 24 vols. (London, 1953–74), 4:262–63. For the sexual aspects of the eye and seeing, see Pietro Pucci's excellent "On the 'Eye' and the 'Phallos' and Other Permutabilities, in *Oedipus Rex,*" in *Arktouros: Hellenic Studies Presented to Bernard M. W. Knox on the Occasion of His 65th Birthday,* ed. G. W. Bowersock, W. Burkert, and M. C. J. Putnam (Berlin and New York, 1979). With his observations we might compare Bronislaw Malinowski in *The Sexual Life of Savages in Northwestern Melanesia* (New York, 1929), 166: "The kidneys are considered the main or middle part or trunk (*tapwana*) of that system. From them, other ducts (*wotuna*) lead to the male organ. This is the tip or point (*matala,* literally eye) of the whole system. Thus, when the eyes see an object of desire, they 'wake up,' communicate the impulse to the kidneys, which transmit it to the penis and cause an erection.

Hence the eyes are the primary motive of all sexual excitement: they are 'the things of copulation.' "

18. Seneca, *Oedipus*, 797.

19. Cesare Musatti, *Artemidoro di Daldi: Degli Interpretazione de' Sogni* (Milan, 1976), 17; see also Robert J. White, *The Interpretation of Dreams: Oneirocritica by Artemidorus* (Park Ridge, N.J., 1975), 81.

20. Ibid., 19 and n. 34; Theodor Gomperz, *Traumdeutung und Zauberei* (Vienna, 1886).

21. See also my *Metaformations: Soundplay and Wordplay in Ovid and Other Classical Poets* (Ithaca, 1985), chap. 1.

22. Musatti, *Artemidoro di Daldi*, 7, 19–20.

23. Fitts and Fitzgerald, *Oedipus Cycle*, 50.

24. Cavander, *Sophocles: Oedipus the King*, 31.

25. *Sophocles, Three Tragedies*, trans. H. D. F. Kitto (Oxford, 1956), 80.

26. Knox, *Oedipus the King*, 66.

27. Dawe, *Oedipus*, 193.

28. A. W. H. Harrison, *The Law and Life of Athens: Family and Property* (Oxford, 1969), 20–21; see also Cynthia Patterson, " 'Not Worth the Rearing': The Causes of Infant Exposure in Ancient Greece," *Transactions and Proceedings of the American Philological Association* 115 (1985):103–23, especially 104–7 and n. 5.

29. Euboulus *fragments* 1, 2, 3 (Edmonds) and Ephippus *fragment* 3 (Edmonds) cited by Athenaeus, *Deipnosophists* 9.370C.

30. Dawe, *Oedipus*, 198, on line 1021.

31. Harrison, *The Law and Life of Athens*, 71.

32. Fitts and Fitzgerald, *Oedipus Cycle*, 51.

33. *Sophocles*, trans. Robert Fagles, 219.

34. Dawe, *Oedipus*, 199, on line 1026.

35. Pucci, "On the 'Eye' and the 'Phallos' and Other Permutabilities, in *Oedipus Rex*," 130; cf. Gould, *Oedipus the King*, 175.

36. See, for example, J.-P. Vernant, "Ambiguity and Reversal: On the Enigmatic Structure of *Oedipus Rex*," in *Sophocles' Oedipus Rex*, edited with an introduction by Harold Bloom (New York, 1988), 112–13; John Hay, *Oedipus Tyrannus: Lame Knowledge and the Homosporic Womb* (Washington, D.C., 1984), 27–33.

37. See Max Sulzberger, " 'Onoma Epônymon': Les noms propres chez Homère et dans la mythologie grecque," *Revue des Études Grecques* 39 (1926): 381–447.

38. Ibid., 431.

39. On etymological figures in *Ajax*, see W. B. Stanford, *Sophocles: Ajax* (London and New York, 1983), 270–71 and his notes on *Ajax* 308–9, 317–18, 430–33, 574, 606–7, 685–86.

40. In Sophocles, *Electra* 836–41, the chorus hails Amphiaraus himself as king of the dead.

41. *Odyssey* 9.365, 408, 455, 460; for more on the echoes of Odysseus, *outis*, and Oedipus, see the next chapter.

42. Knox, *Oedipus at Thebes*, 184.

43. The etymologizing plays in Plato's *Cratylus* are similarly based on the old Attic alphabet: see, for example, *Cratylus* 398C–D.

44. See Cynthia Patterson, *Pericles' Citizenship Law of 451–50 B.C.* (Salem, N.H., 1981), especially 95.

45. Cf. Xenophon, *Hellenica* 3.3.3–4.

Chapter 7. The Witness Arrives

1. R. D. Dawe, *Sophocles: Oedipus Rex* (Cambridge, 1982), 205.
2. Ibid., 160.
3. At *Oedipus* 1029, Oedipus has inferred (though he receives no positive confirmation from the messenger himself) that the Corinthian is a wanderer looking for jobs as a hired laborer. R. C. Jebb, *Sophocles: The Plays and Fragments*, Part I: *Oedipus Tyrannus* (Cambridge, 1893), 136 (on *Oedipus* 1029) adduces Isocrates, *Oration* 14.48 to show the distinction between a *doulos* (unpaid slave) and a *thētēs* (paid worker).
4. R. G. Lewis, "The Procedural Basis of Sophocles' *Oedipus Tyrannus*," *Greek, Roman, and Byzantine Studies* 30 (1989):42.
5. A. R. W. Harrison, *The Law and Life of Athens*, vol. 2: *Procedure* (Oxford, 1971), 147.
6. Ibid., 150.
7. See A. M. Dale's discussion in her review of G. W. Bond, *Euripides: Hypsipyle* (Oxford, 1963) in *Journal of Hellenic Studies* 84 (1964):166–67. Dale points out that the pronoun *hode* "is deictic, evolved by a people used to talking with their hands, and there must be *some* reason for a gesture of immediacy."

Chapter 8. The Palace Messenger and the Coup d'Etat

1. The use of the future optative particularly is worthy of note since it is a form first found in fifth-century B.C. Greek and belongs almost exclusively to indirect speech. See E. Schwyzer, *Griechische Grammatik,* 2 vols. (Munich, 1950), 2:337. Future optatives are *much* more common in the Oedipus than in any other play of Sophocles. They occur only in *Antigone* 414; *Oedipus at Colonus* 945; *Ajax* 313, 727; *Philoctetes,* 353, 376, 612; and *Oedipus* 538, 539, 792, 796, 1271, 1274 (2). In other words, there are as many future optatives in *Oedipus* as in all Sophocles' other plays put together.
2. Central to the lie is a story built on *Iliad* 10.313–465, where Odysseus and Diomedes capture, interrogate, and kill Dolon, a Trojan spy who knows the secret of Troy's salvation: the newly arrived Rhesus and his marvelous horses.
3. For a fuller (and different) treatment of reported speech in *Trachiniae,* see Bruce Heiden, *Tragic Rhetoric: An Interpretation of Sophocles' Trachiniae* (New York, 1989), 43–79, 85–90, 109–19.
4. David Grene in *Sophocles I, The Complete Greek Tragedies,* ed. David Grene and Richmond Lattimore (Chicago, 1954), 65–66.
5. E. F. Watling, *The Theban Plays* (Harmondsworth, 1947), 60.
6. David Grene in *Sophocles I* translates 1265–66 on p. 65: "When he saw her, he cried out fearfully / and cut [rather than untied] the dangling noose."
7. R. D. Dawe, *Sophocles: Oedipus Rex* (Cambridge, 1982), 225.
8. See Pietro Pucci's nice contrast between the Euripidean and Sophoclean hero in this respect in *The Violence of Pity in Euripides' Medea* (Ithaca, 1980), 175–87.
9. Aeschylus, *Agamemnon* 1372–98; *Libation Bearers* 892 and 973; *Seven against Thebes* 848; Euripides, *Bacchae* 1168 and 1216; *Electra* 1172–80; *Hecuba* 663–64, 1085–119; *Hercules* 1029–30; *Hippolytus* 806–10; *Phoenician Women* 1480–84; *Suppliants* 794–97; *Trojan Women* 1119–21; Sophocles, *Ajax* 865; *Antigone* 1257 and 1293; *Electra* 1458–65. In Euripides, *Andromache* 1166–67, Neoptolemus' body is brought onstage even though he himself has not appeared as a living character. The major exceptions to this pattern are *Medea* 1313–22, where Jason's attempt to break into the house and

see his children's corpses is frustrated by Medea's appearance; *Iphigeneia in Aulis* 1532ff., where, in the ending whose authenticity has been disputed (unnecessarily, in my judgment), the dubious, announced apotheosis of Iphigeneia leaves no body to be produced; and *Antigone,* where Antigone's corpse may not have been brought out along with that of Haemon at 1257.

10. R. C. Jebb, *Sophocles: The Plays and Fragments,* Part I: *Oedipus Tyrannus* (Cambridge 1893), 169.

11. Dawe, *Oedipus,* 228.

12. Its closest rival is Euripides' *Hecuba* (1049–53), where Polymestor enters blinded, and with his murdered children.

Chapter 9. Creon Kreon

1. Apollodorus, *Library* 3.5.8 and 3.7.1.

2. See Plato, *Gorgias* 495B. Cf. C. J. Ruijgh's review of M. Meier, *-ιδ-Zur Geschichte eines griechischen Nominalsuffixes,* Ergänzungshefte zur Zeitschrift für Vergleichende Sprachforschung 23 (Göttingen, 1975), in *Mnemosyne* 30 (1977): 436–39.

3. See J. Diggle, *Euripides Phaethon* (Cambridge, 1970), 147–48 and the sources cited there, and my *Metaformations: Soundplay and Wordplay in Ovid and Other Classical Poets* (Ithaca and London, 1985), 129.

4. W. B. Stanford, *Ambiguity in Greek Literature* (Oxford, 1939), 104–5; cf. the comparable wordplays on *outis* in Euripides, *Cyclops* 547–48, 672–73, and 675.

5. See the brief note of James Dee, "Odysseus' Pun Rendered," *Classical Outlook* 65 (1987–88):41: "Could Homer have invented the Outis form for the sake of the *metis* wordplay?"

6. See Stefan Radt, *Tragicorum Graecorum Fragmenta,* vol. 4: *Sophocles* (Göttingen, 1977), 374–78; A. C. Pearson, *The Fragments of Sophocles,* 2 vols. (Cambridge, 1917), 2:105–14; also Carlo Gallavotti, *Aristotele: dell' Arte Poetica* (Florence, 1974), 49n.; C. Whitman, *Sophocles: A Study of Heroic Humanism* (Cambridge, Mass., 1951), 143–44; Dana Sutton, *The Lost Sophocles* (Lanham, Md., 1984), 90–94; Jan Bremmer, "Oedipus and the Greek Oedipus Complex," in *Interpretations of Greek Mythology,* ed. Jan Bremmer (London, 1987), 51–52.

7. Sutton, *The Lost Sophocles,* 91. We should add that a further parallel between the later life of Odysseus and the Theban legend emerges in the story of Euryalus. Eustathius in his commentary on the *Odyssey* (1796.52) says that, according to Sophocles, Euryalus was Odysseus' son by Euhippe, a Thesprotian woman. Euryalus was killed by Telemachus when he grew up and came to Ithaca with tokens of his birth. Parthenius (*Erotica* 3), however, gives a different report of Sophocles' play. In it, he says, Odysseus is tricked by Penelope (who has learned of Odysseus' affair with Euhippe) into killing Euryalus, who, she says, is plotting against him. Scholars now tend to give preference to Parthenius' version; see Pearson, *Fragments,* 1:145–46; Radt, *Fragmenta,* 4:194–95; and Sutton, *The Lost Sophocles,* 46. If Eustathius is right, Telemachus' action makes him a fratricide; if Parthenius, Odysseus kills one son and is killed by another. Euryalus' name, curiously, is identical with that of one of the Epigonoi, the sons of the unsuccessful Seven against Thebes (*Iliad* 2.565–66; Pausanias 2.20.4; Apollodorus 3.7.2). It is this Euryalus whom Homer describes as having conquered all the Thebans in box-

ing at the funeral games for Oedipus, but who is defeated at Achilles' funeral games by Epeius (*Iliad* 23.677–99).

8. See R. F. Hock and E. N. O'Neil, *The Chreia in Ancient Rhetoric*, vol. 1 (Atlanta, 1986), 23 and (for other definitions and ancient sources) 49; see also 5 and 224.

9. Ibid., 194.

10. For the fuller context, see Chapter 5. It is noteworthy that *chreia*, "need, pithy statement," has, as its anagram *cheira*, "hand," which occasionally becomes confused with it in the textual tradition (as in Euripides, *Helen* 420).

11. Hock and O'Neil, *Chreia*, 338–39 and examples 60 and 61.

12. Ibid., 49–50.

13. Ibid., 252.

14. R. D. Dawe, *Sophocles: Oedipus Rex* (Cambridge, 1982), 239.

15. E. Hruza, in *Beiträge zur Geschichte des griechischen und römischen Familienrechtes. I, Die Ehebegründung nach attischen Rechte. II, Polygamie und Pellikat nach griechishem Rechte* (Erlangen, Leipzig, 1892, 1894), 2:165, argues that in the most famous instance of an incestuous marriage, that of Oedipus and Jocasta, the discovered incest does not invalidate the marriage or legally incapacitate the children. But A. R. W. Harrison, *The Law and Life of Athens: Family and Property* (Oxford, 1969), 22–23 (note), argues against this reading on the grounds that *Oedipus* 1214, 1256 refer to the marriage as "a marriage that is not a marriage" (*agamon gamon*) and to Jocasta as a "wife who is not a wife" (*gynaika ou gynaika*); similarly *Oedipus at Colonus* 367 shows that Eteocles and Polyneices are not legitimate heirs, and *Oedipus at Colonus* 830–33 show Creon as having the rights of a head of family (*kyrios*) over Antigone since she is the illegitimate daughter of Jocasta.

16. See the discussion immediately following and notes 20, 21, and 22 for details of the scholarly controversy on the play's ending.

17. See Dawe, *Oedipus*, 245–46.

18. Oliver P. Taplin, *Greek Tragedy in Action* (Berkeley and London, 1978), 46.

19. Dawe, *Oedipus*, 247.

20. Ibid., 245. See also Thomas Drew-Bear, "The Trochaic Tetrameter in Greek Tragedy," *American Journal of Philology* 89 (1969):385–405. The problem with the trochaic tetrameter is that after Aeschylus and the play *Rhesus* (circa 450 B.C), attributed, probably wrongly, to Euripides, it is not found again in Greek tragedy (except in this section of Sophocles' *Oedipus*) until Euripides' *Heracles* and *Trojan Women* (written sometime between 420 and 415 B.C.). Given the small number of surviving tragedies from the third quarter of the fifth century, this statistic may have much less significance than scholars often accord it.

21. Franz Ritter, "Sieben unechte Schlusstellen in den Tragödien Sophokles," *Philologus* 17 (1861):422–36, and R. D. Dawe, *Studies in the Text of Sophocles*, vol. 1 (Leyden, 1973), 266–73; cf. C. P. Gardiner, *The Sophoclean Chorus: A Study of Character and Function* (Iowa City, 1987), 107 and n. 1, and R. W. B. Burton, *The Chorus in Sophocles' Tragedies* (Oxford, 1980), 183–84.

22. William M. Calder, III, "*Oedipus Tyrannos*, 1524–30," *Emerita* 38 (1970):149–61; Brian Arkins, "The Final Lines of Sophocles, *King Oedipus* (1524–30)," *Classical Quarterly* n.s. 38 (1988):555–58; D. A. Hester, "Very Much the Safest Plan or, Last Words in Sophocles," *Antichthon* 7 (1973):11–12; S. Douglas Olson, "On the Text of Sophocles' *Oedipus Tyrannus*, 1524–30," *Phoenix* 43.3 (1989):189–95; cf. Albin Lesky, *Die tragische Dichtung der Hellenen* (Göttingen, 1972), 122n.

23. Plutarch, *Solon* 30.

Chapter 10. Oracular Wordplay

1. W. R. Halliday, *Greek Divination* (London, 1913), 22.

2. Ibid., 50–51.

3. A. A. Long, *Language and Thought in Sophocles* (London, 1968), 1. Long cites Athenaeus, *Deipnosophists* 1.22B who remarks that Sophocles criticized Aeschylus for achieving success without knowing how. But the context of the remark is a discussion of whether Aeschylus was sober when he wrote—a charge of drunkenness was leveled against him by a poet named Chamaeleon. Thus the point of Sophocles' alleged remark appears to be that Aeschylus' genius expressed itself in an unknowing alcoholic haze.

4. Long, *Language and Thought in Sophocles*, 168–69.

5. Ibid., 154 and 161.

6. G. M. Kirkwood, *A Study of Sophoclean Drama*, Cornell Studies in Classical Philology 31 (Ithaca, 1958), 229.

7. Long, *Language and Thought in Sophocles*, 153; cf. 161; also W. Nestle, "Sophokles und die Sophistik,"*Classical Philology* 5 (1910):135; W. Schmid and O. Stählin, *Geschichte der Griechischen Literatur*, vol. 1, part 2 (Munich, 1934), 494; Lewis Campbell, *Sophocles: The Plays and Fragments*, 2 vols. (Oxford, 1871–81), 1:99–100.

8. See J. C. Rijlaarsdam, *Platon über die Sprache: Ein Kommentar zum Kratylos* (Utrecht, 1978), especially 18–22.

9. For a fuller discussion of ancient etymologies and their role in Greek and Latin poetry, see my *Metaformations: Soundplay and Wordplay in Ovid and Other Classical Poets* (Ithaca, 1985), and *"Ars est Celare Artem*: Art in Puns and Anagrams Engraved," in *On Puns: The Foundation of Letters*, ed. Jonathan Culler (Oxford, 1988), 17–43.

10. See C. J. Ruijgh's review of M. Meier's *-ιδ-Zur Geschichte eines griechischen Nominalsuffixes*, Ergänzungshefte zur Zeitschrift für vergleichende Sprachforschung 23 (Göttingen, 1975), in *Mnemosyne* 30 (1977):437.

11. R. C. Jebb, *Sophocles: The Plays and Fragments*, Part I: *Oedipus Tyrannus* (Cambridge, 1893), 119; the forms there are *chrêsimoi* and *chrêtai*; compare Parmeniscus in *Scholia Vetera in Euripidis Medea* 264 (also on 1382) and Joseph Fontenrose, *The Delphic Oracle* (Berkeley and London, 1978), 369.

12. Sigmund Freud, *The Interpretation of Dreams*, trans. and ed. James Strachey (New York, 1955), 264.

13. See J. Diggle, *Euripides Phaethon*, Cambridge Classical Texts and Commentaries 12 (Cambridge, 1970), 147–48. Aristophanes parodies a similar etymology in *Clouds* 1265, where Amynias complains that he has been thrown out of his chariot by his horses: *O Pallas, hôs m' apôlesas*; Aristophanes shifts the play from Apollo to *Pallas*—thus showing, by the way, that a shift of vowel does not cause the wordplay to disappear. Something of the same may be happening in *Oedipus* 153–55 between *pallôn*, "trembling," and an implicit Apollo. Aristophanes also admits a horsey element into the wordplay, since *pôlos* is a common Greek word for "horse," especially a horse that draws a chariot. Indeed, Oedipus himself remembers killing a man who was riding in a *pôlikes apênês*, "a horse-drawn wagon" (*Oedipus* 802). Curiously, Sophocles (fragment 480 Keil) corrects the reading preserved in the manuscript of the scholiast on Apollonius, *Argonautica* 3.1214 from *pôlousa* to *pallousa*. Cf. my discussion in "Amber, Avallon, and Apollo's Singing Swan," *American Journal of Philology* 103 (1982):373–411, especially 390–94.

14. These lines contain the only two instances of *tarbos* in *Oedipus*. *Tarbos* and associated words are not common in Sophocles, except, curiously, in the *Trachiniae* where there are nine of the nineteen instances from the surviving plays.

15. For a discussion of the problem of wordplay involving vowels of different length, see Chapter 1.

16. See my discussions in *Lucan: An Introduction,* Cornell Studies in Classical Philology 39 (Ithaca and London, 1976), 121–30, and "Statius' *Thebaid*: A Reconsideration," *Aufstieg und Niedergang der römischen Welt* 33.5 (1986):2803–912, especially 2822–27.

17. J.-P. Vernant, "From Oedipus to Periander: Lameness, Tyranny, Incest in Legend and History," *Arethusa* 15 (1982): 19–38. On the theme of lameness, see also C. Lévi-Strauss, *Anthropologie structurale* (Paris, 1958), 227–35, and J.-P. Vernant and M. Detienne, *Les ruses de l'intelligence,* 2d ed. (Paris, 1978), 257–60.

18. Apollodorus (1.9.13) gives a rather different account.

19. My argument in favor of a Mycenaean Cadmus in "Cadmus and the Palm-Leaf Tablets," *American Journal of Philology* 88 (1967):188–94, is no longer tenable in view of M. Bernal's *Black Athena: The Afro-Asiatic Roots of Classical Civilization* (London, 1987), and Ruth Edwards, *Kadmos the Phoenician* (Amsterdam, 1979).

20. Hans von Geisau accepts the "labda" etymology for Labdacus' name but explains its application to lameness on the grounds that lambda was written in ancient times with one short leg. He suggests that the characteristic lameness of Oedipus was projected back onto his ancestor (*Der Kleine Pauly* 3.427).

21. Vernant, "From Oedipus to Periander," 22–23.

22. Although Euripides does use *laios* (*Heracles* 671 and 728, for example), he neither employs it in the sense of left-handedness nor makes any suggestion of wordplay on this basis.

23. For example, *Oedipus at Colonus* 741: *pas Kadmeiôn leôs* ("the whole people of Cadmus"); *Trachiniae* 194 and 783: *Mêlieus hapas leôs* ("the whole people of Melos"); *pas leôs* ("the whole people"). Cf. *Antigone* 73; *Ajax* 1100.

24. In the *Odyssey* the sense is somewhat different. To cite simply the description given in *A Greek-English Lexicon* (compiled by Henry Scott Liddell and Robert Scott, revised and augmented by Sir Henry Stuart Jones with the assistance of Roderick McKenzie [Oxford, 1968]): "in the *Odyssey laoi,* more rarely *laos* means men or people; as subjects of a prince, for example." Callimachus (*Epigram* 28.4 = *Palatine Anthology* 3.301) uses the plural vocative *ô laoi* in the sense of the public or the audience in the theater of Athenian assembly, as is pointed out by A. S. F. Gow and D. L. Page. *The Greek Anthology: Hellenistic Epigrams,* 2 vols. (Cambridge, 1965), 2:186.

Conclusion

1. Pietro Pucci, "On the 'Eye' and the 'Phallos' and Other Permutabilities, in *Oedipus Rex,*" in *Arktouros: Hellenic Studies Presented to Bernard M. W. Knox on the Occasion of His 65th Birthday,* ed. G. W. Bowersock, W. Burkert, and M. C. J. Putnam (Berlin and New York, 1979), 130.

2. See René Girard, *Violence and the Sacred,* trans. P. Gregory (Baltimore, 1977), 487–502.

3. For a fuller treatment of Cato, see my *Lucan: An Introduction* (Ithaca and London, 1976), 131–76.

4. For more on poetic polyphony see Maija Väisänen's brilliant study of Catullus, *La Musa dalle Molte Voci,* Societas Historica Finlandiae, Studia Historica 30 (Helsinki, 1988), especially 9–38.

INDEX OF ANCIENT
AUTHORS CITED

Book and line numbers are printed in bold.

Aeschylus: *Agamemnon*, 106; **855**, 105;
1081–82, 248; **1372–98**, 278; *fragment*
122 (Radt), 9, 268; **350**, 37; *Laios*, 9;
Libation Bearers, 14; **892, 973**, 278;
Persians, 32; *Prometheus*, 46; *Seven
against Thebes*, 11; **848**, 278; *Sphinx*,
11; *Suppliants* **90**, 256; **963**, 93
Alcaeus: *fragment* **57**, 144
Alcmaeon: *fragment* **24B4**, 46, 229,
271
Andocides: *On the Mysteries*, 271
Apollodorus: *Library* **1.7.2**, 252; **1.9.13**,
282; **3.5.6**, 252; **3.5.7**, 154, 181, 275;
3.5.8, 117, 279; **3.7.1**, 279; **3.7.2**, 279;
3.81, 55
Apollonius of Rhodes, *Argonautica*
3.1214, 281
Aristophanes: *Acharnians* **215–17, 223–
32, 289–91, 299–302**, 274; **530–39**,
271; *Clouds*, 23, 25, 26, 27, 43, 231;
394–403, 234; **658–66**, 22, 23; **1265**,
281; *Frogs* **569**, 95; **1182–94**, 8, 9, 10;
1323, 51; scholia on *Frogs* **1184ff.**, 8;
Knights, 29; **1–5**, 274; **61, 109–43**, 97;
137, 191–93, 274; **195–210**, 97; **275–
76, 296–98, 392**, 274; **860**, 29; **960–

1096, 97; **1111–20**, 29; *Lysistrata* **757**,
176; *Peace* **637**, 274; **684**, 93; *Thesmophoriazusae* **502–16**, 176–77; *Wasps*,
14, 27, 96; **42, 45**, 96; **592–93**, 274;
1223–37, 1228–29, 274; **1236–37**, 96;
scholia on *Wasps*, 289
Aristotle: *Constitution of Athens* **26.4**, 190;
28.2, 272; **28.3**, 274; *fragment* **102**
[Rose], 144; *Nichomachean Ethics*
1128A20, 23; *Poetics* **1452A**, 17;
1453B, 16, 229; *Problems* **I (861A)**,
276; *Rhetoric*, 33, 78; **1365B**, 210;
1375A, 270; **1377A–B**, 125; **1377B**, 77;
1379A, 81–82; **1380A**, 82; **1382A**, 29,
168; **1400B**, 14, 181; **1408B**, 94–95;
1411A, 41; **1412A–B**, 23; **1415A**, 17;
De Sophisticis Elenchis **170B1**, 76;
183B32, 15; *Topics* **2.6.2**, 181
[Aristotle]: *Rhetoric to Alexander*
1431A7–8, 76; **1432A**, 125; **1433B12**,
24
Artemidorus of Daldi: *Oneirocritica* **1.79**,
49, 168; **4.26**, 169
Astydamas: *Alcmaeon*, 229
Athenaeus: *Deipnosophists* **1.22B**, 281;
2.37E–F, 144; **2.37F**, 52; **2.40D**, 144;
3.99D, 271; **6.222A**, 269; **6.253E–F**,
268; **9.370C**, 277; **11.467D–F**, 180;
13.602, 253–55

GENERAL INDEX

Library of Congress Cataloging-in-Publication Data

Ahl, Frederick M.
    Sophocles' Oedipus: evidence and self-conviction / Frederick Ahl.
        p.   cm.
    Includes bibliographical references and index.
    ISBN 0-8014-2558-1 (cloth: alkaline paper)
    ISBN 0-8014-9929-1 (pbk.: alkaline paper)
    1. Sophocles. Oedipus Rex.   2. Oedipus (Greek mythology) in
literature.   I. Title.
PA4413.07A45   1991
882'.01—dc20   90-55733

Gramley Library
Salem College
Winston-Salem, NC 27108